'*Rescue* gives us hope that we can come together to build forward better and shape societies and economies that are fairer, greener and more inclusive. Ian Goldin's prescriptions for investing in people and the planet, and with strong international cooperation, show us how we can create a world that works for all.'
Kristalina Georgieva, Managing Director
of the International Monetary Fund

'A fresh and penetrating insight from one of the great authorities on globalisation into what's gone wrong with our world and what needs to be put right.'
Gordon Brown, United Nations Special Envoy for Global Education and former Prime Minister of the United Kingdom

'Ian Goldin gives us a bold, compelling account of the lessons of the pandemic: after four decades of neoliberal market thinking, big government is back. Only an activist state can deal with inequality, climate change, and future pandemics. This important book shows that we need not a "reset" but a fundamental rethinking of capitalism if we are to build more just, resilient societies.'
Michael J. Sandel, author of
The Tyranny of Merit: What's Become of the Common Good?

'Essential reading for anyone interested in making the world a better place. *Rescue* provides an urgently needed roadmap for us all.'
Arianna Huffington, Founder & CEO, Thrive Global

'Ian Goldin offers an insightful perspective on the injustices and crises besetting today's world. His book deserves wide readership – indeed one would like to hope that his wisdom will influence the political leaders who confront the challenge of "building back better" after Covid-19.'
Lord Martin Rees, Astronomer Royal

'Ian Goldin's *Rescue* is an optimistic and insightful analysis of the pros as well as the cons of the pandemic and seeks to assess its potential to reshape our lives for the better. To paraphrase his words and the essence of the title – can the pandemic go down in history as the event that rescued humanity? Goldin brings statistics alive in this optimistic analysis of the positive as well as the negative impact of the pandemic – it is a beacon of hope for the future.'
Lord Norman Foster

'This well-researched book shows us what is wrong with our current economic model and provides a convincing clarion call for change after the pandemic.'
Baroness Minouche Shafik, Director, London School of Economics

'Professor Ian Goldin is mapping the short- and long-term consequences of the Covid-19 pandemic in his excellent book *Rescue*. We know that some negative effects will linger for a long time in our societies and economies, but there is also hope of a brighter future. Professor Goldin points out that something better can come out of this if we make a joint effort to reset our communities on a more sustainable path. This well-written book gives hope of a better future.'
Cécilia Malmström, former European Commissioner for Trade

'In this broad-ranging book, Ian Goldin aptly views the West's failure to address at all adequately the Covid-19 virus as emblematic of widespread national failures. To get out of this dystopia, he argues, nations will have to create nothing less than "a different operating system" and they must cooperate far more than in the past. This radical book is a must-read.'
Professor Edmund Phelps, economist and Nobel Laureate

'*Rescue* is a wise and hopeful book. As the world begins to emerge from the Covid-19 pandemic, Ian Goldin has assembled an extraordinary range of data to assess its impact and identify opportunities for transformative change. Just the tonic weary readers need!'
Professor Anne-Marie Slaughter, CEO of New America

Also by Ian Goldin

Terra Incognita: 100 Maps to Survive the Next 100 Years
Age of Discovery: Navigating the Storms
of Our Second Renaissance
Development: A Very Short Introduction
The Pursuit of Development: Economic Growth,
Social Change and Ideas
Is the Planet Full?
The Butterfly Defect: How Globalization Creates
Systemic Risks, and What to Do about It
Divided Nations: Why Global Governance is Failing,
and What We Can Do about It
Exceptional People: How Migration Shaped our World
and Will Define Our Future
Globalization for Development
The Case for Aid
The Economics of Sustainable Development
Economic Reform and Trade
Modelling Economy-wide Reforms
Trade Liberalization: Global Economic Implications
Open Economies
Trade: What's at Stake?
The Future of Agriculture
Lessons from Brazil
Making Race: The Politics and Economics of Racial Identity

RESCUE

From Global Crisis to a Better World

IAN GOLDIN

SCEPTRE

First published in Great Britain in 2021 by Sceptre
An Imprint of Hodder & Stoughton
An Hachette UK company

1

A CIP catalogue record for this title is available from the British Library

Hardback ISBN 9781529366877
eBook ISBN 9781529366884

Typeset in Dante MT by Palimpsest Book Production Ltd, Falkirk, Stirlingshire

Printed and bound in Great Britain by Clays Ltd, Elcograf S.p.A.

Hodder & Stoughton policy is to use papers that are natural, renewable
and recyclable products and made from wood grown in sustainable forests.
The logging and manufacturing processes are expected to conform to
the environmental regulations of the country of origin.

Hodder & Stoughton Ltd
Carmelite House
50 Victoria Embankment
London EC4Y 0DZ

www.sceptrebooks.co.uk

To all those who have suffered from the pandemic;
may it lead to a better world

Contents

From Global Crisis to a Better World

Covid-19 has created a pivotal moment. Everything hangs in the balance. The pandemic compressed into a year trends that would otherwise have taken decades to emerge. It has brought us to an inflection point in history. By seizing this historic moment, we can turn the tide to shape our individual and collective destiny, and in so doing we would rescue humanity from catastrophe and create a better world.

The overused clichés that punctuate many commentaries on Covid-19 are a source of my nightmares. Returning to 'business as usual', or 'bouncing back', means we would be heading in the same direction that brought us to where we are today. Other widely used expressions are similarly worrying. 'Bouncing forward' implies we are leaping ahead along the same tracks. A Great Reset, as called for by the World Economic Forum, or 'reboot', another popular phrase, can suggest that we should go back to what has already been programmed, when what is needed is a different operating system. 'Building back better' – the slogan used by the Biden–Harris Presidential team – is more encouraging but still worrying; if there is one thing that Covid-19 has taught us, it is that our system is built on shaky foundations, and building back on unstable foundations guarantees future collapse.

It is business as usual that led to our disastrous situation. To prevent future pandemics, which could be much more deadly than Covid-19, and to stop catastrophic climate change, we need a radical change in direction. The coronavirus crisis comes on top of escalating climate, inequality, geopolitical and other crises that are tearing our societies apart. The gradual return to normality as vaccines become available will come as an enormous relief. We all no doubt will celebrate the simple pleasures of being able to hug our families, socialise with friends and walk down busy streets. Economies will rebound as the combination of government stimulus and pent-up consumption leads to rapid growth.

The pleasure of reclaiming our past lives should not, however, lull us into complacency. Unless our societies operate in a fundamentally different way, we cannot overcome pandemics or any of the other escalating crises we inevitably will face. The world will be different after Covid-19. The question is will it be sufficiently different?

We are at an intersection with roads leading in irreconcilable directions: it is time to choose whether we continue hurtling down the road that will lead to escalating crises and dystopian outcomes or whether we turn in a new direction that leads to a healthier and more inclusive world of shared prosperity.

The pandemic has brought us to a crossroads in geopolitics, economics, technology, urbanisation, education, globalisation and social relations. Whether we like it or not, Covid-19 has reshaped all of our lives. It has changed our priorities regarding jobs, education and careers. It forces us to rethink where we live and work and to understand how our incomes and prospects have altered. We have all been affected – young and old, wealthy and deprived, urban and rural, employed and retired, in rich countries and in poor countries.

The trends that the pandemic has accelerated and revealed are not new. But the extent and scale of the global disruption has meant that the structural weaknesses in our societies and in international cooperation have become shockingly evident for all to see.

The pandemic has provided a unique opportunity to clarify our priorities. What is needed is radical reform to prioritise the needs of society and sustainability over our acquisitive individualism and self-destructive nationalism. While everyone's creative individuality should be allowed to flourish, and all nations have a right to self-determination, this cannot be at the cost of others and of future generations. The reprioritisation of our individual lives, businesses and governments towards greater solidarity would be reflected in changing political preferences, leading to a realignment of politics to create more inclusive and sustainable societies within countries and internationally. Merely changing who is in power is not enough; deep-seated reforms are required that would address the fundamental weaknesses in our societies.

While the idea of radical reform is worrying to many, what I am proposing is far less scary than the prospect of business as usual, which inevitably would lead to growing instability, and worsening prospects for the majority of citizens. The failure to manage the growing risks from our entangled world would result in future pandemics, as well as escalating geopolitical tensions, with a rising risk of war and ecological and other disasters. Domestically, rising inequality would lead to rising populism and protectionism, with this accelerating the downward spiral of slower growth and worsening of prospects for all but a cocooned minority.

The only certainty arising from a continuation of our current ways would be more nasty surprises. Radical reforms, by addressing the fundamental sources of instability, would create a more predictable world by focusing on policies that promoted equity and sustainability. What seems radical today was not long ago considered mainstream in the US and UK, when high levels of public investment in health, education and social safety nets, funded by highly redistributive tax systems, were regarded as essential tenets of the settlement that followed the Second World War. Indeed, such policies still have broad support in many countries, including Denmark, Finland, Norway, Sweden and the Netherlands. The battle against Covid-19 has been the biggest challenge societies have faced since the Second World War.

Although history does not repeat itself, we can gain vital insights from understanding the historical rhythms. The key question is whether history will judge today's leaders as more like those of the First or the Second World War. The First World War was born out of a tragic accident of history that led to the death of more than 20 million people, about half of whom were soldiers, and wounding of a further 23 million people, which left economies and societies in ruin. Any hope of a better future was soon dashed by the devastating impact of the Spanish Flu pandemic in 1918 and 1919, which killed more people than the war, and then the Great Depression that followed. Rising inequality and joblessness stoked populism and the rise of fascism, which in turn precipitated an even worse war.

H. G. Wells wrote that the 1914 to 1918 conflict would be The War That Will End War. Sadly, it turned out to be a precursor to another. Following the war, the victors forced reparations on Germany, in the form of payments, coal and the detachment of the German Rhineland, which came under the control of France. The extent of the humiliation and impossibility of meeting the payments led to growing resentment, resurgent nationalism and the inflationary printing of money (Germany made its final reparation payment in October 2010, ninety years after the war had ended). In addition, the British, French and Italian allies owed vast amounts to the US, which they were unable to pay and which the US refused to reschedule. On the contrary, US banks provided new loans, adding to the unsustainable debt pile. Growing US protectionism, culminating in the Smoot–Hawley Tariff Act of 1930, which raised tariffs on over 20,000 imported goods, served to reduce trade and growth in Europe and the US, at a time when stimulus was urgently required. These errors were compounded during the Great

Depression by the cutting of government spending in an ill-fated attempt to close yawning deficits, which deepened and prolonged the Depression.

Policy errors in the aftermath of the First World War combined to create a toxic combination of economic decline, rising protectionism and festering grievances that in Germany and Italy gave rise to fascism and the nationalist attacks that triggered the Second World War.

A better world was forged in the fires of the Second World War; not by accident, but by design. The Second World War was the deadliest conflict in human history with an estimated 70 to 80 million fatalities, of whom only approximately 16 million were soldiers. As it came just twenty years after the devastation of the First World War, leaders were compelled by the previous failure to promise soldiers and citizens that this time their sacrifices would not be in vain.

It is difficult to imagine a more hostile environment in which to plant and nurture the seeds of the welfare state, the United Nations, the Bretton Woods Institutions and the Marshall Plan, designed to fund the reconstruction and development of the vanquished as well as the victors. But it was the visionary work undertaken during the war that defined the peace and shaped the fortunes of generations to come. While the British government was fighting on five fronts in a war that it was not yet clear it could win, and while bunkers were being built to repel invaders and their offices and homes were being bombed, civil servants were told to collaborate with economists like John Maynard Keynes and William Beveridge to plan for a better life for all and to ensure that this finally would be the war to end all wars.

The Beveridge Report, published in the UK in November 1942, at the height of the war, provided the foundations for the welfare state, setting out to overcome the 'five giants' of 'want, disease, ignorance, squalor and idleness'. It successfully argued that a 'revolutionary moment in the world's history is a time for revolutions, not for patching.' Churchill was lionised for his victorious leadership during the war, but, within twelve weeks of it ending, his unwillingness to support this radical post-war reform agenda saw him defeated by the Labour Party under 'Citizen' Clement Attlee in the 1945 election. The result was the creation of a cradle-to-grave welfare state, with free health and education offered to all, funded by redistributive taxes and expansionary economic policies that aimed to generate full employment.

Similar expansionary policies, inspired by the writing of Keynes, were adopted in the US, with the Employment Act of 1946 seeking to bolster demand and create full employment. In France, *dirigiste* policies under General de Gaulle's state-led growth heralded the beginning of the *trente glorieuses* thirty-year boom. The European Recovery Program of US aid to Europe, known as the Marshall Plan, provided over $15 billion to finance the rebuilding of European infrastructure and industries, and the newly created International Bank for Reconstruction and Development (later to become known as the World Bank) provided grants and very low-interest loans to France and also to Germany and Japan. In 1948 the General Agreement on Tariffs and Trade (GATT) came into force to prevent a return of protectionism and to bolster trade. State-led investments in social welfare, infrastructure and industry, funded by concessionary debt and higher taxes, together with the establishment of a benign global trading environment and a new world order committed to peace and stability, created the springboard for what has become known as the Golden Age of Capitalism that followed the war.

In June 1944, with the war still raging, President Roosevelt welcomed Keynes, the leader of the British delegation, and representatives from all forty-four Allied nations to the Mount Washington Hotel in Bretton Woods in New Hampshire, with these words: 'Economic diseases are highly communicable. It follows, therefore, that the economic health of every country is a proper matter of concern to all its neighbours, near and distant . . . The things we need to do, must be done – can only be done – in concert . . . I know that you all approach your task with a high sense of responsibility to those who have sacrificed so much in their hopes for a better world.'[1]

Roosevelt recognised that radical reform of national policies and of the international system was necessary and that it can only be achieved by countries working together. Do we?

Seventy-five years later, we are again at a critical moment in world history. The pandemic has presented humanity with a chance to turn the tide that shapes our lives and the course of history. It forces us to make decisions on our individual and collective destiny. The choice is ours.

PART ONE

INEQUALITY: OVERCOMING GROWING DIVIDES

CHAPTER I

Reducing Inequality

Historian Walter Scheidel argues in *The Great Leveler* that pandemics are among the four great horsemen that, through history, have led to greater equality, the others being war, revolution and state failure.[1] Economist Thomas Piketty in *Capital in the Twenty-First Century* similarly points out that the world wars and the Spanish Flu epidemic in 1918 and 1919 contributed to the decline in inequality after 1945.[2] But while mass death by reducing the workforce can drive up workers' wages, pandemics are neither a necessary nor a sufficient basis for reducing inequality. Far from being a 'great equaliser' the coronavirus pandemic has revealed and compounded pre-existing inequalities in wealth, race, gender, age, education and geographical location.

The Covid-19 pandemic of 2020 does not compare to the Black Death which killed one third of Europe's population or the Spanish Flu, which killed around one-third of the world's population. The consequence of the Covid-19 pandemic is rising unemployment, not a shortage of available labour as was the case with these earlier crises. Meanwhile, unlike the Great Depression and previous periods of crisis, during the Covid-19 pandemic stock markets and the assets of the wealthy soared in value, widening the gap between rich and poor. To assume that the pandemic would inevitably lead to reductions in inequality and usher in a better world would be irresponsible. The First World War was certainly no great leveller; far from it leading to better conditions, inequality in many countries peaked in the early 1920s, and by the 1930s with the onset of the Great Depression there was widespread unemployment and destitution in the US, UK and Europe. The contrast with the progress that followed the Second World War reveals that we cannot tell in advance what these cataclysmic crises will bring. It is human actions and leaders that shape societies, not simply events. In this chapter I identify some of the ways in which individuals, businesses and governments could precipitate change to reduce inequality.

Inequality was rising in both Europe and the US before Covid-19 struck and the pandemic has only accelerated this trend. After being relatively stable in the decades following the Second World War, the labour share of total income has been falling in the US, Europe and UK since the 1980s. This is mainly due to the tide of liberalisation that was ushered in when Margaret Thatcher in Britain and Ronald Reagan in the US initiated a race to the bottom in taxation, attacks on trade unions, and a weakening of competition policy, which all allowed for the growing concentration and strength of employers. Now in the twenty-first century, among high-income countries the US is by far the most unequal, followed by the UK. It is in these countries that the neoliberal crusade has advanced the furthest.[3]

Lower levels of inequality in northern European countries and in East Asia since the 1970s are due to both higher levels of welfare payments for those in need and higher public investment in education, health and housing, which are financed by higher levels of taxes on the wealthy. Both require considerable budgetary resources, and since the financial crisis of 2008, with rising unemployment and a deterioration of already weak public finances, southern European countries have been less able to afford the largesse that in Germany accounts for over 20 per cent of government spending. Workers in Italy, Spain and eastern European countries such as Poland and Hungary have not seen anything like the levels of support enjoyed by their northern neighbours. The result has been a rapid increase in inequality in the southern countries and growing divides between southern, eastern and northern Europe.

The pandemic increased both economic and health inequalities due to a range of intersecting factors, which compounded each other. The wealthy were not only able to keep their well-paid jobs, but also benefited from soaring stock markets and rising house prices.[4] Low-paid workers were, however, more likely to have jobs in the sectors that suspended activities, including hospitality and tourism. They were also more likely to work in essential services such as nursing, policing, teaching, cleaning, waste removal, and as shop assistants, in all of which they had a higher likelihood of being exposed to Covid-19. The risk of contagion was further elevated by their living in more crowded homes, living in apartment buildings with communal lifts and entrances, and on their being more reliant on public transport. As Covid-19 peaked in their neighbourhoods, they were more likely to be locked down, which further undermined incomes. Weaker health facilities in their neighbourhoods meant mortality rates were higher, with a higher incidence of pre-existing health problems also increasing their vulnerability.

A higher share of poor workers are in precarious hourly-paid employment, making them less able to access social security, health insurance and emergency benefits that could cushion the decline in income and impact of Covid-19 on their lives. In Italy, more than one in six people work in the informal sector and so could not rely on their companies for sick pay or other support, and in India up to half of the workforce is considered to be informal, with no contractual rights.

Undocumented immigrants who do not have official residence rights are even more vulnerable, as in many countries they are unable to access medical or welfare benefits. They also have among the lowest levels of savings and can seldom afford to be out of work for longer than a week without suffering from shortages of food and other essentials.[5]

The rise of gig workers, who are classified as self-employed by many technology platform companies, has meant that a growing share of the workforce is not able to fall back on corporate employment protection. Employers also invest less in their skills and training, and they are less likely to be represented by trade unions.

The pandemic has come on top of a decade of austerity and stagnating wages, deepening the hardship endured by growing numbers of people. A survey of thirty-seven countries showed that the pandemic caused three-quarters of households to experience a loss in income, with 82 per cent of poorer households negatively affected.[6] Across Europe, poverty increased by 10 per cent.[7] In the US, more than two million additional households reported that they did not have enough to eat as a result of the pandemic.[8] In the UK, by Spring 2021 a staggering one-third of the population – 22.5 million people – are expected to fall below the minimum socially acceptable standard of living.[9]

The more deprived the area, the higher the mortality rate, for all causes of death. In the UK, US and Brazil, the extent of pre-existing inequality led these countries to record some of the highest death rates from Covid-19 in the world, with the underlying inequalities in health and the social conditions that lead to ill health having being revealed and amplified by the pandemic.[10]

BAME Inequality

The pandemic revealed and exacerbated the health and income inequalities experienced by black, Asian and minority ethnic (BAME) individuals. Even before the pandemic the life expectancy of black men in the US was four and a half years less than that of white men.[11] A 40-year-old Hispanic person in the US is twelve times more likely to have died from Covid-19 than a similar-aged white person, while an African American of an equivalent age is nine times as likely to have died.[12] These differences are largely attributable to social and economic inequalities, including crowded housing, reliance on public transport, poor diet and healthcare, and greater exposure to the disease through work, as minority groups are disproportionately represented in jobs that were most exposed to the virus, such as in hospitals, care homes, shops and public transport.

In the UK, 21 per cent of all healthcare workers are classified as being BAME, yet 63 per cent of all healthcare workers who died were BAME. Twenty per cent of nursing staff identify as BAME, but 64 per cent of the nurses who died, and an astounding 95 per cent of the doctors who died in the first months of the pandemic, were black or minority ethnic.[13] The disproportionate impact on BAME medical staff was also reflected in the general population. In England, Black African men were four times as likely to die of Covid-19 and men of ethnic Bangladeshi origin were around three times more likely to die than white English men.[14]

Health inequalities reflect inequalities in other dimensions, including with respect to wealth. Whereas the median white British household has assets worth £282,000, for Black Caribbean origin households in Britain it is less than a third of this (£89,000), for Black African barely 8 per cent (£24,000) and Bangladeshi 7 per cent (£22,000).[15]

During the financial crisis that began in 2008, in the US 60 per cent of businesses run by black people closed and never reopened, and the pandemic is expected to have had a worse effect.[16] In just the first month of the Covid-19 pandemic, 22 per cent of small businesses in the US had gone under.[17] While barely 17 per cent of white-owned businesses went bankrupt, 41 per cent of black-owned businesses and a third of Hispanic-owned businesses failed.[18] The reasons black-owned businesses were more than twice as likely to collapse included that they tended to be concentrated in the pandemic hotspots and in poorer neighbourhoods. They had more fragile underlying finances, fewer reserves, and much weaker contacts with banks and the financial institutions that were given responsibility by the government to administer its emergency grants. Only seven per cent of the companies in the Bronx received grants, with the number of companies in richer counties of New York receiving grants was almost double that.[19]

Gender Inequality

Despite significant advances in the rights of women and girls, gender discrimination has yet to be eliminated in any country. Women everywhere still get lower pay for the same job and are under-represented in powerful positions. The extent of their unequal treatment varies. In most poorer countries, women's opportunities for gainful employment are limited to subsistence farming, and they are often excluded from land ownership. Even in the wealthiest countries, including several oil-rich states, women are confined to home-based production or are forced to work in the informal economy where their incomes are low and working conditions are dismal. Women typically endure the triple burden of paid employment, unpaid domestic work, including cooking and cleaning the home, and reproduction and childcare.[20]

The World Economic Forum 2020 gender index ranks 153 countries on the basis of various dimensions of gender inequality. The best performers are Iceland, Norway, Finland and Sweden, followed by Nicaragua, New Zealand, Ireland, Spain and Rwanda, but even in these top performers gender inequality is predicted by the WEF to persist for the next fifty years, whereas in the worst countries it is predicted to persist for well over a hundred years. In virtually every country for which meaningful data exists, women earn about a quarter less than men for the same job.[21] In the 1960s, women earned about 60 per cent of what men earned; by 2000 this had improved to around 75 per cent.[22] Since then the pay gap in some nations, including wealthy ones such as Italy, has widened again.[23]

According to the United Nations, the pandemic set back our painfully slow progress on gender equality by twenty-five years.[24] In the US, women were twice as likely to lose their jobs, even though they make up less than half of the workforce, and in December 2020 women accounted for all of the 156,000 net jobs lost in the US, while men gained 16,000 jobs.[25] Women in the UK were about one-third more likely to be in a sector that shut down.[26] Their greater loss reflects the fact that women are more likely to work in services such as catering and hospitality, which for large parts of 2020 were closed down due to local and national lockdown legislation.

In previous recessions, men have suffered from more job losses, due to the sensitivity to economic downturns of sectors such as construction and manufacturing. This crisis was different, though, as it hit customer-facing jobs hardest, such as those in shops, restaurants and airlines. The concentration of women in these worst-affected sectors does not entirely explain the job and income loss that women have endured. Discrimination has played its part, as has the pressure on mothers to leave their jobs to take care of children when schools closed and childcare was unavailable.[27]

Evidence from Italy, where the pandemic hit early and hard, highlights the extent to which women have suffered disproportionately. One-third of Italian women stopped working during the lockdowns, and 80 per cent of these women ended up doing on average over an hour more housework a day than their male partners, whereas less than a quarter of the men in equivalent lockdown situations did extra work.[28] With the Italian economy unlikely to recover until 2025, at the earliest, it is likely that the already high levels of gender inequality in Italy will be further increased.[29] Already before the pandemic, Italy ranked 76th out of 153 countries on gender equity.[30] In Italy, as elsewhere, the pandemic has increased gender inequality.

That said, a possible silver lining of the pandemic could be the introduction of more flexible attitudes to work and a reduction in pressure for 'presenteeism'. These changes may be beneficial for those who need to spend more time at home and could lead to a narrowing of gender inequality and higher levels of female participation in the workforce in certain circumstances. Indeed, studies undertaken in Sweden during the pandemic indicated that remote working and more flexible working practices contributed to a narrowing of the gender earnings gap.[31] Remote working may lead to mothers being able to reduce the earnings gap by working more from home, even though this is likely to be at the cost of adding further multitasking pressures.

These findings are, on the whole, atypical. Instead, far from giving women greater opportunities, the pandemic severely discriminated against women. In the UK, it was estimated that over two-thirds of the extra forty hours a week of caring and childcare that resulted from lockdown were done by mothers.[32] And mothers working at home are 50 per cent more likely to be interrupted than men.[33] Even when they could continue working, mothers were twice as likely to stop work as fathers due to the additional pressures the pandemic caused on child and dependent care.[34] In all countries, the needs of children and dependants added additional demands during the pandemic, with these particularly falling on women.

Two in five mothers with children under ten struggled to find the childcare they required, with this becoming even more difficult during periods in which preschool and aftercare facilities were closed. One in six working mothers in the UK – mostly in low-paid jobs – had to reduce the hours they worked.[35] And in the US, up to four times as many women left the workforce as men.[36]

A possible future 'blended working' environment in which people come into the office a few days a week for meetings could result in a two-tier system where women without sufficient childcare are left out of decision-making.[37] Strong action will need to be taken to guard against the advent of hybrid offices further increasing inequality as 'white middle-aged males' who dominate decision-making in the office return, while women and ethnic minorities find it harder to come back.[38]

The reversal in progress made in the participation of women

in the workforce will be exacerbated further by the bias towards the hiring of men in the industries that benefited from the pandemic. In the EU, the US, the UK, Japan and Australia close to a million jobs were created in computer programming and related services.[39] Men are five times more likely to be recruited to jobs in this relatively well-paid sector than women, while sectors that favour the employment of women, such as care homes and healthcare, tend to offer low-paid jobs that often demand irregular hours and cannot be done remotely.[40]

The pandemic led to a major reversal in progress to overcome gender, race and other discrimination. Overcoming this requires that it be central to any rescue package, and that radical reforms of existing policies and practices be adopted. These include the targeting of measures to overcome the impact of the pandemic on the hardest-hit communities and overcoming the biases that have directed bank and government lending to those who already have the connections. Overcoming gender discrimination requires that the jobs that are predominantly occupied by women are better paid and that much greater effort is made to ensure that women who work more flexible hours are not discriminated against.

The Poor Get Poorer

The claim of politicians that 'we are all in this together' has consistently been contradicted by the growing sense of unfairness at the more severe impact of the pandemic on poorer people and their neighbourhoods. The pandemic has resulted in greater geographical inequality, as people in poor places are more vulnerable to both the health and economic impact.

Within rich countries, poor neighbourhoods are considerably more vulnerable. In New Orleans, the same low-lying streets that were devastated by the flooding from Hurricane Katrina in 2005 suffered, during Covid-19, from mortality rates two to three times higher than elsewhere in the city. This is due to higher-density living and a greater dependence on service economy jobs, as well as the continued use of public transport, which exposed these residents more readily to Covid-19 than their wealthier neighbours. People living in this area also suffer from higher levels of diabetes and other chronic diseases, which increased their vulnerability to the virus, but have less access to healthcare, and mental health support is almost non-existent.[41]

In the UK, the death rate from Covid-19 in the poorest areas of the country was more than double that in wealthy areas.[42] In areas of the old industrial north-west and Yorkshire one in three jobs were lost or are at risk.[43] Even in affluent areas, one in five jobs were vulnerable, reflecting the toll that the pandemic had on the entire economy.

Clearly, the pandemic exacerbated existing divides. Child poverty rose fastest in deprived northern towns; in these towns more than 45 per cent of children were in poverty even before the pandemic.[44] Prior to the pandemic, in the poorest parts of London over half of the children were estimated to be suffering from poverty, and although this has not increased as rapidly as in the northern cities, the longer-term prospects for all these places have become even bleaker, with a growing number of people living off welfare and food banks and with few new jobs being created locally.[45]

As many poor areas experienced higher rates of coronavirus infection, they suffered from particularly stringent lockdowns that further reduced the ability to earn incomes, with unemployment in many parts of the north of England rising to the highest levels in over thirty years.[46] The already prevalent sense of injustice regarding their relative deprivation and neglect by authorities has been heightened by the deepening of the economic malaise. Lockdowns interrupted a vital saving grace of these places, which is the sense of community and shared burden. When pubs and social venues closed, the feeling in many communities grew that they live in 'the land that time forgot'.[47]

Cramped homes lead to a higher risk of the spread of the

virus as well as a less viable homeworking environment.[48] All over the world, poorer people do not have separate rooms at home for work.[49]

Migrant workers everywhere are particularly vulnerable; they were among the first to lose their jobs. They often live in crowded dormitories, increasing their exposure to Covid-19. Many were stranded, without incomes or accommodation and unable to get home due to the cessation of flights and closure of borders, placing them in particularly precarious health, economic and legal situations. In Singapore, for example, more than 300,000 foreign workers are housed in dormitories, and 94 per cent of the cases of Covid-19 in Singapore were recorded in this community.[50]

Billionaires

The pandemic has been a boon for the ultra-rich, with the fortunes of the world's 2,189 billionaires increasing by a third during 2020 to more than $10.2 trillion, which exceeds the combined economies of Africa, Latin America and South Asia.[51] In the US, while more than 44 million people lost their jobs and unemployment surged towards 15 per cent, the fortunes of 29 billionaires doubled, with the biggest gains going to those with high stakes in the technology companies that have benefited from the pandemic.[52] Jeff Bezos, the founder of Amazon, saw his wealth almost double, making him the first person in history to be worth more than $200 billion, while the wealth of Elon Musk, the founder of Tesla, increased by more than $160 billion during the pandemic, to $184 billion.[53] In China alone 257 people became billionaires in 2020.[54] Mukesh Ambani's ownership of India's Reliance Industries, which has businesses across a wide range of industries including telecommunications and digital services, saw his wealth increase by a third to $75 billion, while the majority of Indians got decidedly poorer.[55] Globally, the 20 richest billionaires now have more wealth than four billion people, over half the world's population.[56]

As if their wealth bonanza of over $1 trillion dollars was not enough, millionaires and billionaires in the US were major beneficiaries of President Trump's $2 trillion Coronavirus Aid, Relief, and Economic Security Act.[57] This is because a significant part of the package was tax relief, which allowed many of the wealthiest US citizens to avoid paying nearly $82 billion in taxes in 2020.[58] The tax changes particularly benefited property developers and hedge-fund executives.

The lucky few who have big stakes in technology, pharmaceutical, home leisure or other businesses that benefited from the pandemic saw their wealth soar. But it is not that billionaires were suffering before the crisis. Between 1980 and 2020 billionaires in the US saw their wealth increase by a staggering 1,130 per cent, which is over 200 times faster than median wages increased.[59] At the same time, measured as a percentage of their wealth, the tax obligations of billionaires in the US declined by 78 per cent between 1980 and 2018.[60] The wealthiest 1 per cent in the US now own on average $14 million in wealth, and are worth three times more than the entire bottom half of the entire population of the US.[61] Wealth is even more concentrated in the booming stock market than it is in other asset classes – the richest 1 per cent own more than $14 trillion, which is 88 times more than the bottom half of the population own in stocks.[62]

The rising accumulation of wealth in the hands of a very small minority is increasing the pressure to tax the rich and their heirs. Among high-income countries, the US has the highest level of wealth inequality, the second highest level of income inequality, and one of the lowest levels of intergenerational mobility, so an individual's future is largely determined by their parents' income. In 2020 alone, children inherited around $764 billion and paid an average of just 2 per cent tax on this income. By contrast, for working people, the average tax rate is 16 per cent, eight times more.[63] These disparities are further skewed by race, with the racial wealth gap even larger than it was in 1968, at the peak of the struggle for civil rights.[64]

Addressing this needs to begin with overcoming the gross inequities and exemptions from tax. Among the urgent actions required are a closure of tax havens and loopholes, the introduction of wealth taxes on the assets of the top 1 per cent, higher inheritance taxes on the transfer of wealth of the top 1 per cent, and progressive income taxes that exempt the lowest earners and then rise steeply for the highest earners.

In most countries, if the wealthiest 10 per cent paid an annual wealth tax of only 1 per cent of their wealth, it would contribute more tax than the poorest half of taxpayers currently pay.[65] This may sound unrealistic, but the Wealth Tax Commission in the UK, in December 2020, after consulting with over fifty global tax experts recommended a one-off wealth tax on millionaire couples of 1 per cent per year for five years, which it calculated would raise £260 billion to help offset the impact of the Covid-19 crisis.[66] The Commission concluded that wealth should be calculated on the basis of all assets, including homes, and that this tax would be fair, efficient and difficult to avoid.[67] In the US, a wealth tax of just 3.5 per cent would raise as much money as all currently existing taxes in the US put together.[68] Together with the closure of the loopholes that allow companies to avoid their tax responsibilities, taxes on top earners could yield much greater revenue, allowing governments to increase spending in health, education and other areas in urgent need including spending on reducing carbon emissions, thereby creating a much more equitable, sustainable and inclusive society.

Rescue from Growing Inequality

In 2015, Christine Lagarde, then head of the International Monetary Fund (IMF), remarked that 'reducing excessive inequality is not just morally or politically correct but is good economics.'[69][70] The underlying reasons are straightforward: if only a few people gain and distort the rules in their favour through lobbying, corruption and avoiding paying their fair

share of taxes, economic potential suffers and social cohesion
dissolves.[71] Rising inequality is widely associated with rising anger
among the working class and marginalised members of society
at the urban elites and authorities.[72]

The rise of populism and nationalism is one of the most
obvious reminders of how inequality frays the fabric of our societies.[73] Simmering inequality is strongly connected to the Brexit
vote in the UK, the election of Donald Trump in the US and
the rise of populist and nationalist parties across Europe.[74] Rising
inequality also helps explain the elections of Presidents Zuma
(President of South Africa from 2009 to 2018) and Bolsonaro
(voted in as President of Brazil in October 2018). The tragedy is
that the policies implemented by these populist leaders benefit
the few not the many, thereby deepening and entrenching
inequality.

To overcome inequality, we need to decide which inequalities
matter and why. Everyone is unique and we all have different
abilities to do certain things. Some of us may be good at sport
or theatre and others at maths or music. Beyond these latent
abilities, most of our life chances are shaped by where we are
born, our parents' incomes and education, our schooling and
other factors that are far beyond our control. Reducing inequality
of opportunity by, for example, ensuring poorer young people
from deprived neighbourhoods have access to decent schools,
and focusing on giving everyone an equal chance to succeed, is
vital to overcoming inequality. To overcome inequality, it is also
important to focus on outcomes, as deeply entrenched discrimination by race, gender, religion and in other ways means that
even if individuals have the same opportunities, they may still
find they are unable to succeed in the way that more privileged
individuals would and may suffer very different outcomes.

Ensuring that everyone has an equal starting point is not
enough.[75] As Tony Atkinson, the pioneering professor of
inequality studies, wrote, the race of life is unfair. Some people
are running with one hand tied behind their back and may trip

over obstacles placed in their path, while others are sprinting ahead unencumbered. Where winners take all and the losers get nothing, inequality is entrenched.[76] As differences in wealth begin to widen, the opportunities for the next generation become increasingly constrained because children of successful parents have better preparation, training and nutrition. This reinforces and perpetuates a cycle of inequality.

Education is a powerful tool for overcoming inequality. Levels of schooling differ vastly between countries and within them. Children of richer parents are five times more likely to receive pre-primary education than the children of poor parents.[77] Inequality in primary education is carried through to later years. In the UK, 80 per cent of Cambridge and Oxford University students are from the top two social classes.[78] The inequalities of opportunity are even greater. Despite fewer than 1 per cent of the adult population of the UK being graduates of Oxford or Cambridge, they have produced more than half of its prime ministers, senior judges and high-ranking civil servants.[79]

Creating a level playing field for opportunities is not only fairer, on equity grounds, but also essential if the talents of every individual are to be given the chance to flourish. This benefits not only specific people, but also entire societies. The risks are painfully evident in the increased social and political polarisation that characterises fractured societies. Several studies underline the link between widening inequality and a growing range of social and economic challenges, including stagnating economic growth, increased crime, ill health and depression.[80] Rising inequality is also strongly associated with increasing popularity for populist politicians and economic protectionism, as I discuss elsewhere in this book.[81]

For the Nobel Prize Winner Amartya Sen, inequality is above all about inequality of opportunities available to people to lead fulfilling lives, with education, gender and human rights being central. In his book *Development as Freedom*, Sen underlines why inequalities need to be overcome so that everyone can lead fulfilling lives that are both personally satisfying and also support the common good. Sen's writings led to the creation of the influential idea of 'human development', which goes beyond narrow measures of income and economic growth to striving for human flourishing in all its dimensions.[82] The implementation of these ideas has spawned a growing range of policy interventions that seek to address the different dimensions. These range from legal frameworks that promote human rights and equity to those focused on sustainability and access to food and health, education and other services.

Taxes and Benefits Reduce Inequality

The response of many rich people is to say that they give to charity. Although there are many examples of effective philanthropy, these are a complement to but not a substitute for wealthy individuals paying their fair share of tax. Waving a benevolent wand for the lucky recipients who are favoured by the donor cannot substitute for the collective decisions and capabilities of governments to allocate resources to those most in need. Charity can also develop dependency on the largesse of donors. When their priorities change, or they stop giving, the recipients are left bereft.

Governments have a central role to play in overcoming inequality. Inequality reduction is about much more than raising income and increasing economic growth, though this is key. Ensuring equal access to education, health, energy, internet and other services, as well as guaranteeing minimum standards, is equally critical.

In the Golden Age of Capitalism following the Second World War, the US and UK had among the world's highest tax rates for top earners, of around 90 per cent. If the US distribution of income today was the same as it was in the thirty years following the Second World War the bottom 90 per cent of the US population would be $47 trillion richer today than they are.[83] But since the 1970s the US and UK have lowered taxes and as their revenues

have declined so too have expenditures on welfare, public education and investments targeted at reducing inequality. As
government revenues and the potential for redistribution have
fallen, inequality has soared. The growing contrast between
English speaking countries like the UK and US in comparison
to continental Europe, which has maintained its commitment
to redistribution, is evident in the share of taxed national income
that is spent on health, education and social welfare. In Europe
it is 10 to 20 per cent higher than in the UK and US and, as a
result, inequality has not risen significantly over the thirty years
prior to the pandemic.

Taxes that fund redistributive spending, in the form of health
and education, as well as social security, housing, child, disability
and other benefits, can all significantly help overcome inequality.
Before taking account of taxes and government spending,
inequality is almost as high in France as in the US and UK, and
even higher in Ireland, which without redistribution would be
the most unequal of the thirty-four richest countries.[84] However,
in Ireland and France taxation and redistribution have reduced
inequality to levels that are well below that in the UK. Meanwhile,
the failure of successive governments in the US to use taxation
and spending to overcome inequality means that it is the most
persistently unequal of all the rich countries.[85]

Overcoming inequality requires higher wealth and inheritance
taxes for the upper-income families that have seen their wealth
rise dramatically in recent decades. If the billionaires whose
wealth increased by a quarter during the pandemic paid a
5 per cent wealth tax amounting to around $125 billion, they
would still be far better off than before the pandemic. Similarly,
if Jeff Bezos gave all 876,000 of his Amazon employees a $105,000
bonus, he would still be richer than he was at the start of the
pandemic.[86]

Even in poorer countries government policies can make an
enormous difference. Concerted efforts on the part of past
Brazilian governments succeeded in partially reducing their

disparity between the rich and poor, even if levels have crept back up in recent years. The Bolsa Família programme provided parents with a monthly cash payment (of around $35) in exchange for sending their children to school and attending regular health check-ups.[87] The cash given to mothers was typically used to buy food, school supplies and clothes. This pioneering 'conditional cash transfer' initiative reached more than 50 million low-income Brazilians at its peak, a quarter of the national population, and is credited with reducing extreme poverty by half.[88]

An estimated 94 per cent of the funds from the Bolsa Família programme reached the poorest 40 per cent of the population and contributed to a marked reduction in inequality.[89] Originally trialled in Brazil in 1996, in Mexico (under the name Progresa) in 1997, and in Chile in 2002, the success of these and similar variants of the conditional cash transfer model have been adopted by more than twenty countries, including Indonesia, South Africa, Turkey and Morocco.[90] The concept has even been applied in New York with Opportunity NYC.

Even so, good policies require good government and staying power. In Brazil, changes in government, austerity measures and the dramatic reversal of social policies have severely undermined inequality reduction efforts. Effective policies also benefit from a dose of good luck such as the commodity boom that propelled Brazil's economy during the 2000s. More recently, however, the combination of policy failure and a sluggish economy have resulted in over four million people falling back below the poverty line and inequality rising again to among the worst in the world.[91] South Africa, the country of my birth, has the unenviable distinction of being the most unequal society on the planet.[92]

The good news is that the achievements of Brazil and other countries like France, Denmark, Bolivia, Thailand, Cambodia and South Korea show that inequalities can be overcome.[93] Reducing inequality cannot be achieved through empty slogans. The so-called American Dream promises that if people work hard enough, they can succeed no matter how poor they are. This is pure fantasy. One's parents' wealth is a far better predictor of future success than intelligence, education or one's willingness to slog away at work.[94] While we all celebrate the extraordinary stories of those who beat the odds, these are truly exceptional experiences. To overcome inequality, we need to overcome the root causes, not rely on the poor and vulnerable beating the absurdly adverse odds stacked up against them.

Crises increase inequality. This was evident in the financial crisis in 2008, is evident in the starvation and suffering caused by the climate crisis around the world, and was evident in the pandemic when millions of people who had never experienced it before were forced to depend on inadequate welfare systems. Inequality is not a remote or abstract threat. It threatens us all and is dangerous. It must be reduced if we are to prioritise the well-being of people and our planet. To rescue societies from growing inequality will require significant increases in taxes and redistribution, greater investment in public health, education, housing, welfare and transport systems, regulations and incentives that encourage businesses to create decent jobs, and a deep commitment enshrined in law to overcome gender, race, ethnic, religious, age and other discrimination. While no country has achieved all these goals, we can learn from the remarkable progress that has been made to address seemingly intractable discrimination and inequality. The legalisation of same-sex marriage in over forty-two countries, the establishment of a minimum income in France, advances to overcome institutionalised race discrimination in South Africa, and the massive advances in many Scandinavian economies to reduce inequality are testimony to the ability of societies to change. In this as in other areas, actions speak louder than words.

The pandemic, by exacerbating and further revealing the extent of inequality and discrimination, has made the case for addressing these injustices more compelling than ever. In response to the pandemic, governments and businesses have acted in ways that would not have been considered possible in January 2020. The challenge now is to build on these initiatives to reduce discrimination and inequality everywhere.

CHAPTER 2

Solidarity of Young and Old

For young people, everything changed during the pandemic. Generational divides were overturned as social solidarity triumphed over economics. For young people under the age of thirty the chances of dying from Covid-19 were less than the likelihood of their dying in a car accident, and for school-age children lower than being struck by lightning. Yet, they willingly put their education, social lives and job prospects on hold, and inherited massive debts, to follow rules that were designed primarily to protect the elderly and vulnerable.[1] In the US, UK and Europe, the average age of Covid-19 fatalities was around eighty-two, which is also about the average life expectancy.

Young people's prospects have been blighted by their unstinting sacrifice for the elderly. As after the world wars, we owe them a better future. Our societies have done what they can to rescue the elderly. Now we also need to rescue the young people.

Prospects for Youth

Young people aged eighteen to twenty-nine experienced the brunt of the hit to jobs and pay caused by the pandemic. One-sixth of young people in the world lost their jobs in the second quarter of 2020.[2] Young self-employed and gig workers were some of the worst affected, with youth unemployment three times the level of that in the rest of the workforce.[3] Being the least likely to have health and unemployment insurance, they are particularly vulnerable.[4] Even those who have retained their jobs have suffered, experiencing significantly bigger pay cuts than the rest of the population.[5]

In the UK, people aged between sixteen and twenty-six were more than twice as likely than older workers to have lost their jobs during the pandemic, and accounted for 60 per cent of all job losses, with youth unemployment at the end of 2020 approaching 20 per cent.[6] Of the younger people who managed to hold on to their jobs, six out of ten saw their earnings fall.[7]

One of the challenges of the coronavirus pandemic was that there were no easy targets to blame that might have created new bonds of common rebellion within younger generations. Young people were unable to wave protest placards against the virus, like those in support of 'Black Lives Matter' in the summer of 2020. They were forced to be largely passive, often in their parents' houses, waiting for the Covid-19 nightmare to pass, and knowing that what faced them next was the biggest economic hangover ever. As during the financial crisis of 2008, when job offers to new entrants stalled and those most recently recruited were the first to lose their jobs, it has been young people coming onto the job market who have been particularly badly affected by the pandemic.

Young people are stepping from the pandemic into a world that is radically uncertain. Full of promise, but also doubt.[8] While this was already the case before Covid-19, the pandemic has compounded the uncertainties and added to the competitive pressures by disrupting jobs. The emotional impact for many is at least as significant as the economic struggle, and these two can reinforce each other, as economic uncertainty adds to anxiety and makes it difficult to work effectively. Those who lose their jobs lose not only their income, but also their identity, routine and vital parts of their social networks.[9] This particularly impacts on young people, who have yet to establish the confidence and develop the experience, skills, structured work habits, savings and relationships that arise from work.

For many in their late twenties and early thirties, this is the second major crisis of their working lives. Covid-19 has struck barely ten years after the devastating impact of the 2008 financial crisis, when the banking system crashed and global economic activity collapsed. The subsequent Euro crisis, which followed from the financial crisis originating in the US, had an even more devastating impact, with over half of young Spanish jobseekers and 40 per cent of young people in Italy unable to find work.[10] Youth unemployment in southern Europe during the pandemic returned to the levels experienced in the depths of the financial crisis, and in Britain it tripled to 15 per cent, far exceeding the 'one in ten' levels that became the title of a legendary UB40 song released at the height of the austerity-induced British recession of the early 1980s.[11]

Young people were particularly disadvantaged by the number of job vacancies globally collapsing by over two-thirds.[12] In the US in 2020 3.9 million graduates planned on entering the job market, and to start repaying the average $32,000 of debt that they had accumulated after four years of study.[13] Yet the doors to their future careers have been closed. Indeed, over a third of job offers previously made to students in the US and UK were cancelled during the pandemic and, whereas prior to the pandemic an average of 60 per cent of students had secured jobs before graduation, only 18 per cent of the 2020 class found jobs before graduating.[14] The result was that almost half of young people surveyed in the UK said that they were lowering their life expectations; more than half of those from poorer backgrounds said their future goals were 'impossible' to achieve.[15] Even in China, where neither the recession nor the job market has been as severely affected by the pandemic, job vacancies for college graduates dropped by a quarter in 2020 compared to the previous year, despite the extended hiring season and the establishment of online recruitment fairs.[16] For those of the class of 2020 lucky enough to get work, average pay is around 10 per cent below pre-pandemic levels.[17]

One of those who felt fortunate to find a job was Mariel

Sander, who graduated from Columbia University, New York, without enjoying the celebratory rites of passage, as the pandemic reached its peak in May 2020.[18] The only job she could find was as a temporary morgue worker, helping carry dead bodies off hospital beds into refrigerated trailers.

In London in April, Tommy, aged twenty-five, having qualified with a degree in Economics and Management, was made redundant from a job in events. He considered himself fortunate after six months to have found another job, only to have lost it during the second lock-down. None of his former colleagues or his highly qualified brother have managed to find employment. One of his school friends, who had excelled in her exams in his year, applied for over 300 jobs, was shortlisted for seven, but was not offered one.

Not surprisingly, among many young people the pandemic has led to low self-confidence and undermined aspirations, igniting growing mental health concerns.[19] Past recessions have demonstrated the lasting impact on individuals and concerted action is necessary to ensure that the crisis does not permanently scar the prospects – both economic and emotional – of young people.[20]

Prior to the pandemic, young people had already borne the brunt of the stagnation of wages over recent decades and the rise of precarious service-sector jobs, which now employ four out of every ten young workers.[21] The post-financial-crisis pay squeeze further diminished their income, with the median wage of workers under thirty now below the level it was fifteen years ago and hovering just above the minimum wage.[22] Meanwhile the number of women under the age of thirty claiming unemployment benefits in the UK doubled during the pandemic.[23]

Lower wages have reinforced, and will continue to reinforce, the massive pre-existing wealth differences between different age groups. In the US, baby boomers – those born in the two decades following the Second World War – now account for well over half of the wealth, with millennials, born between 1981 and 1996, not having seen their share of wealth increase beyond 5 per cent since the financial crisis of 2008. When baby boomers were as young as millennials are today, they owned a quarter of the world's wealth, five times more than young people today.[24]

Children of school age were severely impacted by the pandemic, too, with over 60 per cent of primary school children globally missing out on their education. School closures have led to fears that children may suffer permanent educational losses. Learning is a cumulative process and missing classes can lead to rapid regression with six-month absences potentially setting students back as much as a year in their abilities.[25] In the UK, the pandemic saw most children slipping back with their learning and even in their social skills, with this particularly evident in the first years of school, where the hardest-hit children lost basic skills such as knowing how to use a knife and fork.[26] The start-stop nature of the return to school, along with complicated new Covid-19 protocols, has also been confusing, particularly for younger children.

A study of school-age children in Germany during the pandemic found that if a student lost a third of a school year this would likely lead to an average loss of 3 per cent of their future income over their entire working life.[27] These averages, however, masked considerable variations, which reinforce existing differences. Low-achieving students mainly spent their time away from school on video games, while high achievers devoted more time to study, with these differences reinforced by socio-economic and other home differences.

As with all other age groups and globally, the pandemic widened the pre-existing gap between rich and poor in education. Children in poorer households were less likely to have computers or the space and privacy to study undisturbed. Children from richer households were more likely to have teachers who provided online classes and parents with the skills to home-school them, as well as access to nutritious meals and gardens and parks in which to exercise. In the UK, a quarter of pupils – about

2.5 million children – had no schooling or tutoring at all during lockdown; indeed, three-quarters of private school pupils had full days of teaching, while barely one-third of state pupils' teaching was uninterrupted.[28] This problem was compounded by wealth discrepancies due to race: BAME children fell furthest behind, as the gap between rich and poor pupils grew by 46 per cent in the 2019 to 2020 school year.

The increase in poverty arising from the pandemic will have an even more devastating impact on children's long-term prospects than the loss of education. Poverty not only impacts on nutrition, which is particularly vital for the development of young brains, but also on the material and social environment in which children develop. In England 1.3 million children from families earning below the poverty threshold are eligible for free school meals during the school year, the absence of which could permanently stunt physical and mental development.[29] Due to the catastrophic effects of the pandemic, an additional 900,000 more children required free school meals.[30] A further 1.5 million children have not qualified but are thought to be in need as 32 per cent of English families suffered a pandemic-induced drop in income.[31] Over the summer of 2020 footballer Marcus Rashford highlighted the importance of this by initiating a campaign to provide a lunch voucher scheme for children to receive free meals in school holidays. The strength of his campaign twice forced the government to back down, first to provide food vouchers during the first lockdown and throughout the summer holidays, and then, after a second public outcry, when the government was forced to extend both the duration and reach of the scheme through the Christmas holidays to Easter 2021.[32] Subsequently, in January 2021, Marcus Rashford again forced a change in government policy, by exposing the inadequacy of the food parcels being delivered for children.

Very few children were killed by the coronavirus directly, but in developing countries the pandemic led to a tragic 45 per cent increase in child mortality due to health-service shortfalls and malnutrition.[33] The provision of school meals, bed-nets to prevent malaria, and vaccinations against childhood diseases were cut back as budgets and scarce medical resources were reallocated to address the new needs of the pandemic. Around the world, Covid-19 resulted in a 15 per cent increase in child poverty, with 150 million more children suffering from deprivation, bringing the total to a staggering 1.2 billion.[34] Even in the US, one in six households with children reported not having enough food to eat, and among those earning below $25,000 over a third of families were not able to meet their basic needs, with many relying on charity food banks to survive.[35] Food insecurity in the US doubled because of the pandemic, with the problem becoming worse following the expiration in July 2020 of the supplementary payments that had been provided under emergency unemployment relief.[36]

More than 1.6 billion children in 192 countries were excluded from school by lockdowns, with more than half of these in developing countries and more than 462 million children having no opportunities for remote learning.[37] In poor countries the long-term impact of school closures was more severe than in rich countries because there was less opportunity to continue studies remotely without the technical resources and because there is a greater likelihood in poor communities that children will not resume their studies. Fewer than 1 per cent of children from poor households have access to the internet. In Brazil and Nigeria, for example, under half of the children from the poorest regions were able to continue their studies during the pandemic.[38]

The vast underlying inequalities in teaching and educational facilities have been compounded by the economic collapse of many poor countries, with their educational systems even less able to meet the needs of the rapidly growing school-age population. Class sizes in many African countries exceed fifty pupils and less than a third of the schools have handwashing or other facilities, which made social distancing and pandemic safety procedures to return children to school during the pandemic impossible to achieve.[39]

In many poor countries the closure of schools and loss of income by family members led to a return to child labour as desperate families sought to supplement their meagre incomes by putting millions of children to work. Even when classes resumed, more than 24 million children in 40 countries were unlikely ever to return to school.[40] Up to 2.5 million more girls around the world are at risk of being forced into child marriage over the next five years, with Covid-19 unwinding twenty-five years of progress in reducing numbers of child brides and adolescent pregnancies.[41] The irreversible setbacks and lost progress have rolled back the painstaking progress of recent decades to achieve the Sustainable Development Goal of universal education.[42] The wide-ranging individual and societal consequences include an estimate that missing half a year in education means that globally students will forgo $10 trillion in lost earnings.[43] Clearly, the pandemic has permanently scarred young people's prospects. Their loss is also a societal loss. When the younger generations are poorer, so are we all.

Debt Time Bomb and Pensions Crisis

The pandemic has led governments to take on an additional $12 trillion in debt. At some point in the future the mounting interest payments due on the expanding debt mountain need to be paid. The diminished prospects and incomes of young people due to the unprecedented education and jobs challenge they face make them ill-equipped to shoulder this additional financial burden they have been saddled with.

The ticking financial time bomb of national debt comes on top of that of the growing financial burden of elderly people on societies. The rapid ageing of European, North American and East Asian societies, all of which are seeing a sharp increase in median ages from around twenty-five to over forty in a generation, has placed a growing tax burden on the young, who have to pay for the pensions and care of their parents' generation. The pension system was already unsustainable prior to the pandemic, with declining fertility and increased life expectancy reducing the number of workers relative to dependants. By increasing unemployment, the pandemic reduced the number of contributors to pension schemes, leading to a decline in government taxes and revenues, while the number of people who depend on taxpayers has increased due to rising joblessness.

The pensions crisis has been aggravated by the collapse in interest rates. The combination of record low returns on low-risk investments and rising expenditures has created an explosive mismatch. As individuals set aside more for their retirement, they will spend less. More savings will keep downward pressure on interest rates, while less spending will reduce demand and slow the recovery. As people save more, industries and services sell less and employ fewer people. The result is a long period of what the Harvard economist Lawrence Summers has called 'secular stagnation', which is characterised by very low or negligible economic growth and stagnating average incomes.[44] The implications of this for the young are manifold: not only will their prospects be blighted, but they will also have to sacrifice a growing share of their earnings in taxes to repay rising government debt and to prevent the older generation from becoming destitute.

The mismatch between the needs of elderly people for retirement pensions and the sums available in pension funds to pay has been aggravated by the collapse of many businesses, which cuts the value of their pension funds. In the UK, the collapse of British Home Stores in April 2016 left a £571 million pensions deficit, and during the pandemic the bankruptcy of Debenhams and the Arcadia retail groups similarly left thousands of long-term employees dependent on meagre government pensions.

The age at which citizens are eligible for state pensions has been creeping up in all the high-income countries as governments have attempted to address the looming pensions crisis. In the

UK during the pandemic it was lifted to sixty-six for both men and women, having risen for women by one month for every year since 2010, and with further increases planned for the coming years.[45] Individuals entering the workforce today are likely to work well into their seventies and will need to contribute to national insurance for over forty years, compared to the current requirement of thirty-five years, to be able to claim their full pension.

In the US, the pensions system is even less generous and requires private contributions, and the accumulated savings are totally inadequate for all but the richest 1 per cent of the population to sustain a decent lifestyle. Over 60 per cent of working-age individuals in the US have no savings set aside for their retirement and those who are approaching retirement have an average of only $40,000 in assets for the rest of their lives. Assuming the average retiree lives for twenty years after retirement, this means living on less than two thousand dollars a year, which in the US is well below the breadline.

The pandemic led many people to postpone their plans for retirement, as lower returns on investments and a growing need to support their dependents places increasing pressure on household incomes. In the US, almost three-quarters of those due to retire before 2025 have been forced to rethink their plans, and in the UK a third of older workers suffered a significant deterioration in their finances and were rethinking their plans.[46]

A decade-long rise in the number of over-fifties in employment has been brought to an end by the pandemic. In the UK, over a quarter of workers over fifty-four years of age were furloughed, and as the economy collapsed and lockdowns prevented tradespeople from visiting homes, only a fifth of self-employed elder workers were able to sustain the employment they had before the pandemic.[47] As was the case during the 2008 financial crisis, many of these workers were forced into early retirement, leading to permanently lower incomes, compounding their anxieties and vulnerability to both mental and physical ill health.

The economic turmoil arising from the pandemic has had a persistent impact on older workers. Older individuals who lose their jobs are less likely to secure re-employment, and if they do it is likely to be on lower wages. Being unexpectedly out of work, or having wages reduced, undermines their future ability to sustain their livelihoods and fulfil their ambitions for retirement. The combination of job loss, involuntary retirement and financial pressures is known to have adverse effects on health and to significantly reduce life expectancy.[48]

To rescue older workers from the consequences of the pandemic, state pensionable allowances should be increased so that, together with any benefits received from private pension schemes, they are above the minimum living wage. Mentoring and voluntary schemes and activities that encourage a sense of self-worth and community among elderly people should also be encouraged, including through the provision of funds for these purposes. By supporting the elderly and reducing the burden they will place on society, governments also are supporting the young. There is widespread political support for schemes that support the elderly, but this urgently needs to be turned into practical measures that seek to redress the dire consequences of the pandemic. The acknowledgement of the sacrifice the young have made for the old also needs to be reflected in concrete actions that advance their interests.

Rescue the Young

Meeting the short-term needs of young people for education, employment and income and the long-term requirement that they live in a safer and less risky world requires a concerted effort by people of all ages. Employers should be more open to employing and creating more paid internships for individuals who may be lacking experience or whose grades may have suffered due to the hiatus in schooling. Governments should be prepared to invest additional resources in tutoring and catch-up classes as well as in youth employment schemes and tax incentives that reward companies that take on more young people. Youth organisations which provide life-saving support for young people need urgent public support.

In the UK, over two-thirds of the youth centres closed over the past decade due to chronic underfunding and of those that remain a third are not expected to survive the pandemic without urgently required public funding.[49] Government support is also required to subsidise on a temporary basis young people commuting long distances or relocating to other cities to find a job and escape from places where they are too often confronted by the choice of working with gangs or being sucked into a downward spiral of drugs and despair.

For school-age children most in need the provision of school meals and nutritional supplements throughout the year, as well as the funding of one laptop per child, is a modest investment that will be repaid through a more productive and engaged citizenry of the future. Overcoming the short-termism of governments to ensure that investments are resilient to political cycles and can focus on longer-term objectives is vital when it comes to the welfare of children, as it is in other areas.

The obsession with university degrees in the UK and to a lesser extent in the US needs to give way to a greater focus on technical education. The mass adoption of university education in recent decades and increasingly widespread requirement by employers that applicants have degrees have come at the expense of an unhealthy downgrading in the status of and interest of students and employers in vocational training. Only 10 per cent of adults in the UK have a technical certificate as their highest qualification, compared to 17 per cent in the US, 20 per cent in Germany, and a third in Canada.[50] In the UK, there are fifty times more university students than those studying for vocational qualifications, and less than a quarter of school leavers have done any technical training, whereas in Switzerland 59 per cent of sixteen- to eighteen-year-olds have technical qualifications, and 41 per cent of eighteen-year-olds in Germany have technical skills.[51] The result is a growing mismatch between the skills needed and those available, which needs to be addressed to create vibrant societies and employment opportunities.[52] In the UK, for example, even before Brexit placed further limits on recruiting immigrants, there was an acute shortage of skilled people in engineering, building, construction and related trades, as well as in paramedic and healthcare occupations requiring technical training.

The creation of meaningful employment opportunities for young people simultaneously serves to improve the prospects of the elderly as it increases tax revenues and the sustainability of pensions as well as increasing the provision of services on which elderly people depend. The creation of viable pensions systems and reducing the debt burden on young and old requires that they are not made to suffer from misguided austerity programmes that lead to a contraction in services and employment on which both the elderly and the young particularly depend.

The issues facing the young and the old cannot be separated from those facing the rest of society. All generations have a shared interest in a brighter future. But for the young, who could live well into the twenty-second century, there is the most to lose by or to gain from the irreversible decisions we are taking today. If societies commit to actions now that address joblessness, inequality and the environmental and other emergencies, the collective sacrifices of the elderly and the young will prompt reforms that will lead to a more sustainable world.

CHAPTER 3

Overcoming Global Poverty

Covid-19 caused the biggest development setback of our lifetimes, reversing seventy years of progress. Low- and middle-income countries suffered negative growth for the first time since the 1950s. Many more people died of starvation and poverty-related causes than from the direct health impact of Covid-19, with the pandemic resulting in as many as an additional 150 million people falling into extreme poverty, and acute hunger doubling from 130 million people in 2019 to 260 million in 2020.[1] In many poor countries education and health systems have collapsed. Without a massive rescue package, achieving the universally agreed Sustainable Development Goals is impossible.[2] The seventeen interlinked goals were set in 2015 to be achieved by 2030, including the elimination of extreme poverty and hunger, and achieving ambitious targets for improvements in health, education, employment and gender equity for all of humanity, as well as addressing climate change and reversing environmental degradation.

The pandemic not only destroyed jobs, but because it was global, it simultaneously disrupted the ability of working migrants to send money back to their home countries, a financial lifeline on which many poor families depend. Opportunities to do informal work, eke out a living on market stalls, or even beg to top up incomes also disappeared in this crisis due to stay-at-home orders and the collapse of the informal retail market. In poor countries government safety nets are threadbare, where they exist at all; whereas richer countries can raise debt and increase spending to mitigate the worst impact of the crisis.

Rising Poverty, Inadequate Action

Migrant workers and those on informal contracts were particularly vulnerable everywhere as they were not eligible for even the meagre support that some cities and governments put in place. About two-thirds of workers worldwide – around two billion people – are engaged in informal work that has no formal contractual basis. These jobs range from subsistence farming to street vending, to running self-employed microbusinesses. The pandemic threatened the livelihoods of over 80 per cent of these informal workers – 1.6 billion people – of whom over 90 per cent are in developing countries.[3] In developing countries, a much higher share of the population works in informal jobs than is the case in rich countries. In India, for example, it is estimated that half of urban workers are in informal jobs and went without any work or pay during the lockdowns.[4] Fewer than one in four unemployed Indian workers received any government support, so aggregate incomes were halved during the pandemic, with the poor experiencing an even greater loss.[5]

Developing countries do not have the financial resources to provide adequate welfare, and even those that previously provided emergency relief, such as Brazil and Peru, were unable to sustain the payments. In Latin America alone more than 45 million people fell back into poverty in 2020 as the regional economy contracted by over 10 per cent.[6] In China, the poorest, who tend to be those in remote rural areas and living on the margins of society, suffered more than others. The bottom 40 per cent of the Chinese population cannot last for three months without income and so rely on work and the government's meagre payments.[7] China's expenditure on social security is barely 3 per cent of GDP, which, while not out of line with other developing countries, is far lower than the average of 12 per cent in developed countries, highlighting the limitations of even relatively better-off developing countries' ability to sustain their populations.

Many people who managed to climb out of a poverty trap have found themselves back in it in 2020. Jeff, whom I met in the Philippines, is a good example. He worked for a scuba-diving company and, from carrying tanks, had worked his way up in the company to become a dive instructor. He was proud of the fact that he could send money home for his children's education. When the pandemic precipitated the end of tourism in March 2020 the scuba company closed and he has returned to his home village, where he is attempting to make a living as a fisherman, as his father did before him. His wife has also lost her job in a nearby hotel and they can no longer pay for their children's education. While they are just about managing to get by with help from me and others, he is desperately worried for other people in the village who he sees wasting away and dying of hunger.

In all developing countries, the pandemic led to a sharp contraction in revenues from tourism, exports, taxes and remittances sent home by migrants abroad. Panicked investors also transferred their savings to less risky markets, leading to a flight of capital. Before long, countries previously in good economic health became vulnerable. The poorer the country the less they have been able to support their populations, but some middle-income developing countries (including India, Brazil, Malaysia, South Africa and Thailand) that can issue debt domestically have done so, to close the gulf between their collapsing revenues and their emergency increases in health and social welfare expenditures. The widening budget deficit in these countries comes at a severe cost, as it not only depresses their currencies, making imports and foreign debt payments more expensive, but also makes it more likely that a greater share of future budgets will need to be allocated to payments of interest on the debt, and that there will be fewer resources for education, infrastructure and other much-needed investments in the future. While spending to fight the Covid-19 health and economic emergency has been necessary, the long-term health of societies has been severely compromised.

The stringency of the lockdowns in developing countries matched and, in many cases, exceeded those of the rich world, even though poorer governments were far less able to support their citizens and businesses. All countries around the world faced the torturous choice between the need to contain the health risks of the pandemic through lockdown and the devastating economic consequences of doing so, but this dilemma was much more acute in poorer countries, as the economic costs and suffering exceeded anything previously experienced.

South Africa had one of the most stringent early lockdowns. As a result 2.8 million jobs were lost, with an estimated 40 per cent of these losses permanent, reversing decades of job creation.[8] Those in the poorest quartile were ten times as likely to have lost their jobs than those in the richest quartile, with poor, female, less educated and rural workers the most at risk.[9] With only 32 per cent of working age people in rural areas finding jobs, and barely 40 per cent in towns and 49 per cent in cities, more than half the working population in this country of 60 million were made unemployed.[10] Of these, only 4.4 million people were able to access the government's Covid-19 grant of rand 350 ($20) per month, insufficient to cover even the barest food necessities.[11]

Anne works as a cleaner for households in Cape Town. Despite having worked for some families for more than twenty years, she was not paid when lockdown stopped her working. As a result her daughter, who was in her second year of a computing course, had to drop out and her grandchildren, who depend on her income, were told they could not go to school as they could no longer afford the writing materials required for attendance.

Failure of International Solidarity
The IMF, renowned for its conservatism, called for an additional $2.5 trillion to support developing countries in countering the

impact of the pandemic. And yet in 2020 they received barely $100 billion, less than 1 per cent of the $12 trillion that the rich countries made available to support their own economies. Less than half of this support went to the countries that need it most, with these countries less able to lobby for aid and the donors applying criteria that did not reflect the extent of poverty and need. High- and middle-income countries such as the Bahamas received $464 for each of its citizens and the Seychelles $389 per citizen, whereas much poorer and more populous Zambia, Kazakhstan, Cameroon and Tanzania received less than 20 cents per citizen, despite the pandemic having a far worse impact on these much poorer economies.[12]

To make matters worse, at a time of unprecedented need, aid budgets in 2020 contracted, as they are calculated as a share of the rich nations' national income. When the donor economies contract, so does aid. UK aid, for example, in 2020 was down £3 billion on the previous year.[13] The inability of governments to sustain their economies and the failure of the international community to lend support threatens the collapse of many developing countries. This is disastrous for their citizens, and inevitably also has wider regional and global repercussions, including increasing the number of refugees and raising the number of failed states which are potential sources of terrorism or new pandemics.

The reason why poor countries particularly need foreign assistance in responding to the pandemic is that, whereas rich countries can print money and increase their deficits and debts in response to crises like these, poor economies become unsustainable when they do this. Poor people do not have sufficient domestic savings to invest in government bonds and so their governments are compelled to rely on foreign lenders and have to repay their loans in foreign currency. When their currencies decline, the cost of these debt repayments rises. Whereas rich countries have been able to find on average 20 per cent of their GDP to support businesses and workers, middle-income countries on average have been able to raise only 6 per cent and poor countries just 2 per cent of their much smaller national output to stave off the consequences of the pandemic.

Their already meagre resources have been further depleted by foreign bondholders repatriating their holdings and wealthy citizens sending their cash abroad. This capital flight has meant that more money has been flowing out of developing countries than has been coming in, draining government coffers. As a result, many emerging market currencies have collapsed during the pandemic, with South Africa's rand and Brazil's real losing over a fifth of their value relative to the US dollar.[14] As foreign debt has become more expensive relative to domestic currencies, countries are less able to repay their loans. Worsening prospects have led to countries being downgraded by the credit rating agencies, creating a vicious downward spiral of rising costs of debt and countries becoming less able to escape their predicament.

The countries in the worst situation are those with limited domestic savings and large pre-existing external debts. Since 2010, external debt has risen faster in sub-Saharan Africa than in other regions, from 40 per cent of GDP to over 60 per cent in 2019, when the IMF classed eighteen countries as high-risk.[15] The countries with the greatest risk of default include Egypt, Zambia, Angola, Ethiopia and Ghana, but South Africa, Nigeria, India and Brazil are also in the high-risk zone and Turkey, Indonesia and Mexico are next in line.[16] To allow these countries some breathing space to address the urgent needs of their citizens, a lowering of their debt repayment obligations is required, as was achieved with the Heavily Indebted Poor Country Initiative.[17] The initiative was launched in 1996 by the World Bank and IMF in response to sustained pressure from campaigning groups, and provided debt relief to thirty-nine heavily indebted countries, thirty-three of which were in sub-Saharan Africa.

Whereas in the past multilateral institutions such as the World Bank, IMF and regional development banks were the primary creditors for developing countries, now African governments mainly owe money to other governments and commercial banks. The actions of these bilateral and commercial creditors will be vitally important in determining whether poor countries can free up resources to address their economic and health emergencies in the short term and restore their development prospects for the long term.[18]

China now accounts for almost two-thirds of the lending to the seventy-three poorest countries, which owe it over $744 billion.[19] African countries owe $146 billion to Chinese institutions, and well over $115 billion to other foreign private banks and bondholders.[20] Zambia, for example, has $11 billion in external debt, of which, as of 2020, $426 million was owed to China.[21] Without Chinese banks agreeing to a moratorium, other creditors are concerned that any relief offered will be used to repay China rather than to address the pressing domestic needs of the highly indebted countries. Cooperation with China is therefore vital to address the debt and development crisis, the extent of which has been exacerbated and revealed by the pandemic. To demonstrate that it has come of age as a donor that is deeply committed to development, China needs to write off, or at least reschedule on more favourable terms, the debt owed to it by highly indebted countries, as it is now too large an economy to argue that it requires the repayments of these funds for its own development purposes.

The commitment by the World Bank to lend $160 billion in emergency financing until the end of 2021 as part of its fast-track Covid-19 response for 111 countries is a good first step, as is the IMF's allocation of $100 billion for temporary budgetary relief. Yet, the only coordinated action has been the G20's Debt Service Suspension Initiative (DSSI), which has allowed seventy-three of the poorest countries to postpone repayments of debt owed until June 2021. And $30 billion still had to be repaid by struggling developing countries to commercial creditors. Finding the extra resources when economies were collapsing compounded the hardships many faced. The reason that countries continued to repay their official and commercial loans was because not to do so imperilled their hard-won credit ratings; yet this came at a severe cost for their population in the short term.

In the decade prior to the pandemic, twenty-one African countries were able to access international credit markets by issuing bonds, most of them for the first time; and eight of these managed to secure thirty-year money, which was testimony to their rising standing in international markets. However, the private credit rating agencies threatened to downgrade the credit ratings of countries that accepted the G20's offer to postpone official payments.[22] Downgrades have severely negative consequences, as they limit the access of countries to capital markets and raise the cost of future borrowing.

The IMF's emergency loans to more than 100 countries and the G20's agreement to postpone official bilateral debt repayments from seventy-three of the poorest countries were no doubt helpful, but do not go nearly far enough and were undermined by the actions of the credit rating agencies.[23] The risk posed by downgrading has meant that within eight months of the initiative being launched only forty-three of the seventy-three eligible countries had applied for debt suspensions. This covered barely $5.3 billion in interest payments – less than half of what was due – pointing to the need for a much more ambitious and comprehensive solution to the problems the pandemic has caused in developing countries.[24]

The actions of the credit rating agents are unfair because they penalise countries that have got into difficulties through no fault of their own. The pandemic is a *force majeure* external occurrence. The downgrading by the credit rating agencies of emerging market credit ratings is short-sighted as it compounds their difficulties and has reduced their access to finance and, when they are able to get loans, leads to higher interest rates, thereby increasing the cost of repayment, leaving less to invest in urgent domestic needs. This makes it more difficult for countries to borrow to meet their legitimate needs to address their health and economic emergencies, and by undermining their recovery it reduces their future growth prospects and makes them even less able to repay their loans.

The law governing sovereign debts places a responsibility on countries to repay their foreign creditors before spending money on their own citizens. As a result, even the poorest countries are required to pay foreign debts, with so-called 'vulture' funds pursuing countries in courts even when other creditors may not. International agreement to allow for debt-write-offs and partial payments is therefore essential to reduce the burden on poor countries. This needs to go well beyond the G20's DSSI. One option would be to shield low-income countries from litigious creditors, as was done by the UN Security Council at the instigation of the US following the invasion of Iraq to stop the country's assets being seized by foreign banks that were owed money.[25] Once again – this time for a good cause – forceful leadership by the US is required, and it also requires global cooperation to protect the interests of the poor and vulnerable.

From Disaster to Opportunity

Developing countries together owe $17 trillion, about a quarter of the total amount of outstanding global government debt.[26] To create light at the end of the debt tunnel requires that the stock of debt be reduced rather than interest payments simply being deferred, as that interest continues to compound, leading to ever-rising debts. A reduction in the debt due to all creditors is required, and private banks and countries like China need to be part of the solution. To date, the G20 has agreed to reschedule payments that were due during 2020 and the first half of 2021 to the second half of 2021. Much more action on the part of creditor countries is needed, however, including ensuring that this postponement of payments does not lead to high interest charges. In 2021 and 2022 emerging markets will have to repay over $300 billion a year in maturing bonds, which is $100 billion more than in 2020 and previous years. Prior to the pandemic, this would have been challenging but achievable, but Covid-19 means that at least some creditors will have to accept the debt being rescheduled. With sovereign debt repayments in eight poor countries accounting for over a third of their entire budgets, higher than was the case when rich countries agreed to debt write-offs, an urgent resolution of the debt crisis facing highly indebted countries is essential to stop their populations being sacrificed on the wall of repayments.[27]

Zambia is the sixth country in 2020 to have defaulted on its payments and the risk is growing of debt defaults and a return to the financial patterns of the 1970s and 1980s when poor countries were at the mercy of international institutions. While the IMF recommends further fiscal stimulus and greater indebtedness for the rich countries, heavily indebted poor countries cannot take on more debt and so are being told they need to revert to 'fiscal consolidation' – also known as austerity as a condition of further lending.[28] A condition of IMF and World Bank bailouts is that tax increases and expenditure cuts be implemented by 2023.[29]

The risk with this solution is that poor countries would be forced to suffer further from the greatest economic contraction in history, with potentially tragic consequences. To enforce austerity on these fragile economies would be catastrophic. The lesson of the doomed structural adjustment programmes of the 1970s and 1980s is that, far from restoring a country's growth prospects, austerity – cutting investments in education, health, infrastructure and state capacity – reduces future growth and development by undermining its economic foundations. From the statements of the Managing Director of the IMF, Kristalina Georgieva, it is clear that these lessons are being digested and that a very different approach is now being contemplated. But this requires that creditor countries, who also are the dominant shareholders of the international institutions, agree to write off debt.

Rescue Development

For the greatest development disaster of our lifetimes to be turned into an opportunity requires a comprehensive package of debt relief that would reduce borrowing costs and allow the countries in trouble to meet the needs of their people, while respecting the legitimate necessity of private lenders to be repaid their loans.[30] What is required is a writing off of debts, not simply the postponement of repayments; the latter means that interest accumulates. The priority should be to help the poorest countries, whose situation has deteriorated through no fault of their own, on the sole condition that the funds released from debt repayments are spent on supporting their citizens in need through investing in health, education and basic services. Making this happen requires the coming together of the US, European Union, China, the IMF and World Bank. The G20 and G7 meetings in 2021 provide an opportunity to launch a fresh initiative, reviving the bold ambitions associated with the 2005 G7 Summit in Gleneagles, Scotland, which campaigners hoped would 'Make Poverty History'. If only out of self-interest, rich countries need developing countries to succeed to create investment and trade opportunities and to reduce the risks posed by geopolitical insecurity and the growing threats of pandemics and climate change.

In developing countries carbon emissions are rising rapidly. But it is not too late to ensure that the billions of people who are gaining access for the first time to electricity and buying their first cars and fridges do not add to the already catastrophic global increase in carbon emissions. Directing a small part – less than 10 per cent – of the $12 trillion that the rich countries have raised for themselves in response to the pandemic to a green new deal with developing countries would rescue these countries from their dreadful predicament and reduce carbon emissions by allowing their citizens to benefit from clean electricity and transport. Poverty reduction can and must be part of the creation of a more sustainable and inclusive world where growth is reconciled with environmental and climate concerns.

Developing countries have been devastated by the pandemic and are urgently in need of help. Increases in foreign debt that poor countries have incurred due to the pandemic should be written off by international agencies and creditor governments to place these countries on a sustainable financial path and restore their creditworthiness in international markets. One solution would be for the shareholders of the IMF to agree to the issuance of a trillion dollars in Special Drawing Rights (SDR), which is a relatively costless way of creating new money and one which can be allocated to developing countries. SDR is effectively money issued by the IMF, with the value based on a basket of major currencies; once countries are allocated an amount they can swap it into one of these currencies. The IMF last issued SDRs in response to the financial crisis of 2008 and could do so again if its board votes for this. In practice this means the US and European countries must agree, as together they have more votes than the rest of the 190 member countries represented on the IMF's board.

The United Nations has estimated that at least $2.5 trillion more in aid is required to address the health and economic repercussions of the pandemic for developing countries. This is about a fifth of the $12 trillion that rich countries raised to address the fallout in their countries from Covid-19. Yet, to date the rich countries have allocated less than 1 per cent of what they have raised for themselves to developing countries. To make matters worse, their national aid budgets contracted along with their economies, so less aid was provided during the pandemic, when it was needed more than ever before, than in the previous year. The UK, which was among the leading agencies in terms of aid contribution, in 2020 made the short-sighted decision to cut its aid budget by a third, setting a terrible precedent and undermining its ability to provide leadership at the 2021 G7 and climate summits. As I have argued elsewhere, this reinforced the view that far from Brexit leading to what Boris Johnson has trumpeted as the arrival of Global Britain, it has led to Britain becoming an increasingly insular island.[31]

There are moral reasons as well as reasons of self-interest to support poor countries. But even for countries not convinced by the ethical arguments for supporting others if their suffering can be relieved, mitigating hunger and overcoming the humanitarian disaster faced by many countries should be a priority for all countries seeking a better future world. Without such support Covid-19 cannot be eliminated, global growth cannot be restored, and the challenges posed by growing movement of refugees and from climate change, as well as from the security threats posed by failed states, cannot be addressed. Addressing these needs requires increased aid, debt relief and, to stop the pandemic, an equitable global distribution of the vaccine.

Whereas in previous crises the International Monetary Fund has been subject to criticism, in 2020 it was praised for the rapidity and scale of its response to the crisis. Loans to more than eighty countries were approved in record time and without the usual stringent conditions and lengthy processes of negotiation, with countries told they needed simply to spend in response to the pandemic 'but keep the receipts'. However, the Fund's rapid financing instrument is constrained by its country quotas, which are far too small given the needs.[32] During the 2008 financial crisis IMF support for European countries such as Greece, Iceland, Hungary and Portugal broke all the quota rules and dwarfed current giving, and yet today Hungary is among the most conservative voices on the IMF board, preventing the IMF giving more active support to developing countries.

Placing developing countries on a sustainable financial footing requires the adequate resourcing of the international institutions and reforms in their governance to ensure that they are not once again the instrument of austerity, which undermines rather than fosters development efforts. It also requires that the governance of the institutions be reformed. The absence of leadership from the World Bank, which suffers from the crippling defect of having its leader appointed by the President of the US rather than being chosen through an open competition, has been evident in its failure to mobilise the level of funding required and for that funding to reach those most in need in poor countries. An analysis by Oxfam showed that nine out of ten World Bank projects in seventy-one countries failed to remove the financial barriers of user fees, which limited access to healthcare facilities, and two-thirds lacked any plans to increase the number of healthcare workers.[33]

For countries to prosper, broadly speaking most of the responsibility lies within countries themselves; yet the creation of a supportive external environment and assistance from abroad is essential, too, and lies behind all successful development experiences. Poor countries and poor people are the most vulnerable to risk and so overcoming destabilising global risks, especially pandemics and climate change, is essential for their future prosperity. So too is the exchange of ideas, trade, finance, technologies and people. Vibrant and inclusive globalisation is required for developing countries to prosper. This requires that sustainable jobs are available in developing and high-income economies. Creating sufficient decent work around the world was a critical challenge before the pandemic, and this need has subsequently become even more urgent. To rescue development we must rescue the world of work.

CHAPTER 4

Work for All

Covid-19 destroyed more jobs than any past event. More than half the workers in the world, an astonishing 1.6 billion people, suffered losses to their livelihoods, with one in six being forced to stop work and over 400 million people or 14 per cent of the global workforce losing their jobs entirely.[1]

Talking to people I have met around the world, the breadth and depth of the devastation has become abundantly clear. Unemployment is indiscriminate and has affected people everywhere: there's the desperate plight of Jeff and his wife Sara in the Philippines; and my nephew Blaise, living in Utrecht with two young children, who managed events and whose wife Lindi worked in a clothes store – both of them lost their jobs. So too did Thomas, a conference organiser in Paris. As did Joe, a DJ in London; Sara, a wedding photographer in San Francisco; Josef, an osteopath in Berlin; Gopal, a highly experienced Himalayan Sherpa in Kathmandu; Momo, a previously overworked Uber driver in Cape Town; Jean-Paul, who managed a restaurant in Washington, D.C.; Leo, who worked as a ski and hiking guide in the French Alps; and Emmanuel, who supports an extended family of twenty dependants, and once took me to the top of Kilimanjaro. In a normal year Emmanuel would do forty ascents; 2020 was very different. All of them despair of the future.

What all these people have in common is that they were self-employed. They have no job security and when unemployed or sick have to rely on their own meagre resources or government benefits – which for my friends in poor countries were non-existent. Even in rich countries safety nets are thread-bare. In the US, more than 57 million self-employed people have no recourse to sick pay. In the UK, over a million self-employed people received no benefits during the pandemic, with a third indicating that they had trouble paying for basic necessities.[2]

As economies recover so too will jobs. But many will never return; the pandemic not only led to the worst economic collapse and loss of jobs on record, it also accelerated an economic transformation that is permanently changing the nature of work and societies. The greater reliance of companies on outsourcing and on casual or 'zero-hours' freelance contracts for their workforces is not new, with up to a quarter of workers in many countries already being in this precarious situation prior to the pandemic, but Covid-19 has accelerated this trend.[3]

The pandemic crystalised the divide between insiders and outsiders, and extended it as new fault lines in the labour market emerged. Whereas previous recessions hit manufacturing and construction hardest, this time it is the hospitality, leisure and tourism sectors that have been hardest hit, while individuals working in online services and delivery, as well as government and health practitioners, found they were more secure. The financial crisis was far less severe in its impact than the pandemic, and yet it led to a decade of austerity, widening inequality and the rise of populism that brought us Trump and Brexit. To ensure that the pandemic does not do even more severe and lasting damage requires that the lessons be learnt and that radical reforms be introduced to help heal the wounds it has inflicted. In particular, to prevent permanent damage to livelihoods as well as social and mental well-being requires new approaches to the world of work and an understanding of how the pandemic has accelerated its transformation.

Different Worlds

During the pandemic upper-income groups further increased their wealth while the poor became worse off. The stock market soared, but so too did hunger and homelessness. The result is a widening divide between Wall Street bankers, Silicon Valley tech companies and those investing in stock markets, which enjoyed record profits, and Main Street small business, workers and consumers, who were devastated by the pandemic and face a bleak future.

Employment in the bottom fifth of income earners in the US plunged by 35 per cent, with 42 per cent of these job losses considered to be permanent.[4] And as the UK economy suffered its worst decline in 300 years, the income of average working households dropped at double the rate experienced during the 2008 financial crisis.[5]

Since low earners are more vulnerable to losing their jobs, their decline in income has been much steeper than that experienced by high earners. In the US, the income of the bottom half of workers fell by a fifth during the pandemic, while the top half of income earners only suffered a 4 per cent decline.[6] In the UK, low earners were seven times more likely than higher earners to work in a sector that was forced to shut down during lockdown. Businesses employing one-third of employees in the bottom tenth of the earnings distribution generally had to close, whereas barely 5 per cent of the top 10 per cent of income earners experienced a loss of earnings.[7]

The ability of the wealthy to escape to second homes was underscored during the pandemic when many big-city neighbourhoods emptied out. The sight of shuttered windows and deserted well-to-do streets became commonplace, with over 40 per cent of the residents of the wealthy New York neighbourhoods of the Upper East Side, West Village, SoHo and Brooklyn Heights having fled the city – roughly 420,000 people – whereas very few residents with median incomes of $90,000 or less had the wherewithal or opportunity to leave.[8] In Paris,

record traffic jams stretched a cumulative 420 miles (700 kilometres) as residents of the Île-de-France or Region Parisienne
relocated to their second homes ahead of the second lockdown
in late October 2020.[9]

In the UK during the height of the lockdown the Prime
Minister's powerful former advisor Dominic Cummings went
from London to his second home in the north of England, while
the Prime Minister's father Stanley Johnson left for his villa in
Greece, reflecting their privileged status as well as apparent
immunity from the rules prohibiting travel that governed those
who felt less entitled (though both maintain they were travelling
for 'essential purposes'). The sense of injustice this engendered
was reinforced during the second wave in October 2020 when
the hardest lockdowns were imposed first on poorer northern
cities, yet many low-paid essential workers were forced to leave
home to go to work, whether or not they lived and worked in
areas of high risk.

Remote Work and Incomes

Covid-19 has revealed and amplified the wide gulf in opportunities for remote work. Top earners are five times more likely
to be able to work from home than the lowest earners, many
of whom lost their jobs.[10] In the US, fewer than one in ten of
the lowest earners can work from home while well over half of
higher earners and 80 per cent of the top income earners can.[11]
In the UK, the overwhelming majority of the highest-paid
employees can work from home, but less than 10 per cent of
the bottom 40 per cent of wage earners.[12] As a result, while the
pandemic has barely impacted on the income potential of higher
earners it has radically reduced that of individuals who have to
physically work in factories, construction, cleaning, hospitality,
health, security, retail and other jobs that require their physical
presence; and while higher-paid jobs can generally be done from
home, those individuals working for generally lower wages have
no option but to travel to work.

Remote working has profound implications for inequality and reinforces many prior biases. Whereas only 5 per cent of high school dropouts can work from home, two-thirds of people with a graduate degree can do so.[13] While the working-from-home revolution has been predicted for over forty years, prior to the pandemic only around one in twenty Europeans worked from home.[14] The pandemic changed this dramatically, leading to between a quarter and a half of Europeans working remotely. Across Europe, three-quarters of the highest-paid quintile could work at home, but only 3 per cent of the lowest quintile could do so.[15] The result was that not only were inequalities exacerbated within countries, but also between countries. Luxembourg, which has the highest average income in Europe, saw more than half of the population working from home, whereas in Romania, one of the poorest European countries, barely a quarter of the population was able to do so.[16] It is estimated that at the height of the pandemic, two-thirds of US GDP was produced in peoples' homes, and that a record 42 per cent of the US workforce was working remotely, double the number of those at their work premises, while a third of the workforce was not working at all.[17]

In the last wave of significant automation in manufacturing, mainly blue-collar manual jobs were outsourced to countries where labour was cheaper; yet the pandemic has revealed the potential for the outsourcing of administrative and professional office jobs. Having demonstrated that professional services can be done remotely, what is to stop these services being moved overseas, rather than simply to nearby suburbs? The benefits of employing a costly lawyer or banker located in an expensive big-city office will increasingly be weighed against the benefits of employing someone in a cheaper location or even another country, if they are able to do at least part of the job for a fraction of the cost.[18] Specialised brokers will offer services that meet the language and regulatory requirements of clients, for example in English law, US accounting standards or French building regulations. One-to-one virtual meetings with these experts will take place from home offices, which increasingly will be in another town, or a distant country.[19]

The overall result is that people doing remote work will increasingly be competing with a global talent pool that is available 24/7. Platforms such as TaskRabbit, Upwork, Fiverr and Amazon Mechanical Turk, which allow for global competition for specific tasks, are proliferating. Like other gig workers, participants on crowd-work platforms are paid by the job and have no employment or contractual rights.[20] These platforms typically have no minimum wage, with the 'requesters' of jobs paying a small piece rate per job. Prolific, which is a UK-based online research and survey business, does have an hourly pay floor, but this is still 40 per cent below the UK minimum wage for over-25s.[21]

A rare study in 2017 of online work auctions revealed that the median wage was $2 per hour, with only 4 per cent earning more than $7.25, which was the US minimum wage at the time.[22]

The unpredictable nature of future demand has discouraged businesses from entering into long-term commitments with workers and suppliers. The result has been that a growing number of companies are employing workers on temporary contracts. This is exploiting the desperation of workers who are prepared to accept short-term and freelance work, bringing the gig economy from the fringes of economies to its core. High levels of unemployment also place strong downward pressure on hourly rates and starting salaries for all categories of jobseekers are as a result likely to remain below pre-pandemic levels for years to come.[23]

While the pandemic had a catastrophic impact on jobs everywhere, the immediate impact on incomes was intermediated by government policy. In the US, more than 22 million people lost their jobs, and only about half had regained employment six months later. The government was not prepared to subsidise continued employment but instead allocated $3 trillion to temporarily boost unemployment benefits and gave $1,200 to most taxpayers. But in the absence of agreement on renewing the stimulus and support, unemployed and low-income earners in the US have had to fall back on the tattered social security system, with many failing to qualify for even meagre benefits. In January 2021, President Biden unveiled a $1.9 trillion emergency response to the pandemic, including giving $1,400 in additional direct payments to individuals and increasing unemployment insurance from $300 to $400 per week until September 2021. European countries, by contrast, from the onset of the pandemic developed strategies to pay at least part of the wages of workers to keep them on payroll or to sustain a basic income. These include the UK's furlough scheme, Germany's *Kurzarbeit*, France's *chômage partiel*, Italy's *cassa integrazione* and Spain's minimum income guarantee. France and Germany have committed to continue these emergency payments to 2022.

The disaster relief funds in the US and furlough schemes in the UK, and their equivalents in Europe, have not deterred jobseekers from applying for jobs.[24] In the US 9.3 million workers returned to a job before federal support ended, demonstrating that unemployment benefits are unlikely to have been a disincentive to work.[25] Jobseekers understood that the emergency responses were temporary and that during a recession one cannot afford to be picky, as long-term unemployment and loss of income could have devastating consequences.[26]

Jason, a relative of mine, had for twenty years managed a restaurant in Vancouver, which closed permanently in August due to the Covid-19 lockdowns. He now, at the age of fifty, is washing dishes in another restaurant, glad to have any job at all. Similarly, Michael, who delivered my online order today, explained that he had worked for British Airways as aircrew for the past fifteen years and after losing his job in May 2020 applied for over sixty jobs before getting a job delivering parcels.

In the UK individuals who were kept in employment for at least a third of the time had their salaries topped up through a government furlough and job support scheme that extended to

September 2021. But the stop-start nature of the scheme, which supported more than three million workers, and the requirement that it be linked to ongoing employment and contributions from employers, has meant that more than two million additional jobseekers are anticipated to join the ranks of the unemployed in the spring of 2021.

Young workers were much more likely to have been furloughed than older, more experienced workers, and when they ceased to benefit from the scheme they were much more likely to have lost their job. With youth unemployment at its highest level in four decades, getting a job has become a daunting task.[27] One example is Gemma, a 29-year-old graduate, who was made redundant from her job as a journalist in Manchester and has applied for more than 200 jobs all over the UK, to no avail. It is difficult to imagine the effect on her self-confidence and mental health.

High unemployment is not only crippling for the unemployed, but also significantly reduces spending in the economy, leading to a further downward spiral in growth as well as rising poverty. Three million people in the UK were estimated to be going hungry because of the coronavirus pandemic.[28] As the furlough and job support schemes were wound down, the number of people dependent on food banks was anticipated to double, with hundreds of thousands of households becoming dependent on food banks for the first time.[29] The Joseph Rowntree Foundation found that existing welfare support, through the universal credit and tax credit scheme, is 'not at a level to sustain a minimum quality of life'.[30] Analysis of food bank use showed that black families were disproportionately worse off.[31] With the number of redundancies in the US and UK over double that at the height of the 2008–9 financial crisis, the pandemic has led to rising hunger and has exacerbated existing inequalities.[32] Of the world's high-income countries the US and UK provide among the least generous unemployment benefits, compounding bleak prospects for many.[33] The weekly allowance in the UK, at £59 for under

25-year-olds and £74 for older claimants, is barely 10 per cent of average weekly earnings.[34]

Covid-19 also exposed the brutal disconnect between what people do and what they are paid. Essential workers, on whom we have all relied, have been called heroes, yet they work in many of the lowest-paid and, when it comes to the virus, most high-risk professions. To the police and fire services we should add hospital and care home workers, nurses, retail employees, delivery drivers and rubbish collectors. The growing recognition of how vital these jobs are and the risks involved could lead to a redefining of how we compensate these individuals. We could think them more akin to the military, who have status and pay more fitting for the risks they take on our behalf. For firefighters, police officers, teachers, carers and other essential workers who have been on the frontline of the pandemic, the public sector pay freeze announced by the UK chancellor in November 2020 sends precisely the wrong message. The poor treatment of workers who keep the rest of us going is a reflection of how the pursuit of an indi- vidualistic market economy has imposed its values on the rewards given to individuals and jobs. Radical reforms in this will not only provide much-needed fairness in compensation but will also contribute to reductions in inequality. By increasing the attractive- ness of vital jobs our societies will become more inclusive as well as more resilient and prepared to withstand future shocks.

Hierarchies and Creativity

Workplaces provide a vital source of human contact and friend- ships and these face-to-face relationships will remain a powerful magnet for employees, particularly for young people. There is a risk that remote working undermines not only the building of team spirit but also creativity and transparency. To retain corporate cultures and encourage networking and creativity, the more staff work remotely, the more time and money needs to be devoted to get-togethers offering a combination of formal and informal interactions with colleagues.

Offices in the future will increasingly be viewed as hubs which offer more than simply a place to work, with an increasing focus on the vital role that social interaction plays in innovation, the development of talent and the building of diverse teams. Consulting, law, journalism, investment banking, academia and many other professions use an apprenticeship model characterised by young recruits working with more seasoned staff to develop their skills, which allows the profession to be renewed by a constant infusion of new people and ideas. Communicating with and challenging colleagues is more difficult online than in person, as the risk of miscommunication and taking things out of context is greater. Much of learning is informal and spontaneous and takes place on the margins of meetings, and during corridor conversations and over drinks and meals, all of which are lost during structured online meetings. Remote work reinforces existing hierarchies and friendship networks, with the formality of remote meetings hindering or even excluding the chance encounters and social opportunities that allow more junior staff and new recruits to integrate.

Whether remote working will lead to an increase in productivity remains to be tested. It does however appear to lead to more efficient meetings, with the average length of a meeting having declined by around 15 per cent (even before taking into account the time savings of not having to get there and back).[35] The ability to multitask without it being apparent to colleagues also can increase productivity, not least during long, boring meetings. However, distractions due to childcare and other needs, and lack of privacy, may undermine productivity.

Among the few studies that look at this systematically are some from Chinese call centres, where home-workers processed more calls, worked longer hours and were less distracted by noise.[36] These results are consistent with those for the US, where workers who spent more time at home were paid slightly more for the same tasks, suggesting higher productivity, which was attributed to fewer meetings and distractions and less fatigue from commuting.[37]

The pandemic-induced shift to working from home lowered commuting time in the US by 60 million hours per workday, with cumulative time saved estimated at over a billion hours a month.[38] A third of the time saved was spent on work and the balance on other tasks, including household chores, childcare and exercise. While there appears to be little variation by gender and race, there is considerable variation by education and whether the respondents have childcare responsibilities.[39]

The short-term improvement in productivity from home-working may come at the cost of longer-term improvements that arise from engaging fluidly with colleagues and sparking off their ideas in ways that lead to breakthroughs and innovation. None of the companies I interviewed had started major new initiatives remotely, reinforcing the conclusions of surveys which have pointed to a decline in creativity. The impromptu conversations, external stimuli and new experiences which nurture innovative ideas have been radically curtailed by remote working.[40] It is no accident that researchers and scientists who work together in laboratories and universities have a higher share of collaborative ground-breaking papers and patents.[41] The vaccines to stop the pandemic are unlikely to have been developed at all, let alone at record speed, if the scientists had worked on their own and only connected remotely.

Accelerating Automation

While viruses don't discriminate, the pandemic revealed the stark inequalities that underpin the accelerating transformation of work and incomes due to automation. Research by my Future of Work team at the Oxford Martin School found that in the US 83 per cent of workers in occupations paid less than $20 an hour are at risk of being replaced by machines, whereas only 4 per cent of workers paid over $40 an hour are vulnerable. High-income jobs are not only harder to automate, they also are more pandemic-proof as these earners are five times as likely to be able to work remotely.[42] In total we estimate that about half of US jobs could be automated.[43]

The acceleration of automation has dramatic consequences for globalisation and supply chains. Around the world, globalisation has historically involved outsourcing parts of production processes to distant locations to take advantage of cheap labour. A growing range of repetitive manufacturing production processes have been automated, starting in the car industry and now increasingly evident in electronics production as well as clothing and shoe manufacturing. Digital payment and processing systems have already replaced the back offices of banks, accounting, law and administrative services.

The pandemic added to pressures on industry, particularly the rise of tensions between China and the US with former President Trump championing America First trade policies. Other trends that were already changing the market include the acceleration of online consumption, where customers in Europe, the US and China are increasingly choosing suppliers who offer quick delivery by locating production nearby to major markets. To take advantage of this, US companies are projected to invest in the coming decade over $5 trillion in automated systems.[44] Automated factories that can deliver products to consumers more quickly and more cheaply pose a growing threat to workers in retail and manufacturing.

In the past, governments have responded to automation by increasing their investment in education. When tractors and threshing equipment transformed farming jobs in the early 1900s the US government facilitated the transition from the countryside to urban employment – in 1910 a third of employment in the US was on farms, while today this sector accounts for under 1 per cent of employment. A large part of the focus was on retraining individuals and expanding access to public schools. After the Second World War this accelerated and by 1956, the GI Bill had sent 7.8 million US veterans into further education.[45]

Since the 1970s the expansion of education in the US has been largely privatised and has become a one-off experience before work, rather than a mid-career opportunity to retrain. Spending by governments to ease job transitions today amounts to a tiny 0.1 per cent of GDP, less than half what was devoted to retraining thirty years ago.[46] To make matters worse, the government incentivises companies to automate by giving tax breaks for purchases of machines and software. A business that pays its worker $100 pays $30 in social security and other taxes every payday, but if it spends $100 on a machine, it pays only $3 in tax as a one-off cost.[47] As workers lose their jobs to the pandemic and to automation the need for retraining and business taxes that reward employment rather than automation has never been greater. This requires reducing the depreciation allowances given to companies that invest in machines and providing tax allowances to companies for investing in training new staff. It is necessary to provide the unemployed with government-funded vouchers to pay for retraining, as well as to cover travel and accommodation for a period in other locations where new jobs are to be found, as in most instances the places where jobs are being lost are not within commuting distance of those where new opportunities arise.

The great difference between the current and previous periods of technological change is the speed of the transition. Slower adoption rates in the early 1900s meant that individuals could move and be trained for new jobs that were being created faster than the old jobs were being destroyed. The adoption of steam engines and electricity took many decades even in the countries where this technology was invented and only slowly percolated around the world. Indeed, there are still billions of people in Africa, Asia and Latin America who do not benefit from these centuries-old technologies. Yet there are more mobile phones than people in the world and more than five billion have access to the internet. Moreover, now the pandemic has accelerated a technological leapfrogging of the digital economy.[48]

Call centres are introducing chatbots that can respond to 10,000 queries an hour, whereas an efficient call-centre operator can answer six. Industry insiders predict a race to the bottom on costs, with staff numbers being cut by 90 per cent.[49] In the UK more than 1.3 million people, or about 4 per cent of the workforce, are employed in call centres.[50] Prior to the pandemic, barely 10 per cent of these people worked from home, and operators taking payments over the phone were legally required to be in the office. The reconfiguring of systems so that calls can be done from home happened rapidly, with the closure of centres in South Africa and India during their lockdowns increasing the urgency of this reorganisation.

The introduction of learning algorithms in call centres has meant that automated responses are already getting higher customer satisfaction ratings for all but the most complex questions or unusual accents. This includes using chatbox and voice recognition technology which is already available in iPhone's Siri and in Amazon Alexa, Google Home and other smart devices.[51] The linking of voice recognition to artificial intelligence provides the potential for 90 per cent of call centre jobs to be automated within ten years. The fallout in terms of employment will be severe. In India, Bangalore has been at the forefront of call- and data-centre outsourcing and employs millions of Indians, contributing over $100 billion to the national economy. In the Philippines, more than 1.2 million people work in this industry, which is now worth $25 billion.[52]

It is not only the private sector that is seeing the advantages of replacing people with machines. Automation is taking off in the public sector, too. Faced with their staff not being able to work in recycling centres, municipalities are using AI-assisted robots to sort through rubbish, with one manufacturer of these robots reporting that demand increased fivefold during the pandemic.[53]

The pandemic has further eroded already inadequate government revenue at the national, state and local levels. As revenue generated by taxes declined in recent decades, the incentive to reduce headcount and find savings through automated systems was increased. The pandemic made the establishment of auto-mated e-government services more urgent, as individuals now required online services. In response to the pandemic, IBM adapted its Watson question-answering computer system to do the work of civil servants, and artificial intelligence-augmented systems are being developed to emulate a growing range of jobs. Long before autonomous vehicles are delivering our online orders, service platform companies will have replaced bricks-and-mortar shops and supermarkets, with cutting-edge robotics systems filling orders. Indeed, Ocado in the UK and Kroger in the US already deliver food from warehouses that are almost entirely automated.

The World Economic Forum projects that over the five years to 2025, 85 million jobs will be taken by machines, with admin-istrative, accounting, factory and mechanical jobs being worst affected.[54] This process has been accelerated by the pandemic, but while the WEF claims that 95 million new jobs will be created by artificial intelligence and automation, its reassurance 'Don't fear AI. It will lead to long-term job growth' will not be a conso-lation for those losing jobs; even if these new jobs materialise, they are unlikely to be in the same places as those being lost and do not require the same skills.[55]

Rescue the Arts
A growing share of work in the coming age of automation and robotic work will be in knowledge and creative jobs. We are living in a new renaissance in which innovation and ideas are flourishing but so too are the risks associated with the more rapid spread of technologies. As artificial intelligence and auto-mation forge ahead, humans will be increasingly replaced in repetitive tasks that do not require dexterity, empathy or crea-tivity. This means that societies should give more attention to the development of tasks that humans are uniquely capable of

performing: in the arts, entertainment, creativity and caring as well as in teaching and research. The pandemic has shown that schoolchildren require a class environment for optimum learning and that the quality of teaching matters enormously to their development.

During the Great Depression, President Roosevelt paid artists to paint and write for their country. Artists who later became famous and paid back much more in taxes than they had previously received from their government included Mark Rothko, Willem de Kooning and Jackson Pollock. Subsequently, the income generated by museums and the hundreds of thousands of visitors who travel to see these and other artists' work has repaid the investment thousands of times over and, through both the income and the creative inspiration generated by their work, spread the benefits much more widely.

The contrast between Roosevelt's visionary response and that of today could not be greater. Around the world, the closure of venues and restrictions on movement led to a collapse of arts and entertainment. Artists, actors, musicians and other self-employed people bore the economic brunt of the pandemic, with creative and cultural industries contracting by around double the rate of the rest of the overall economy.[56] In France, where GDP declined by around 10 per cent, the cultural sector contracted by a quarter in 2020 and in Germany by a fifth, while the country's economy declined by around 6 per cent.[57] To offset the potentially catastrophic impact of the pandemic on the arts, in Germany the government set aside a €1 billion (£900 million) 'restart culture' programme on top of its many state and other aid packages, and in France €5 billion (£4.5 billion) was provided, along with a guaranteed minimum wage for all workers in the creative industries, including those out of a job.[58]

In the UK, by contrast, out-of-work actors, musicians and artists and workers in the galleries, theatres and music venues that were closed, many of them permanently, found that not only were they out of work but many were not able to access government emergency payments. The Chancellor gave little hope, encouraging those in the creative industries to seek work elsewhere in 'viable' sectors, and adding insult to injury by failing to recognise their contributions to society or alleviate their dire predicaments. Echoing Margaret Thatcher's lieutenant Norman Tebbit's 1977 statement that unemployed people should 'get on your bike' to find work, the UK Chancellor in October 2020 suggested that musicians and people working in the arts, along with others unable to find work, should retrain and find other jobs.[59] Already, in 2019, the government had supported a major advertising campaign to encourage young people interested in the creative industries and other sectors to 'Rethink. Reskill. Reboot.' and to learn cyber skills and more practical expertise, using the image of a young ballet dancer as an example. The resulting outcry, including from the photographer of the image, who denounced the misuse of her photograph, eventually led to the withdrawal of the advertisement.[60]

One of the most moving experiences I had in 2020 was attending the final exquisite concert that Tasmin Little, the renowned violinist, gave in her garden for the maximum permitted thirty close friends and family, before selling her precious Guadagnini violin. We will never again hear her extraordinary live perform-ances, though fortunately her superb recordings remain and will continue to inspire young musicians in the future. Even famed musicians failed to get any government support whatsoever and while Tasmin is fortunate to be able to forge a new career as a radio presenter and giving masterclasses, many free-lance performers were forced to take on jobs such as driving delivery vans and stacking shelves in supermarkets, if they were able to find jobs at all.

It is not only globally renowned artists who give back. Investment in the arts pays off in the short term. In the year before the pandemic struck, the UK arts and culture industry grew by £390 million and directly contributed £10.8 billion to the economy, paying £2.8 billion in tax. It also generated a further

£23 billion in associated areas including services and hospitality, creating 363,000 jobs.[61] On average, each person employed in the arts added £62,000 to the economy in 2019, compared to £46,000 for other workers.[62] The loss of up to a quarter of the UK's artistic talent during the pandemic severely undermined the potential of the creative industries to contribute to the future growth, dynamism and contribution of Britain to the world. This extraordinarily productive sector should not have been allowed to wither.

The actors union Equity, the Musicians Union and Writers' Guild of Great Britain all found that around 40 per cent of their members failed to qualify for any support from the government's self-employed or other schemes designed to minimise the impact of the pandemic.[63] Inadequate government support has led to a haemorrhaging of creative talent. Performers, make-up artists, instrumentalists and others have been forced to survive on meagre Universal Credit social security payments that seldom even cover their rent, forcing many to resort to food banks to survive.[64]

The deep wounds suffered by all those associated with the arts and entertainment industries need urgent attention. Additional resources are required to ensure that museums, theatres and music venues that were closed can be reopened, those who have been cast out can return to the industry, and young people are encouraged to take the place of the many who have been unable to make ends meet and have left permanently for other jobs.

A society that kills the arts kills its memory and soul. Music, film and entertainment nourished people in lockdown and kept loneliness at bay. As we hurtle into a future where machines will undertake a widening range of tasks, uniquely human attributes such as creativity and empathy are becoming more important and, increasingly, will set us apart. The arts rescue us by taking us beyond our practical needs and resonating with our minds and emotions in a manner that goes beyond the material.

To rescue the sector requires government funding for individuals and organisations in the arts, support for live events, payment for copyright fees and for recordings and, most importantly, that we respect and encourage artistic creativity in our societies.

Rescue Work

Not since before the industrial revolution, over 150 years ago when piecework was still routinely undertaken in homes, has as much time and economic activity been spent at home. This is likely to have profound implications for the future of work.

Conscious steps need to be taken to ensure that remote working does not entrench existing hierarchies and networks and discriminate against groups of workers, for example women, who are more likely to be forced to work at home while juggling child minding and caring responsibilities, and poorer employees who live in smaller homes and lack a personal workspace and the privacy needed for focused work.

The pandemic may in some ways have rescued us from the drudgery of the working week, but the new flexibility comes at the cost of blurred boundaries. Workers have been freed from the tyranny of presenteeism and being seen to arrive early and leave late with the bosses, but now need to be vigilant that home offices do not lead to a new tyranny, as work is ever-present when it's at home, and to resist feeling like they are constantly 'on' and being observed. Employers and employees alike need to establish firm boundaries.

Flexible hours are desired by many but a nebulous working week comes with the risk of employees being unable to switch off at the end of the working day, whatever hour that is. Remote workers now need to ensure that their work life does not invade their home life. To meet this challenge, work schedules can be altered, for example, to take time off during the school run or at mealtimes, and in order to align with the schedules of part-ners, children or other dependants.

One possible, and perhaps even likely, model for an improved work-life balance could be some sort of blended or hybrid work structure. Hybrid models, though, can create the danger of a two-tier workforce, where those who are present in the workplace are better known and networked and also better trained than those who are mainly remote, who might find their careers stagnating. This would particularly disadvantage women, who are often less able to commute, along with those who do not already have an established network at their workplace. Clearly, the rethinking of working patterns needs to go well beyond practical questions such as how often people come in and where they sit, and consider also hierarchy and how hybrid work patterns can be vigilant about and overcome discrimination.

Clarity on when employees are expected to come into the office, their days and hours, is going to be needed. So too is guidance with regard to the rights and responsibilities of employees at home: who is responsible for the installation and maintenance of furniture, equipment and connectivity? Who is responsible for privacy, data protection and security, as well as the insurance of data and corporate materials?[65] How businesses contribute to heating costs and to covering the costs associated with space allocated to home-working also needs to be resolved.

Living conditions for poorer and junior workers are likely to be more cramped, particularly in high-density city environments. The average Londoner between the ages of twenty and thirty-nine has just 9.3 square metres of personal space to themselves (the average size of a prison cell in Norway is ten square metres).[66] Four out of ten Londoners have been working and sleeping in the same room during lockdown.[67] For these people going out to work may be the only way for them to have some space away from their bedrooms or the people they live with. Future hybrid models need to be flexible and sensitive to the particular needs of individuals in different localities, many of whom may far prefer the office to a cramped or noisy home environment. One option may be a hub and satellite model, where instead of bringing people together in a city-centre headquarters, companies give workers access to shared workspaces closer to their homes, allowing for some socialising and dedicated spaces but also shorter commutes. This may also serve to bring new life to the main street and other neighbourhoods that are suffering from shuttered shops and excess commercial space.[68]

As we have seen, workplaces offer an opportunity for chatting and sharing information informally, as well as relieving anxieties and addressing questions ranging from the trivial to deeper insights that may be beneficial to both the employees and the business. It is not only workers who benefit from this; so too do managers, who are able to pick up sentiment and proactively address concerns before they bubble over. Offices also provide a vital source of friendships and allow colleagues to develop empathy and mutually supportive relationships, which are much harder to develop through remote connections. Creating ample informal opportunities for engagement will be vital to building a hybrid corporate culture that is healthy, and also to engendering dynamism and learning and developing a creative and supportive working environment. Work friendships are important not only for the establishment of dynamic work environments but also to overcome the growing dangers of isolation and loneliness associated with home-working.

Increasingly, the skills required for the future are behavioural rather than technical.[69] Many businesses operate what is in effect an apprenticeship system of training in which younger recruits are partnered with the more experienced. This is vital not only for the growth of individuals but also for knowledge exchanges which provide a constant challenge within organisations. We are in an information and service economy in which distinctly human skills such as listening, learning, helping, persuading are what are required.[70] The product part of businesses is transforming into an online and increasingly automated service – we get what we need delivered by service delivery companies, such as Amazon or Deliveroo.

Digital skills are taken as given, and soft skills have surpassed them in importance. As the half-life of technical skills continues to shrink, regular retraining to fill these skills gaps is vital. This requires an attitude of curiosity and adaptability as well as constant commitment to learning, with the estimated requirement for training per year rising from three days to thirty-six days over the past decade.[71] This in turn requires new organisational cultures that foster new ways of working and the critical appraisal of skills held by individuals at all levels of seniority and longevity in businesses. Indeed, as Zoom fatigue sets in, remote work will lead to increased demand for succinct, clear written documentation, to complement spoken performance. People who are able to communicate effectively in writing are likely to shine, whereas initially it was the most verbally articulate and succinct employees who shone in remote settings. It is only a matter of time before we see significant improvements to overcome the challenges with remote work, as evidenced by the share of patents that support work-from-home technologies doubling during the pandemic.[72] The soaring valuation of firms that sell products to increase the efficiency of remote work, such as Slack a workplace software company that was bought by Salesforce for $27.7 billion in December 2020, has energised innovation in this area.

Along with innovation and change in work-orientated technology, there needs to be a change in the rights afforded to employees. The pandemic revealed that as formal-sector jobs are lost and people enter into informal, gig and precarious employment, more and more workers become more and more vulnerable. This places a growing responsibility on employers and governments to ensure that these workers are not exploited.[73] Measures that would support this future system include offering the same protection and employment conditions – even if work is via a global crowd-work platform – that would be acceptable for a full-time employee in a worker's home market. Gig and informal workers should receive minimum wages and have employment rights that recognise their hours, health and safety protection and other minimum employment standards. Businesses and governments should invest in the training and retraining of these workers to allow them to retool and advance their skills in rapidly evolving job markets. Indeed, government recognition that the larger the informal sector the stronger the safety net needs to be is key, as workers will be more reliant on the availability of public health, education and training, as well as on unemployment, welfare and pension benefits. Finally, the larger the share of workers in precarious employment the more imperative it is that governments avoid austerity, as informal workers are the first to lose their jobs when economies contract and are thereafter the most reliant on publicly funded services.

Rescue from our Digital Bolt-holes

The pandemic has accelerated the transformation of working practices and rescued many workers from the drudgery of offices and commuting. At the same time, it poses new risks of undermining not only the innovation and relationships that come from being together physically but the role that workplaces play in breaking down misconceptions regarding people from different backgrounds. Working from home risks not only growing loneliness but also, through lack of exposure to experiences different from one's own, to the consolidation of mental silos. To overcome the risk of digital isolation leading to more rigid silos in our world Sir Tim Berners-Lee, the mastermind behind the internet, has proposed an initiative to encourage building networks within work: random meetings of three or more people, where workers would spend time speaking with colleagues who they may not previously have been in contact with. This would be relatively simple to organise on the web and could well be expanded beyond work to wider social and political engagements. In this way digital meetings could be used to overcome rather than reinforce divides.[74]

To counter the potentially negative impacts of remote work,

the focus now should be on ensuring that the rethinking of work rescues our economies from stagnating productivity and serves to flatten entrenched power and pay hierarchies, and overcome deeply engrained gender and race discrimination.

But what may have started as an outcome of remote work has much wider implications. It is likely that the lockdown in our minds will linger far longer than that imposed by governments. After crises, habits of trust need to be relearnt and confidence restored. This takes active will. The presumption has been that the spring will uncoil as soon as the pressure is released, and we will be able to jump back into our prior states. But as journalist Rafael Behr has observed, we will have to consciously 'reach out of our digital bolt-holes'.[75]

A sustained recovery requires the confidence of consumers to leave their screens, as continuing anxiety poses a significant hurdle to the restoration of sustained growth. The same applies to businesses, which is why it will be some time before private investment returns to pre-Covid-19 levels. Following the Great Depression, economist Maynard Keynes chose to increase government expenditure and not raise taxes paid by working people, to encourage citizens to overcome the fear of starting personal spending again.

It is not enough to simply ask for trust and confidence. They need to be built by convincing citizens that risks have been reduced and that they won't be lurching from crisis to crisis in the future. This requires both competent governments at home and cooperation with other countries to address shared threats.

Behaviour changes that were forced on us by lockdown are likely to have a permanent impact not only on where and how we work, but also on our mindset. Having learnt that we can do things more efficiently and cheaply at home, and at times even better, many of us will need to be actively encouraged to go back to gyms, cinemas and shops.

To entice us away from the comfort and safety of our homes, these activities will have to offer something special. This is likely to lead to less frequent but more enjoyable experiences that are not easily replicated at home.

Encouraging employees who can work effectively remotely to leave their home will require more than a workstation in a far-away office. Meetings with colleagues or clients in a manner that cannot easily be replicated remotely, team-building and creative discussions will be necessary. Intermediary solutions, such as a few hours a day spent in neighbourhood meeting places and workspaces, including restaurants, cafes and pubs, are likely to prove popular, allowing the opportunity for a change in environment without a long commute or commitment to a day in the office.

Rescuing work requires a fundamental transformation in our attitudes not only to where and how we work, but also to pay and reward and to our willingness to flatten hierarchies and work in a more egalitarian environment. Work for all requires that training and the health and safety of workers is prioritised and discrimination overcome. Work for many of us takes up most of our time and defines our lives and identities. Too often it lacks meaning, offers inadequate pay and is precarious or even dangerous. But having work is a necessity not a choice for most people of working age, and being deprived of work is a recipe for despair. The pandemic has led to the most dramatic transformation of work in our lifetimes. By accelerating and revealing the growing threats of widening pay differentials, discrimination, and precariousness of work, as well as by causing rising unemployment, it forces us to think anew. Rescuing work requires a commitment to decent work for all. This demands a rethink of our social contracts, to include discussions on for example a shorter working week, the payment for jobs which rely on voluntary contributions, increasing pay for essential workers and those in the creative industries, stricter measures to overcome discrimination, and greater attention to retraining and mobility to get to work.

After the Second World War, in both the US and the UK,

work for all was central to the vision of reconstruction. The devastating impact of the pandemic on jobs means that now is the time to bring this aspiration back onto our agenda for radical reform and action.

PART TWO

INTERVENTION: FROM HANDS-OFF TO HANDS-ON

CHAPTER 5

Economies for Shared Prosperity

The pandemic has made the task of rescuing our economies more urgent. Never have so many countries and individuals simultaneously been knocked back economically so quickly and so hard. The result will be a lost decade of weak growth and spiralling debt. Without urgent action escalating unemployment, inequality and new crises are inevitable.

British economics journalist Martin Wolf has warned of the threat of 'long economic Covid', with long-lasting debilitating scarring long after the pandemic has passed.[1] This needs to be overcome by avoiding the mistake of austerity that followed the 2008 crisis. In the decade that followed Greece, Italy, Spain, Ireland, France, Portugal and the UK sought to rapidly reduce the deficit, which had expanded during the crisis as tax revenues fell and unemployment and welfare expenditures rose. As part of their agreements to secure fresh funding from the European Central Bank and IMF, all countries introduced sustained reductions in public spending on social services, housing and welfare payments. In the UK, despite promises to 'ring-fence' education and health, their budgets fell in real terms over the decade to 2019. These austerity programmes undermined recovery from the financial crisis, increased inequality and undermined the capacity of health systems to cope with the Covid-19 pandemic. Now, following the pandemic, it is essential that the lessons be learnt and that the stimulus not be withdrawn too fast.

We know the world is changing when the IMF calls on politicians to do more to rescue economies and 'scale up public investment', noting that low interest rates made 'more borrowing to invest desirable' where countries can do so at low cost, which is the case for all high-income and most middle-income countries.[2] On the basis of its modelling it estimated that each 1 per cent of GDP increase in government investment raises private investment by individuals and companies by 10 per cent and would boost economies by an average of 2.7 per cent.[3] It particularly recommends investments in healthcare, housing, digitalisation and the environment, estimating that for every 1 per cent increase in government investment in high- and middle-income countries more than 27 million jobs would be created, laying the foundations for a more resilient and inclusive global economy.[4]

In the US alone, Covid-19 cost over $16 trillion, which is almost its entire annual economic output and equivalent to a loss of roughly $200,000 for every family of four.[5] Although the health-related costs have been lower in many other countries, the economic costs have been proportionately higher, especially in countries that are unable to take on new debt to sustain businesses and workers.

In order to rescue individuals from destitution guaranteed income schemes need to be expanded and sustained. In the US in April 2020 the government gave a one-off transfer of $1,200 to every adult earning below $75,000. As a result, average household incomes actually rose in the first half of 2020, despite the pandemic.

Guaranteed minimum income schemes should not be confused with universal basic income (UBI) as universal means that everyone gets it, whether they need it or not. The problem with UBI is that limited government resources are distributed more widely, and therefore too thinly and every citizen gets the same amount – so billionaires and other high earners who don't need more support receive payments unnecessarily, and those in great need may get less than they previously received in targeted welfare payments. For this reason, universal basic income schemes can actually increase inequality and poverty, and despite their claim to be fairer they are not necessarily redistributive. World economies aren't fair and welfare needs to account for that.

In 2020, one of the American Democratic presidential candidates, businessman Andrew Yang, proposed a scheme that would provide all adults with $12,000 annually. This is an income that would be below the poverty line yet which, because it would be given to 210 million people, would cost the public purse $2.8 trillion – the amount the US government spends on pensions, healthcare and other social services combined.[6] In the UK, a universal income at the level of the living wage would cost more than all social services, education and health expenditures combined. The answer is to target assistance to those who require it and not make payments to those who don't. We should not subsidise the rich by taxpayers providing them with additional income; we should instead focus government welfare expenditures on those who need the funds to live a decent life.

The pandemic has put to rest the conservative myth that minimum wages undermine the incentive to work. The creation of safety nets in Canada and Europe in recent decades did not reduce job-search activity and by sustaining demand in fact increased the number of jobs. And, as has been shown in Denmark, low levels of inequality and strong social safety nets raise productivity as people are prepared to take more risk by trying new jobs and creating new businesses without fearing that if it does not work out they would be destitute.[7]

Raising productivity is vital to rescue our economies from sclerosis, and this requires greater investment in education and training. This benefits the recipient, the company and the whole of society. Increasing investments in education and training at work as well as creating positive work environments is not only good for the profitability of companies, and for the employees, it also has wider benefits for society.

The pandemic strengthened the bargaining power of companies relative to workers. With spiralling unemployment and thousands applying for each job, many of them overqualified, employers know that there will be a bigger pool of potential recruits desperate for work who would be prepared to be recruited at lower salaries. The automation of a widening range of manufacturing and services jobs will exert further downward pressure on wages. Enforcement of minimum wage legislation is needed to protect workers from poverty.

The contraction of employment opportunities due to automation and sluggish economic growth in the US, Europe and East Asia will be offset in part by the decline in the working-age population due to the collapse in the birth rate In 2020 the US population grew at its slowest pace in a century as Covid-19 prevented young people from meeting and meant weddings and starting families were postponed.[8] Immigration has also been curtailed by the pandemic and in the UK this has been compounded by the post-Brexit restrictions. Two-thirds of the EU citizens employed in the UK – about 1.3 out of a total of 2.1 million – do not qualify under the skilled visa points system, which threatens to exacerbate the existing critical staff shortage in social care and nursing.[9]

Despite the contraction of the workforce and lower immigration, unemployment has reached levels last seen in the Great Depression. To address soaring unemployment and to kick-start economies governments should create jobs directly, creating a green new deal, inspired by Franklin Roosevelt's New Deal to create jobs after the Great Depression. In Roosevelt's scheme more than eight million unemployed Americans were hired by the government to build 500,000 miles of roads and nearly 100,000 bridges.[10] In response to our twenty-first-century crisis governments should invest resources to prepare for our future, mobilising the unemployed in the battle against climate change.

Countries should invest more to achieve their growth and decarbonisation goals simultaneously.[11] Between two and eight jobs are generated directly for every additional million dollars spent by governments on traditional investments, and even more jobs, between five and fourteen, are created when the same amount is spent on clean energy and other investments that reduce carbon emissions.[12] In the UK, a green new deal would create tens of thousands of jobs, many of them local and employing technical skills, such as those required to insulate homes and install solar panels.

With negative real interest rates, lenders are paying us to borrow from them. Borrowing to fund growth to create more equal and prosperous societies makes economic as well as environmental and societal sense. Without resolute government action the economic recovery will be bifurcated, with remote and high-income workers benefiting while the growing number of low-income and unemployed people suffer further losses.

Overcoming inequality and addressing societal needs will require an end in the competition among countries to reduce their rates of tax, which they do to attract international companies and rich individuals. The downward spiral could be stopped by an agreement to close tax loopholes. In the US an estimated $1.6 trillion is forfeited through tax exemptions, which allow powerful businesses and individuals to reduce their tax exposure.[13] The closure of tax havens and low-tax or tax-free jurisdictions, such as the US state of Delaware, the Cayman Islands, Monaco, Dublin, Luxembourg and Liechtenstein, which offer tax residence to companies and individuals who maintain a ghostly presence in order to avoid tax obligations, would yield another $600 billion a year in lost corporate taxes and an additional $200 billion in income taxes globally.[14] Of this, more than $200 billion a year in taxes that have been avoided by individuals and companies from developing countries relocating to offshore havens could then flow back to developing country governments as tax. This is about twice what they received in 2020 in aid.[15]

The big technology companies have been particularly aggressive in their use of tax havens to reduce their tax burden and should be subject to taxes as other companies would be in the countries in which they accrue revenues and profits, not as phantoms resident in a tax haven. Platforms such as Facebook and Google make most of their money from advertisements and mining the data of their users. They and other companies and wealthy individuals who have profited greatly from the pandemic should be subject to a one-off windfall tax to help pay for the recovery and to contribute towards those whose lives and incomes have been destroyed by the pandemic. In the US, this has become the basis for a campaign led by Senator Bernie Saunders, who introduced the Make Billionaires Pay Act to Congress. The Bill aimed to introduce a tax of 60 per cent on the gains of US billionaires during the pandemic, which would raise more than $400 billion.[16] In the UK, the Royal Society for Arts, Manufactures and Commerce (RSA) has called for a modest sales tax levy on what it terms 'pandemic profiteers'.[17]

Other tax reforms, not least with respect to inheritance tax, are needed. The revelation during the height of the pandemic that the billionaire Donald Trump paid a mere $750 in US taxes in two years and none in ten out of fifteen years has highlighted the gross inequities of the tax system and increased the appetite for major reform. The contrast between the terrible suffering and loss of income many are experiencing and the extraordinary boost the pandemic provided to the incomes of a fortunate few, together with revelations regarding tax avoidance by President Trump and others, has given fresh impetus for national and global efforts to reform taxation. This in the coming years is likely to be translated into concrete actions in the US, European Union and through international organisations.

The growing intolerance of tax avoidance has led the Paris-based Organisation for Economic Cooperation and Development (OECD) to work with 135 countries on an agreement to reduce tax 'base erosion and profit shifting', which, with a Biden presidency in the US, could now be ratified. This highly significant initiative aims to stop tax-planning strategies that exploit gaps and mismatches in tax rules to allow profits and income to be shifted to low- or no-tax locations where there is little or no economic activity. Already, a number of European countries have given assistance to companies that have sought help as a result of the pandemic, conditional on the contractual assurance that they are paying their fair share of taxes and that they agree not to use tax havens in the future.

Rescue Economies

The rising support for the closure of tax loopholes is indicative of how the pandemic is altering the language of public policy and revealing a wider range of economic options.[18] This has been associated with a healthy break from the one-dimensional capitalism versus communism and government versus free market spectrum of alternatives. A spectrum that was seen to range from free market Thatcherism in which 'There is no such thing as society' at the one end to communism, where only societal interests dominate, at the other end.

In 1937 President Roosevelt argued that 'heedless self-interest is . . . bad economics' and that 'freedom from want' should be an essential goal in guiding public policy.[19] This indeed is the case today in many societies that would still certainly be defined as capitalist, not least Scandinavian countries.

As Professors Wendy Carlin and Sam Bowles have noted, this restrictive binary description of the options limits the political rhetoric that shapes public policy. What is missing from the state versus market debate on ownership is that key dimensions of life cannot be valued monetarily. The environment, civic responsibility and trust are all crucial to our well-being and that of happy and healthy societies, but in economic calculations these non-pecuniary elements tend not to be measured and to be excluded.

The pandemic has led to a wider appreciation of the extent to which people make selfless decisions that go beyond economics. Societies with higher civic commitments such as New Zealand,

South Korea, Taiwan and Singapore, and in Europe Finland, Norway and Denmark, have done noticeably better. Fairness and solidarity are proving themselves more powerful in guiding human behaviour than market forces, providing a positive sign of the evolution of policy debates in a direction that will encourage more inclusive and sustainable societies.

As Andy Haldane, the Chief Economist of the Bank of England, has noted, volunteers are the often invisible army fighting the invisible enemy.[20] Community and neighbourhood groups, charities and individual volunteers are doing what they can to plug the holes left by governments and the private sector. In the UK the centenarian former British Army officer Captain Tom Moore raised more than £32 million in donations for the National Health Service by walking laps of his garden. He had aimed to raise one thousand pounds. His demonstration of public commitment, like that of the footballer Marcus Rashford, whose campaigning petition to end child food poverty quickly attracted over a million signatures, highlights the extent to which the public are ahead of government in their sense of fairness and desire to address the needs of society.

What Haldane calls the 'institutional immune system of the social sector', was recognised by Beveridge as it had been by de Tocqueville before, in his highlighting of the importance of social and community actions in the building of democracies and the dangers associated with societies of strangers, in which individuals do not support each other.[21] The spontaneous responses of people like the late Captain Sir Tom Moore, Marcus Rashford and of volunteers and charities to helping the left-behind and left-alone during a crisis like the pandemic reflect the depth of social capital in our societies. Economist Raghuram Rajan of the University of Chicago highlights social capital as a neglected dimension that complements financial, physical and human capital, which by contrast are well known and frequently discussed.[22] The 750,000 volunteers in the UK who supported the NHS, and the many millions of track and trace volunteers in the US and elsewhere, will not figure in the national accounts and are invisible in economic statistics.[23]

While the outpouring of volunteerism has provided an inspiration and filled major gaps in health and welfare systems, it is not a substitute for more effective benefits funded by taxpayers. In fact, although their services were in much greater demand, the ability of charities to step up to support those in need during the pandemic was undermined by a collapse in their own income. As street collections, sporting or other neighbourhood or office charity events, and sales through high-street shops were disrupted, normally reliable sources of revenue disappeared. In the UK, this was estimated to mean that the 170,000 charities would suffer a combined £6.4 billion loss and that one in ten would be threatened by bankruptcy.[24]

The pandemic placed complex trade-offs between lives and livelihoods and short-term and long-term responses centre stage. Values are at the heart of many of these debates, at least implicitly, leading citizens and policymakers to reflect on how we value our lives and freedoms and those of others.

We need to move beyond the sterile debates about capitalism versus communism. All countries combine private enterprise with state control. Russia overthrew communism only to replace it with a capitalist autocracy. It offers far less freedom to the private sector than supposedly communist China, where private business accounts for well over half of economic activity and nine out of ten new jobs. In many European countries state enterprises account for a more significant share of economic activity and jobs than is the case in China. The key question is how different models of capitalism perform, not least in whether they generate shared prosperity and offer individuals and businesses the foundations and freedom to grow.

The pandemic tested the merits of different models of capitalism. The more liberal market economies such as the US and UK have done far worse than coordinated market economies such as Germany, the Scandinavian countries, Austria, the

Netherlands and South Korea. Since 1843 *The Economist* magazine has championed liberal democracy, but it now accepts that countries with greater state intervention did better in the pandemic. It claims, however, that states where governments are less powerful will win out in the long run as stronger states will be less flexible, and insufficiently nimble to adjust their economies to the changes coming.[25] I disagree; competent and well-resourced governments are needed to overcome the great threats we face in the future, including further pandemics, climate change and rising inequality.

Effective governments are necessary to invest in and then harvest and share the benefits of improvements in health, clean energy, science and innovation and ensure that they are not captured by predatory elites. The challenge is not to build bigger and more powerful governments, but rather smarter and more accountable governments, able to learn from their citizens, experts and international best practice.

We know that a strong state does not guarantee success, as Russia today and numerous historical examples have shown. It is the quality of institutions and their accountability that determines outcomes. While many democracies – and particularly those led by women – did exceptionally well during the pandemic, others such as the US, Brazil, Mexico, France and the UK performed badly. Those that did worst have in common arrogant imperial leaders who are disconnected from their civil servants and think they are cleverer than the experts. Their inconsistency and apparent immunity from the rules destroyed trust. Those that did well have followed international guidelines from the WHO, have been frank with their populations about the challenges and the hardships, and haven't flouted the rules. By following these simple rules, even relatively poorly-endowed countries, such as Mongolia, Vietnam and in Europe, Greece, Latvia and Estonia excelled in their management of the pandemic, whereas the wealthiest countries, notably Switzerland and Luxembourg, were among the worst performers in terms of the per capita infection rates.

The pandemic exploded the myth of the more liberal economies enjoying greater competence. It also highlighted how democracy is neither a necessary nor a sufficient condition for ensuring success. What both the democracies and autocracies that managed the pandemic effectively had in common is competence in key areas, especially in their health systems. Part of the reason for the muddled and ineffective response in the more liberal democracies was that after years of austerity and budget cuts they no longer had the necessary capacity to undertake basic tasks. The outsourcing to private companies of urgently needed activities, such as testing and tracing, exposed the frailties of the businesses as well as the inadequacies of the processes by which they had been hurriedly selected, which served to further undermine trust in government. In the UK, the British Medical Association has stated that 'severe public health cuts left the UK more vulnerable to COVID'.[26] The decade of austerity between 2010 and 2019, which saw public expenditure as a share of GDP fall by 20 per cent, led to 'dangerously low' spare capacity in hospitals, and a lack of crucial equipment such as ventilators and personal protective equipment, such as gowns and masks, while the number of communicable disease consultants available in 2020 was one-third below pre-austerity levels.[27]

The pandemic has demonstrated that just-in-time delivery and lean management systems are not compatible with resilience. The cutting of costs in supply chains and competition to reduce taxes as part of the neoliberal model of capitalism has proved to be unsustainable. So too have the negative spill-overs of unfettered consumption such as greenhouse gases and pollution. The offloading of risk to others is a critical limitation of liberal market systems. These rising negative consequences of private activities need to attract increased scrutiny by regulators whose role is to ensure that private companies act in the public interest. But stopping companies from undertaking harmful practices will not stop unsustainable activities. This requires that we as consumers also change our ways. As individuals we each have a responsibility to consume less plastic, to reduce our carbon footprint and to choose products and services that are produced by companies that genuinely follow best practice. If we do not change our behaviour and turn away from the individualistic creed of consumption at any cost, we cannot expect companies and governments to do so.

British Prime Minister Boris Johnson in his October 2020 Conservative Party conference speech invoked the wartime spirit of solidarity and vision that led to a new world. But he added that while the pandemic had 'forced' the government into massively expanding the role of the state, it would 'go against our instincts' to conclude that this was for the longer term. He argued that the UK would once again become more competitive, and would reduce taxes and regulation to ensure that the recovery is led 'not by the state but by free enterprise'.[28] The return to the old normal of neoliberal principles and austerity would add further misery on top of that which has been caused by Covid-19 and Brexit. It's a recipe that will ensure that the UK is not only an increasingly unequal country, but also even less resilient in the face of future shocks.

The illusion of supremacy of the US capitalist system has been shattered by its failure to manage the pandemic. Even when people did not like what the US was doing, they thought it was capable of doing what it wanted due to its superior power and wealth. That belief has now evaporated. The unevenness of the global response to the pandemic provided an unprecedented natural experiment, which revealed what works and what does not. The need to rescue capitalism has become starkly evident in many countries. Trying to replace capitalism with another ism should not be our ambition, as it is not the label but rather the content that matters. Our focus should be on what form of capitalism and what type of society and future we want.

The Golden Age of capitalism, seventy-five years ago, introduced visionary and radical reforms that today offer an inspiration for a new age of capitalism, in which capitalism is steered to achieve the goals of our times, to stop climate change and global crises, overcome inequality and poverty. A form of capitalism that places business and finance at the service of the whole of society, rather than serving a tiny minority. At a minimum, in high-income countries citizens should expect their governments to ensure they have universal public services and jobs. The ambition should be to harness capitalism to serve people and not the unfettered pursuit of profits. This radical reform of capitalism is essential if it is to rescue our societies from increasing inequality and the growing risks arising from climate change and pandemics. A key part of this is the reform of businesses to ensure that they become the engine of job creation and shared economic prosperity.

CHAPTER 6

Better Business

During the pandemic competition gave way to corporatism, with government mandarins in many countries deciding whether companies should live or die. Citing 'strategic interests', governments directed food and health services to remain open – even against their will – while instructing most other businesses to close. Subsequently governments determined the sequence of when and how businesses could resume operations. Whereas in February 2020 competition policy would have made it illegal, by March companies were asked to collaborate to build ventilators and vaccines or, in the case of Google and Apple, to work together to devise track and trace apps. As President Trump sought to intervene across the board, including in businesses that had no relation to the pandemic, Nobel laureate economist Ned Phelps warned that he was emulating Mussolini's doctrine of corporatism, in which the President as puppet-master pulls the strings of companies.[1]

Governments around the world provided lifelines to prevent widespread corporate collapse, even if it was not on the scale of the $500 billion provided to businesses by the US government. Corporate leaders now owe politicians a growing number of favours as the survival of their companies depends on the goodwill of political masters. Lobbying and access to power is a means of survival and as a result large incumbents and well-connected businesses have been able to access funding, while small businesses have not. In the US and UK, tender processes have been set aside in the name of expediency, with nameless officials awarding lucrative contracts without the customary due diligence. This means less competitive challenge to established companies. It is also bad for consumers as it results in higher prices, less choice and slower innovation.

The failure of governments to adequately manage the conflicts of interest that can arise when normal procurement rules are short-circuited in the name of emergency needs was highlighted by the neglect of due process in the UK. The National Audit Office revealed that more than £17 billion in pandemic contracts were awarded without competitive tender and that a 'VIP lane' was created through which friends and family of government ministers were ten times as likely to get government contracts.[2] Less than a seventh of more than a thousand contracts entered into by government on pandemic-related purchases was open to public scrutiny.[3] This led to outsourcing of emergency ferrying to a company with no ferries, awarding track and trace contracts to companies with no prior capacity in app development, the purchase of dangerously substandard personal protective equipment (PPE) from a pest control company and a jeweller with no record of sourcing PPE, the awarding of a $44 million deal for hand sanitiser to a dormant company, and the opening up of the National Health Service to private provision with opaque terms and conditions.[4] The pandemic has revealed the extent to which the entangled relationship between politicians and business means that governments are hijacked by their business connections and are prepared to defend narrow private interests at the expense of national needs.

In the US, pay-to-play politics has been taken to the extreme and the pandemic provided an unprecedented opportunity for politicians to make life-and-death decisions that determine the fate of companies. The 2020 US Presidential elections cost the candidates a staggering $14 billion (which exceeds the combined economies of sixty countries), resulting in enormous indebtedness of the candidates to their political paymasters.[5] Every year, over \$3.4bn is spent in the US on lobbying.[6] Ending the interdependence between politicians and companies is vital if governments are to serve in the national interest and not be snared by business. This requires not only the ending of corporate financing of campaigns in the US but also, as the UK and other countries where this has been restricted shows, the enforcement of strict standards that prohibit political involvement in the awarding of contracts, punishable by disqualification from politics and prosecution.

Bigger businesses are more politically connected and have received the largest share of government bailouts. These dominant incumbents also have larger cash reserves and a more diverse range of suppliers and customers and hence have been more able to withstand the disruption caused by lockdown than small businesses.

Globally, the pandemic led to millions of small businesses being made bankrupt and forced to close permanently.[7] In the UK, an estimated six million small businesses supporting about 17 million jobs were placed in a financially precarious position and nearly two-thirds indicated that they were unlikely to survive the pandemic pressures.[8] By accelerating the decline of small businesses, the pandemic raised the market share of larger ones, undermined competition and created a more concentrated business environment. This is despite the fact that around the world, many workers who were laid off energetically explored new options and registered as self-employed, leading to a surge in entrepreneurship and start-ups. In the US in 2020 applications for new business licences rose at their fastest rate since 2007.[9] This mainly reflects the accelerated transition to the gig economy of self-employed and more precarious workers, rather than a new challenge to established businesses.

Being young and lean is advantageous in terms of the health risks associated with Covid-19, but the opposite is the case when it comes to economic risks, as the youngest and smallest businesses without the savings or connections to tap into state resources are threatened the most. Indeed, the pandemic has considerably increased the power of some of the biggest companies in technology, pharmaceutical and online retail, wellness, home improvement and healthcare.

The biggest beneficiary of the pandemic has been Amazon, with the lockdown generating an additional $10,000 per *second* in revenues.[10] Amazon's revenue rose by over 50 per cent in 2020, and the company's value increased by $500 billion in the first six months of the pandemic, as its share of the US e-commerce market increased to 40 per cent, with Walmart a distant second with 6 per cent.[11] With Zoom and e-commerce demanding more and more cloud services, Amazon Web Services has become the largest single source of income for Amazon, with an operating margin of 26 per cent that now accounts for over two-thirds of its income.[12] Meanwhile, Apple's valuation rose to over $2 trillion, which is more than the total of all the economies of sub-Saharan Africa or the top 100 companies on the London Stock Exchange (the FTSE 100).[13]

Digital Business Boom

[handwritten: tech-celeration .]

The pandemic turbocharged the arrival of the digital age, leading to increases in the use of digital services that previously were not anticipated until 2025.[14] Many companies experienced a ten-year evolutionary leap, as what were previously slow-moving transformations, like remote consultations with doctors, were achieved within a matter of weeks. This tech-celeration of changes that were already under way has meant that some who may have thought they were immune to the digital world have now become converts.

The transformation of demand into no-touch and home-based consumption has led to the most rapid restructuring of consumer behaviour and of businesses in peacetime. Not only is the customer experience being transformed, but so too are products, factories, service centres, offices and payment systems. The pandemic has destroyed many businesses but those associated with the digital economy, automation and robotics are thriving. According to the CEO of one leading robotics manufacturer, demand for robots has 'skyrocketed', with the pandemic encouraging businesses to experiment with new approaches that reduce the reliance on people, accelerating the transformation of jobs and adoption of new technologies.[15]

Digital businesses were able to rapidly take advantage of the explosion of new opportunities for remote fitness, music, wellness and online classes. Many of these are asset-light platform businesses that, due to the introduction of automated systems, do not employ many people or require much space. So, for example, the indoor cycling company Peloton saw its value climb by over 200 per cent during lockdown to over $25 billion, with more than a million subscribers registered for its cycling and other streamed workouts.[16]

One result of the pandemic is that it has accelerated the shift to intangible capital and asset-light operating models.[17] This in turn has fuelled the growth of online companies, whose market power has grown. The strength of the online service providers, relative to their suppliers, means that they effectively control the market and have exercised a growing grip on suppliers and dampened their wages and profits. This is bad for workers but keeps the lid on prices and inflation, which may be expected to remain at all-time low levels for years to come.[18]

The deflationary pressure has many negative side effects, though, particularly for savers and pensioners, who rely on positive interest rates to provide a return on their investments and finance their retirement. Excessively low interest rates also suppress productivity by sustaining zombie companies that although unable to make money are kept alive by taking on more debt at very low cost. Low interest rates also encourage businesses to invest in capital equipment such as robots, rather than people, and this increases unemployment.

The growth in digital businesses also poses major regulatory and statistical challenges. While the measurement of physical buildings, machines and products follows long-established protocols, measuring the value of data, content, intellectual property and other intangible capital is fraught with uncertainties. The growing pervasive accumulation of data also accentuates questions of privacy and ownership of data limits.

Companies that accumulate our data make money from selling it to advertisers. In 2020 Facebook made 99 per cent of its revenue of about $100 billion from advertising and Google's holding company Alphabet made more than 83 per cent of its revenue of almost $200 billion in this way.[19] And yet users who give away their data are most often not aware of it and are never paid for it. How we own our data, when and where it is collected raises many questions, including with respect to informed consent, not least by minors. In the European Union, the General Data Protection Regulation (GDPR) has made major strides in the regulation of data to protect the rights and privacy of citizens. In its insistence that businesses pay taxes if they are to receive support from the European Union governments, the European Commission has demonstrated that despite its reputation in the UK as a slow-moving bureaucracy it has managed more effectively than others to keep pace with the rapid evolution of digital businesses in order to hold them accountable.[20] Given these businesses' growing power and the pace of change, the need for regulatory catch-up is more urgent than ever.

A decade of change has been compressed, sometimes taking place almost overnight. At the start of the pandemic, citizens initially hoarded cash, as they had during the feared Y2K computer crash at the turn of the millennium and during the 2008 financial crisis. The smooth operation of digital payment systems, the rise of online shopping, concerns regarding venturing out and touching ATMs, together with fears that the Covid-19 virus could be carried on banknotes and coins, soon however led to the rejection of cash payments.[21] In Spain withdrawals from ATMs declined by 90 per cent and in the UK by

60 per cent during the pandemic.[22] Mobile banking in the US rose by 85 per cent in the first month of the pandemic, with a fifth of US citizens using digital payments and digital exceeding cash payments for the first time.[23] The pandemic reinforced Sweden's commitment to be the first truly cashless society by 2023. In China, while digital payments were already commonplace before the pandemic, they now have replaced cash almost entirely, with over 80 per cent of the population using digital payments. This led to record valuations for Tencent's WeChat and Jack Ma's Alipay, Alibaba and Ant Group, which account for over 90 per cent of transactions on mobile devices, raising concerns regarding the domination of digital sales by a couple of private firms.

The pandemic accelerated the transition from physical to virtual banking, and with this the widespread closure of tens of thousands of bank branches around the world. Cash transactions now are increasingly limited to a declining minority of the elderly who are not comfortable with smartphones or computers, and to those who have ulterior motives to avoid digital payments and prefer the anonymity of cash. Those wary of digital payments may be motivated by libertarian ideologies and distrust of government, a fear of being tracked by repressive states, or a wish to evade authorities by those engaged in illegal activities and avoiding tax. Whereas in China and Kenya digital payment systems have been in common use for years, for even the smallest transactions in informal markets, in the rest of the world the pandemic has accelerated the adoption of digital payments, with levels of adoption in 2020 that were only anticipated to arise after 2025.[24]

The share of traditional banks in global financial transactions declined by over 10 per cent during the pandemic, with fintech companies like PayPal and China's Ant Group accounting for 11 per cent of all payments.[25] Visa and Mastercard, which together account for 94 per cent of all plastic card payments outside of China, saw a 40 per cent rise in transactions during 2020 as shoppers turned to online and contactless purchases.[26] This rapid ascent of digital payments is a permanent legacy of the pandemic, leading to a markedly altered financial landscape.

Winners and Losers

In the 11 years following the financial crisis of 2008 work consumed more and more of our time, with increased office hours and late-night screen time leaving less time for leisure. For many people, the pandemic compounded this problem, as working from home blurred boundaries and meant they were in effect living at work, without privacy or an ability to escape, while sacrificing friendships and the benefits of being able to go out and engage in social activities.

As circumstances forced people to spend more time at home and they were prohibited from or felt uncomfortable going to restaurants, cinemas, gyms or on holiday, home spending soared. The greater focus on home and the need to address the physical and mental health risks posed by Covid-19 led to a boom in online purchases in the areas of well-being, leisure, gardening and pets. With demand exceeding supply, customers had to contend with long delays, even for rescue pets that previously could not find homes. Home baking led to shortages of flour, while home grooming created shortages of hair dyes and equipment normally used by barbers and hairdressers. Outdoor leisure demand created price spikes and delivery delays for purchases of sports equipment, home improvement and gardening tools and beehives. According to the Royal Horticultural Society more than 3.5 million Britons took up gardening for the first time in 2020, leading to shortages of seeds and plants.[27] Online plant sales increased by around 500 per cent, with demand for medicinal plants such as echinacea reportedly rising 3,000 per cent.[28] As winter approached attention shifted from gardening to how best to stay warm outdoors. This led to unprecedented demand for fire pits and outdoor heaters, with one China-based manufacturer doubling its output and resorting to airfreight to meet the demand of less price-sensitive customers.[29]

Books, podcasts, home movies, music streaming and video games have all seen a boom in sales. The content is also changing. On Spotify, an analysis of 17 trillion songs showed people are turning to nostalgia to beat the lockdown blues; as people's anxiety levels rose, they appeared more likely to escape the moment by listening to songs from happier times – there was a sharp increase in downloads of songs that were at least three years old. Online booksellers similarly reported rising interest in historical novels, fantasy, romance and poetry, with non-fiction after years of growth being the only category to report declining sales as readers sought to escape the horrible pandemic reality.

An analysis of winners and losers underlines the extent of the difference between the catastrophic collapse of revenues for hospitality, travel, entertainment and city-centre retail services, and the soaring profits of the technology and healthcare companies that account for three-quarters of the 100 global companies best placed to benefit from the pandemic.[30]

Not every big business benefited. The behemoths of the travel industry, such as airlines, hotels and retailers, suffered shocking losses, as did digital platforms that require the physical presence of customers, such as Airbnb, Uber and WeWork. Despite the tech hype that accompanied its listing, WeWork offers physical office space. Its valuation just before the pandemic was $8 billion and Covid-19 knocked it down below $3 billion, less than half its previous value.[31]

The pandemic has been good for virtual rather than physical, material or people-intensive businesses. The new wellness platforms can cater for thousands of participants for each instructor, who can operate from home. Food services that are home-delivered employ far fewer people than restaurants or grocery shops and have much cheaper overheads.

The companies that have sustained their growth have been those that generate revenues without adding costs for each additional customer. This is achieved by relying on automated software systems that can scale effortlessly, whereas for physical assets each extra customer brings an additional cost. Platform companies that require physical presence, like Airbnb, saw a collapse in their revenues, but as their costs are so low the pandemic consolidated their hold on the market by driving smaller competitors out of business and increasing the need for individuals to rent out their space to earn additional income.[32]

The big household brands have benefited too as consumers shopping online return to the products they have known for decades. Dettol disinfectant, Heinz baked beans, Dove soap and similar recognised everyday products consumed at home have seen record demand, reversing years of sluggish performance from Unilever, Nestlé, Procter and Gamble and other big brand manufacturers.[33]

Not surprisingly, reinsurance companies that provide the back-stop for insurers by underwriting their risks are profiting from the disasters befalling others. Long before the pandemic, the increased incidence of hurricanes, floods, droughts and fires resulting from climate change led to a rise in the number of individuals and companies seeking insurance. The increase in demand led reinsurers to impose double-digit increases on their premiums, and over time these get passed through into insurance premiums. Meanwhile the increase in fraud during the pandemic, due to the increase in digital transactions and introduction of new customers and systems, together with a simultaneous growing focus on sexual harassment, discrimination in the work-place and other unethical behaviour, is increasing reputational risk and liability. The combination of greater scrutiny of boards and CEOs, as well as a growing recognition of the extent of fraud, has led to a tripling in the cost of directors' and offices' liability.[34]

Restrictions and health concerns led to airlines, airports, suppliers and contractors losing up to 90 per cent of their busi-ness overnight. The pandemic sounded the final death knell for

British Airways 747 planes and deepened the crisis affecting the Airbus and Boeing duopoly, with both the iconic Airbus 380 and Boeing Dreamliner construction programmes suspended. A number of airlines have gone into liquidation, while others such as American and United Airlines are being kept aloft by the income derived from their loyalty credit cards, which prior to the pandemic accounted for up to half of their profits and in 2020 provided the bulk of their revenues.[35] During the pandemic, private jets escaped the business travel carnage as wealthy individuals and companies chartered planes to avoid contact with the travelling public on commercial flights.[36]

For many airlines, business travel is the most profitable part of the industry and although it accounts for under 10 per cent of the passengers it accounts for between half and three-quarters of the big commercial carriers' profits.[37] This is likely to be permanently reduced as the cost and time saved by holding remote meetings, and growing concerns regarding the carbon footprint and environmental damage caused by flights, lead to a permanent curtailment of business flights. My interview with a top executive of one of the biggest banks revealed that he is budgeting for a post-pandemic 90 per cent cut in the budget for business flights, with travel restricted to meeting clients for the first time and closing deals.[38]

The airline industry was already under great strain, and in this sector as in others, the pandemic has accelerated trends that were already apparent before the coronavirus crisis. Companies with high cash buffers that were highly rated (in terms of the risks associated with their debt), and those with the strongest operating margins have tended to do better, or less badly, in the pandemic.[39] The businesses that have done well were already outperforming others prior to the pandemic, with this reflecting both the sectors that they were in and the market rewarding more resilient businesses with lower exposure to risks from disasters.[40]

While the pandemic elevated the technology and biomedical

sectors, it also pushed others towards obsolescence. Predictions in the past on how home-working and entertainment would kill businesses proved exaggerated. Videos, DVDs and Netflix did not kill cinemas and nor did CDs, iTunes and Spotify kill live music, even though digital streaming services have diminished performers' income stream as they are not adequately compensated. Cinemas, clubs and live entertainment were suspended during the pandemic and many of these businesses became bankrupt, but for those that survive the future is bright.

Peloton and Zwift diminished demand for spin classes, but gyms that offer state of the art equipment, wellness and social areas where people can meet up will thrive. Equally, a new generation of restaurants and cafes will emerge that are able to cater for our desire to socialise while working remotely and remaining nearer to our homes.

After the horrors of the First and Second World Wars, night-life and hedonism thrived. The pent-up desire to party, socialise and travel means that the pandemic will similarly give way to an ecstatic boom of normalisation that will benefit what remains of the hospitality and leisure travel industries.

Boom and Bust

One of the most surprising phenomena of 2020 was the disconnect between record stock market returns and the collapsing economy associated with a widespread failure of businesses. In November 2020, as the US recorded its highest ever number of new coronavirus infections and even while the outcome of the US Presidential election was unclear, the stock market had its greatest ever monthly increase.

Not even the most contrarian pundits predicted that a major pandemic would lead to a stock market bubble and record new listings.[41] The disconnect between the moribund economy and the record highs in stock markets was not simply attributable to the markets' notorious irrational exuberance. The volatility of stock markets was evident in the dot-com bubble that, due to speculation in internet companies, saw the technology-heavy Nasdaq stock index rise 400 per cent between 1995 and March 2000, before it crashed and lost four-fifths of its value. This time the boom may have a more solid foundation, even if the ephemeral valuations attached to some businesses, such as Tesla, as its founder Elon Musk has noted, defy logic. The ability of the FAANG companies – Facebook, Amazon, Apple, Netflix and Google – to cash in on isolation in homes and the acceleration of the digital economy underpins their rise. The extent to which digital companies now dominate the stock markets is evident in the fact that the $28 trillion attributed to these companies is five times greater than all the physical assets owned by all the other 500 companies in the S&P 500 stock index. During the pandemic intangible assets that you cannot count or see, notably algorithms and brands, were worth a record 12 times tangible material assets.[42] Some of this is due to the decline in the value of some companies, with oil and natural gas producers and cruise lines and airlines contracting by over 20 per cent. This decline was more than offset by the rise in value of digital businesses, with just the five FAANG companies now accounting for a quarter of the stock market, and whereas the rest of the market has on average stagnated over 2020, the values of the FAANG companies have more than doubled.

The repricing of assets is likely to give way to a rush of mergers and acquisitions, as private equity companies seek to find ways to gain returns from their accumulated $1.5 trillion mountain of cash. With dividends down and interest rates negligible or negative, mergers and acquisitions remain one of the few ways for investors (and their bankers and lawyers) to make money. Initially the lockdown led to a collapse in activity, to half of what it was in 2019, but given the economy-wide and global changes in the value of different companies that the pandemic has exposed, the hunger for deals is now greater than ever, with banks generating a record $125 billion in fees in 2020.[43]

There are two aspects of the Covid-19 economic crisis that

are different from previous recessions, though. Firstly, because of government bailouts, the number of bankruptcies has actually gone down, not up as occurred in all previous crises, in the US, Germany, France, UK and all major economies.[44] This has simply bought time and when government support ends in 2021, there will be a tidal wave of delayed bankruptcies, which are going to extend the recession and add to unemployment. Secondly, there has been a burst of entrepreneurship across all major economies, with more new start-ups in the second half of 2020 than in any prior series of quarterly periods. The number of applications for sole trading in 2020 was 50 per cent higher than the previous year.[45] A significant share of these were people trying to benefit from cheap government loans and to find ways to restart their lives after having lost their jobs.

Government and Business

Covid-19 has led to a rewriting of the rules of capitalism. For the influential Austrian economist Joseph Schumpeter, writing between the wars, the constant churn of newer companies replacing those that cannot keep up and the resulting process of creative destruction was a defining characteristic of a capitalist system. During the pandemic, governments in the high-income economies suspended bankruptcy for large businesses by instead offering bailouts and subsidised loans, at the cost of well over $4 trillion.[46] Competition policy was also weakened, as governments circumvented tender processes in response to the crisis. Stronger and bigger companies benefited from the disappearance of many small competitors; while large companies have been bailed out, in most countries small businesses have been allowed to go bankrupt.

The politicisation of the business environment, in the name of security concerns, has added to the return of a corporatist view of enterprise in which the interests of governments and business are intertwined. A key example of this came in the summer of 2020 with Donald Trump's war with Huawei. The

White House chose to disinvest it from the US and forced the
company to retreat from other markets, with a growing range
of suppliers and customers facing legal threats from the US
government if they failed to comply.

In the UK, as debt increased, so too did the power of the big
four banks with large balance sheets and connections to government, including through the many former ministers they employ
as advisors. Barclays, NatWest, HSBC and Lloyds Bank provided
more than 80 per cent of the government-backed loans to
support businesses during the pandemic.[47] In contrast, the four
largest US banks provided just 12 per cent of their government's
loans to business in the same period.[48] In both markets the big
banks are gaining market share, and smaller challengers such as
Monzo, Revolut, Tide and Starling are struggling as the small
businesses they support are closing and their young clientele are
losing their jobs, resulting in a need to cut back on staff and
marketing budgets while they watch the big incumbents being
given lucrative government contracts.[49]

The pandemic reinforced the growing domination of economies by big companies. Large companies benefit more than
small ones from access to power and also from access to capital
markets. While corporate debt increased faster than ever in 2020
and now exceeds the total size of the global economy, almost
all this increase was due to lending to large companies.[50] In the
US, lending to small companies went down in 2020 as banks
concentrated on bigger borrowers, including through bond
issues, which typically have a minimum size of $200 million and
so are out of the reach of most businesses.[51]

Already before the pandemic there was growing evidence that
low interest rates and cheap credit had allowed non-profitable
companies to survive even with rising debt. This reduced Joseph
Schumpeter's 'churn' by which more productive companies
replace less productive ones. As my research group in Oxford
has shown, the unusually low interest rates have contributed to
stagnating productivity.[52] By freezing economies, preventing

bankruptcies and making credit even more widely available at lower cost, the response in rich countries to the pandemic compounded this. All of this increased the zombification of economies, providing a further drag on productivity and future growth prospects.

Companies that have not been able to benefit from the pandemic but have managed to survive emerged deeply weakened. While their long-term prospects may have improved, due to many of their competitors having gone bust, in the short term they suffered from a drain of cash as lower sales meant they were unable to offset ongoing costs.[53] Many surviving companies ran down their equity and are saddled with higher debt. It will require years of lower dividend payments to shareholders for companies to rebuild their working capital, reduce their debts and invest in new opportunities. While patient shareholders will be rewarded, those seeking quick returns will be disappointed as higher payouts will undermine much-needed investment and reduce future prospects and profitability. The implication for pension funds and investors who are already suffering from lower returns on income will be having to accept poor returns for years to come. The alternative is to concentrate a higher share of their portfolios in a narrower set of mainly high-tech companies, which will increase volatility and risk.

Government intervention to preclude foreign companies and suppliers on the basis of strategic national interest risks fragmenting global commerce and igniting a new mercantilism, promoting exports and penalising imports. As history shows, this is enormously costly for citizens, who face the prospect of higher prices, less choice and paying higher taxes to subsidise domestic business. It also increases the prospect of corruption and bribery, as businesses exchange favours with politicians to gain privileged access. In the US, during the pandemic President Trump forced the Chinese company ByteDance to rule out Microsoft's stronger bid and sell the social media app TikTok to Oracle, whose CEO Larry Ellison was one of the few tech moguls to resolutely back him, reflecting the dangers of ruling by decree.[54]

Since the 1970s the hallmark of conservatives has been to argue that governments should not be involved in business and should 'get out of the way'. Yet the pandemic has legitimised intervention as a core value of conservatism on both sides of the Atlantic. It is not only conservative governments that are rewriting the rules of capitalism; so too are business leaders. A growing number of CEOs are embracing the language of stakeholder capitalism and calling for governments to play a stronger role in society. These trends were already emerging prior to the pandemic, but rather than taking decades to emerge, they are now being crystalised. Covid-19 accelerated the transformation of economies, with governments intervening more actively than at any time since the Second World War.

From Shareholder to Stakeholder Capitalism

Covid-19 brought to an end five decades of belief in the virtues of unbridled free market forces and provided impetus to the transition from shareholder to stakeholder capitalism. During the pandemic demand for Environmental, Social and Governance (ESG) data increased fivefold, which, according to David Craig, CEO of the financial data company Refinitiv, reflected a deepening interest in values.[55]

Fifty years ago, Milton Friedman, the Chicago professor and apostle of neoliberalism, proclaimed that the business of business is to increase profits, and that this is their sole responsibility to shareholders. Friedman pushed the intellectual pendulum away from government to the unbridled pursuit of private enterprise. He provided the intellectual justification for President Ronald Reagan in the US and Prime Minister Margaret Thatcher in the UK to attack trade unions, weaken anti-trust law, undermine consumer protection, neglect the environment, lower taxes and, in all areas except law and order and the military, reduce the role of the state relative to the private sector.[56] The consequences of this rule by the market have become abundantly clear, as profits have come at the cost of our health and that of our planet.

Since the 1980s, in the UK and US the increased focus on shareholder value maximisation has led to a more single-minded pursuit of short-term profits. This has driven businesses to reduce investment in longer-term objectives, such as new product lines or the loyalty and training of workers, in favour of paying dividends to shareholders and engaging in mergers that provide quick pay-offs to the owners. In countries like Germany and Japan, where it is harder to buy and sell companies than it is in the US and UK, businesses tend to have a longer-term focus and are more concerned with their broader social impact.[57]

Increasing environmental destruction, stagnating wages and rising inequality in recent decades have led politicians and citizens to place growing pressure on businesses to reframe their ambitions. Today, only 8 per cent of the citizens in a wide range of countries believe that the purpose of business is simply to generate profits, with 92 per cent indicating that companies should consider the interests of all stakeholders.[58] Long before the pandemic, business associations such as the UN Global Compact, The B Team and Business Roundtable were established to provide a shared platform for businesses that recognise that not only shareholders but also employees, customers, suppliers and environmental and ethical standards should guide corporate activities.

Covid-19 has highlighted the failure of many of the signatories of these laudable manifestos to live up to their commitments for social and environmental change or to protect their workers. Indeed, several firms are primary beneficiaries of tax havens and the source of rapidly rising inequality, as their executive salaries and value of shareholdings have rocketed, whilst the wages of their lowest-paid employees have stagnated. The companies that signed the US Business Roundtable Statement of Purpose regarding their commitments to a wide range of stakeholders on average operated no differently during the pandemic from those that had not signed the statement, leading commentators to question whether these activities are done for public relations rather than genuine transformative purposes.[59]

Covid-19 has highlighted the imbalance between the legal obligations and accountability of businesses to shareholders, who can remove CEOs, and other stakeholders such as employees and customers, who have no power. There is a risk that businesses that claim they are working in the interests of all stakeholders in fact are accountable to none; there is a need to enshrine worker protection – and environmental protection – in law to prevent this.[60] As is the case with public benefit corporations and charities, the responsibility of company directors should be mandatory and universally applicable rather than individual private companies being free to choose the jurisdiction in which they operate in order to minimise tax and avoid regulatory compliance.[61]

Whether the pandemic will lead to a radically new social contract in which businesses are held accountable to a wider set of stakeholders has been the subject of much discussion in the European Commission in Brussels, as it has been in financial circles. The *Financial Times* in a series of articles on 'The new social contract' argued that 'Coronavirus has exposed frailties in our economic and social model', reflecting widespread dissatisfaction with the status quo, even in the business community.[62]

Rescue Business

Ensuring that the values and actions of companies are aligned with those of consumers requires greater clarity on standards, including regarding labelling and packaging. The pandemic has made us more sensitive to working conditions and consumers should be able to easily identify the content, origin and cradle-to-grave environmental footprint of everything they consume.

The pandemic allowed governments to operate by stealth in order to address pressing national exigencies. Large government purchases of medical and other equipment were not subject to normal tender processes, allowing contracts to be awarded to friends and family of government ministers and key advisors. The lack of transparency means that we must assume that what we learn about is only a very small fraction of the questionable deals.

As businesses become more dependent on governments for survival, the risk of bribery and capture is growing. The pandemic undermined the global crusade against corruption, with the US and UK retreating further from their lofty attempts to improve the governance of business at home and abroad. Increasing geopolitical tensions and protectionism create a permissive environment for the blurring of corporate and government interests.

The pandemic provided an additional pretext for rushed back-room deals. Rising geopolitical tensions also reduced the international cooperation that is needed to investigate and prosecute corruption that crosses national borders.

To rescue procurement from allegations of cronyism requires, even in times of crisis, transparency, including through cross-party scrutiny. Auditing companies should not be given responsibility for vetting if there is a conflict of interest, as was the case in the UK, where the big four audit and management consultancy companies (KPMG, EY, Deloitte, and PwC) were beneficiaries of the pandemic, taking on numerous tasks that previously would have been assigned to civil servants. Profiteering from meeting emergency needs was banned in the US and UK during the world wars. It similarly should not be allowed during a pandemic or any other national emergency.

Without more action the pandemic could well mark the end of concerted global efforts to improve corporate and country governance; but it is not too late to rescue business from the black hole of cronyism and corruption. To do this, and thus create a better world, it is essential that these efforts be redoubled. Government frameworks need to be developed and enforced to ensure that the pursuit of profit is aligned with the needs of people and our planet. Multinational companies should be at the forefront of spreading and raising standards globally, and should be compelled to contribute their taxes in proportion to the net revenues generated in different jurisdictions.[63]

Business – including in China – accounts for nine out of ten new jobs. We are all consumers and many of us are shareholders, even if only unknowingly through our savings being invested by pension funds. This power is too seldom used to hold businesses accountable for their employment practices, environmental footprint and behaviour. The growing acceptance by companies that they need to move beyond shareholders to engage with a wider range of stakeholders could lead to greater accountability. But it also risks diluting accountability by allowing businesses to choose between the growing number of conflicting demands.

If businesses are serious about their commitment to serving the interests of society and not simply to reward those who make money from them, this needs to be enshrined in laws that specify their obligations.[64] On rare occasions businesses are held criminally responsible for their actions, but more often than not they collapse behind a veil of bankruptcy proceedings, while their owners are shielded from prosecution. So, for example, Purdue Pharma in September 2020 pleaded guilty to criminal charges of promoting the use of OxyContin, which has led to widespread addiction and hundreds of thousands of deaths, and has gone bankrupt; none of the Sackler family, who own the company and have earned more than $10 billion from it, have been personally charged though the family did agree to pay $225 million in a civil settlement with the US Department of Justice.[65]

The move from shareholder to stakeholder capitalism should not be an empty slogan; it needs to be reflected in companies actively engaging with their employees, communities, suppliers and customers. Radical reforms are needed to ensure that business contributes to creating more sustainable and inclusive societies, both at home and abroad. Big businesses and their billionaire bosses who currently escape tax should be compelled by consumers and regulators to pay their fair share. We need to hold companies and their owners accountable and judge them by what they did during the crisis and have done in the past for their employees and customers, just as individuals and political leaders should be judged by their actions. To rescue society we need to rescue business from short-term profit maximising and encourage it to be incentivised to serve the wider long-term interests of our societies – doing well by doing good.

CHAPTER 7

Governments that Serve

Big government is back. In the 1980s Margaret Thatcher, the Prime Minister of the UK, President of the US Ronald Reagan, and like-minded evangelists for free enterprise in Germany and elsewhere, rolled back the system that had been in place since the Second World War. Their neoliberal agenda involved a revolutionary programme of privatisation, deregulation, attacks on trade unions, tax cuts and reductions in government spending on education, health, and welfare benefits. The pandemic has led to a counter-revolution.

As befits this time of change, conservative governments in the US, UK, Germany and France have gone furthest, beyond even Maynard Keynes's arguments in the 1930s that governments needed to spend their way out of the Great Depression. A 40-year-old commitment to balanced budgets and non-interference of governments in markets has been jettisoned overnight to provide lifelines for individuals and companies caught up in the Covid-19 tsunami. Notions that were unthinkable in January 2020, such as banning bankruptcy or providing a basic income for all citizens, have now become mainstream. Even the most obsessively prudent governments, such as Angela Merkel's Christian Democrat-led coalition in Germany, are now living beyond their means. The result has been an explosive creation of debt, to bridge the widening divide between soaring government spending and collapsing tax revenues.

The question now is how this will be sustained and whether

the growing debt mountain will be countered by a new wave of austerity. A century ago, the debt mountain generated during the First World War was followed by belt-tightening austerity and punitive reparations for Germany, leading to the Great Depression, nationalism and another world war. Similarly, in 2008, after the government fire hoses sprayed cash to douse the financial crisis, crippling austerity followed. This led to stagnating wages and rising inequality, political populism and, in 2016, the vote for Brexit in Britain and the election of Donald Trump to the presidency in the US. Austerity also led to national health services and the World Health Organization (WHO) being starved of much-needed resources, making a pandemic more likely and societies less prepared.

In 2020, the cost of these short-sighted policies became dreadfully apparent. In a desperate attempt to sustain their battered economies, rich countries provided over $12 trillion of fiscal stimulus, increasing their deficits to an average of 17 per cent of their GDP.[1] In 2020 the UK government borrowed more than four times the amount it had in 2019, taking its accumulated debt to over £2.1 trillion, the highest level on record and more than the total size of the British economy. To pay this back, an extra £40 billion per year will need to be found by the Treasury and, with the Chancellor promising that 'this Conservative government will always balance the books', a return of austerity is a deeply troubling prospect.[2]

Austerity is not a necessary response to higher debt. Governments are not like households, needing to tighten their belts when times are tough. Cuts and reduced spending will only serve to kill the already dismal prospects for job creation. Rather, productive investments are required to overcome the economic destruction. Other means can be found to reduce debt, including through governments taking equity stakes in businesses they are bailing out and in allowing for renationalisation of industries, which the Conservative government in the UK has finally accepted is required for the railways, three decades after they were privatised.

In response to the pandemic, the bastions of economic orthodoxy began preaching the virtues of more spending and offered
almost unlimited government guarantees. The US Federal
Reserve effectively underwrote a significant amount of corporate
debt, Germany offered loan guarantees worth a quarter of GDP,
and the IMF abandoned its role as the guardian of fiscal restraint;
instead, in a marked shift in its policies it encouraged countries
to continue the fiscal stimulus after the pandemic has passed,
recognising that restoring growth and investing in the transition
to a zero-carbon economy is going to require governments to
continue to spend more than they raise in taxes.

Since the early 1970s, when countries needed support from
the IMF and World Bank to overcome the impact of surging oil
prices and growing indebtedness, these institutions have sought
to implement neoliberal policies in what became known as the
Washington Consensus, which included a commitment to
balanced budgets and reduction in government spending.
Although these 'structural adjustment' policies fell out of favour
in the 1990s, it is only now, with the pandemic, that the IMF has
called on countries that can afford it to take on more debt. In
these high-income countries, debt is likely to keep growing until
well after 2025. This policy makes sense for the high-income
countries, who are unlikely to suffer debt crises as long as interest
rates remain low, but it is not an option for developing countries,
who are unable to raise more debt without incurring a collapse
in their credit ratings and risking a financial crisis. The implication is that the gulf between the prospects for rich countries
and for poorer ones, which has been closing over the past decades,
now – tragically – will widen and along with it global inequality.

Activist States

History tells us that global crises have permanent ramifications
for governments everywhere. Prior to the pandemic, overall
government spending in advanced economies accounted for
about a third of total economic activity. Since the pandemic this

has climbed to over 40 per cent, as expenditure has soared at the same time as economies have contracted. In capitalist economies, this level of government activity has been exceeded previously only during wars. The fact that even the most fiscally conservative governments, such as Germany, now see this as necessary marks a revolution in attitudes.

Tearing up their previously sacrosanct rule books, central banks have undertaken to print money to keep down government borrowing costs, with both the US Federal Reserve and the European Central Bank breaking with past practice by refusing to set any limits and stating that they will do 'what it takes' to resurrect moribund economies.[3] The unprecedented scale of government borrowing has been matched by ballooning bond purchases by the central banks, which are effectively financing deficits by the creation of money. Central banks are also providing new lines of credit to companies and banks, and by directly propping up the system are going way beyond their previous mandate, which was confined to controlling the money supply.[4]

Prior to the pandemic, about 8 per cent of businesses in the rich countries would fail annually and 10 per cent of workers would lose their jobs.[5] With the onset of the pandemic, in most European countries leaders declared a moratorium on bankruptcies and provided credit to prop up businesses. Furlough and similar job retention schemes were also introduced to prevent a rapid rise in unemployment, although in the US companies were saved, but not workers.

Even among economists, who are renowned for their inability to agree, an unprecedented consensus emerged, with debate focused not on whether governments should do more, but on how long the measures should last and how they should be financed. While falling short of the 'Hamiltonian' moment, in which the first US Secretary of the Treasury in 1790 famously engineered a deal that allowed the new federal government to take on the debts of the former warring states and thereby giving them shared responsibilities in a fiscal union, the precedents of a new European Union deal are profound and long lasting. The agreement in the deal allows the EU to borrow on behalf of its members for the first time.

Government tax and revenue collapsed during the pandemic but expenditures soared on health services, welfare benefits and lifelines to public transport utilities. Funding furlough and similar schemes by massively increasing public debt would have been regarded as a revolutionary political act during normal times. However, during the pandemic it was rightly launched overnight without consultation with citizens.

The twenty-seven countries of the European Union for the first time allowed the Commission to incur €750 billion of collective debt. These actions overcame the prior unwillingness of northern countries to accept a pooling of risk with southern European countries. They also allowed for payments to companies that breached the previously sacrosanct rules on state aid, allowing for interventions that in normal times would have been unacceptable. Far from revoking this resurgent activism, the European Commission is promoting it. Europe is aiming to create its own champions that can compete with US or Chinese companies, particularly in artificial intelligence and information technology. The spirit that informed the creation of European bastions of national and business cooperation, such as the giant CERN particle physics laboratory and the Airbus collaborative airline construction project, has been given a fresh impetus by the pandemic.

While in the US states habitually provide tax incentives and subsidies to attract private companies, in Europe this practice is outlawed to prevent wealthier countries attracting investment that otherwise would have gone to poorer countries. Covid-19 however has changed practice on this. Prior to the pandemic, strict European Commission rules on what governments can do with state aid to businesses required on average at least six months of lengthy – and often fruitless – submissions. These exemptions now tend to be approved by Brussels within twenty-four hours. Similarly, whereas budget discussions normally take years of negotiations in the European Commission, the new fast-tracking of decision-making has led to the approval of a €1.8 trillion ($2.2tr) package within three months, far faster than had been previously achieved.[6]

The landmark 2020 budget goes beyond anything previously imagined possible in Brussels. It ties financial support to rule of law principles, including upholding the independence of the judiciary in Hungary and Poland, to investments in renewable technologies and jobs, and to €390 billion's worth of grants to poorer southern and Balkan countries to offset the impact of the pandemic on their economies. The scale of this support is highly significant, with grants worth around 10 per cent of the size of their pre-crisis economies for Croatia, Bulgaria and Greece, and significant amounts for Portugal, Spain and Italy.[7]

For the European Union, the pandemic marks a watershed and has empowered its members to explore new possibilities for social solidarity and transformation. Within Europe, it aims to use its greater economic muscle to force companies to pay tax and uphold higher standards of environmental, social and governance principles. It has also introduced new legislation that seeks to challenge the near monopoly power of big technology companies such as Google and Facebook, seeking to modernise competition policy for the digital age and tighten rules on data privacy and usage as well as illegal and harmful content, threatening fines of as much as 10 per cent of a company's European turnover for breaches.[8] Internationally, it has committed to embed environmental and labour standards in its trade deals and is exploring legislation that would hold its multinational companies legally accountable for actions that would break European laws in areas of bribery, conflict minerals, illegally harvested timber, child labour and human rights. The challenge for the future is to ensure that this lifting of standards during the pandemic is sustained and part of a wider global trend.

Keynes Returns

The pandemic has brought the ideas of John Maynard Keynes back to life despite repeated efforts by Milton Friedman's disciples to bury him. Among Keynes's most influential ideas was the notion that governments had a key role to play in promoting growth by increasing the ability of people to spend money and buy local goods and services. Governments could stimulate demand and economies, he suggested, by borrowing money and increasing investments in infrastructure and services, and could increase expenditure and consumption by giving poor people, who had less capacity to save, money through welfare payments and other forms of redistribution.

Keynes argued that as economic growth recovered government tax revenues would rise and debts could be repaid. His ideas underpinned the success of the UK and other economies in the 1950s and 1960s, but in the 1970s his theories were discredited. Throughout this decade increasing expenditure failed to reduce unemployment and instead created inflationary spirals, with increased spending leading to prices but not production going up. In this context, Friedman and other monetary theorists focused on the need to reduce the amount of money in circulation and with it the size of taxes and governments. The primary focus of government policy became maintaining price stability and raising interest rates to choke off demand and control inflation. Three decades of benign economic growth appeared to support these theories, but at the cost of rising inequality, a growing concentration of economic and political power in metropolitan elites, and the building up of systemic risks, which culminated in the financial crisis of 2008.

After the financial crisis successive cuts in interest rates failed to restore growth. The pandemic has crystalised the failure of monetary theory and austerity and thrust governments back onto the central stage. Having pulled all their increasingly ineffective monetary levers, governments have been forced to fall back on fiscal policy, which focuses on spending and taxes.

Increased debt has led to neither higher interest rates nor inflation. The resurrection of Keynes is complete.

Keynes warned that economic crises can damage economic prospects for the long term. He showed how the Great Depression in the US had led individuals to spend less, and argued that a boost to the economy was needed to convince citizens to part with their savings. Economic crises make people more cautious in their habits and less able to afford investments in the future. A review of nineteen pandemics reveals that that they have depressed longer-term growth because nervous households increased savings at the cost of consumption, which sustains demand and jobs.[9] Policies that avoid this 'belief-scarring' could underpin a sustained recovery and avoid permanent damage to economic growth.[10]

Governments to the Rescue

The impact of the pandemic will persist long after the health emergency itself has passed. Higher levels of unemployment, inequality and debt will leave permanent generational and geographical scars, with many countries failing to achieve their pre-pandemic levels of economic output for years to come. When total output does eventually return to pre-pandemic levels, its composition will be different, as the impact of changing trade patterns, automation, demographic shifts and stagnant productivity will place a drag on growth and reinforce the divides that the pandemic has so starkly revealed. To counter these negative effects and create sustainable and inclusive societies will require a significant expansion of the role of governments in all countries.

This is not about more omnipotent governments, but rather more strategic and smart ones. By accelerating the diffusion of digital technologies and surveillance, the pandemic made more urgent the need for data governance and standards to be implemented at the national and international level. Currently, this is governed by an inconsistent patchwork of rules, with major gaps within countries and internationally. In the US, the tech giants and various states are seeking to go their own separate ways, with no national framework. Europe is the most advanced, setting its own standards; most other countries, not least poorer countries, are either operating in a wild west unfettered by rules, or subject to draconian state controls, as is the case in Russia, China and other autocratic countries. The pandemic has accelerated the arrival of the digital economy and surveillance state, leading to a widening gap between our dependence on digital tools and their governance. It is this gap that now needs urgently to be closed.

We must learn from the governments that have been effective, like Taiwan, Estonia, New Zealand and Finland, that their achievements have not been made by being bigger or more oppressive but rather by being smarter. The pandemic has broken taboos about what governments can spend, how they can regulate and how they can learn. Overconfident imperious powers – the US, UK, France and Russia – have done particularly badly, while smaller governments and those willing to learn from international best practice and be guided by expertise have done much better.[11] If the pandemic accelerates improvements in governments and their ability to build cohesion within their societies and cooperation globally it will have provided a vital building block for a better world.

CHAPTER 8

Cities for the Future

Covid-19 has posed the greatest threat to cities since the aerial bombings of the Second World War. The destroyed British, European and Japanese cities recovered from that, as they and others did from previous catastrophic events and pandemics. Pandemics always hit cities hardest due to rapid contagion in their crowded environments, and Covid-19 was no exception. However, following even the most devastating pandemics, such as the great plagues of the fourteenth and seventeenth centuries and the 1918–1919 Spanish Flu, big cities have recovered fastest and pulled further ahead of rural and declining regions. New York was rocked in the 1970s by crime and near bankruptcy, again in 2001 by the Twin Towers attack, and in 2008 by the collapse of Wall Street. For New York and all other cities this time is different.

The rapid adoption of remote working across large swathes of the global population has changed our relationship to cities like never before. Significant changes in home-working, freelance lifestyles and self-employment were already under way, but by accelerating and compressing slow-moving trends into a single year, the pandemic has had a seismic impact on the future of offices and cities.

Although people value cities for many reasons, including that they are more accepting of differences and offer more entertainment, culture and amenities, the centuries-old attraction of cities as places of work is breaking down. As a result, the pandemic will permanently reshape not only cities but, as people relocate, also suburbs, small towns and rural areas, creating a more diffuse landscape. The growing share of remote work will accelerate the movement of families and older professionals out of cities. The result is that cities will become increasingly cosmopolitan hives for people who choose to live there for lifestyle reasons, rather than the necessity of work. They also will be home to those who cannot afford to move elsewhere.

The shift to more flexible work arrangements is one of the most significant workplace transformations since the industrial revolution and is much more rapid.[1] The industrial revolution led to a seismic shift away from small-scale homeworking in the countryside and small villages to large-scale manufacturing in cities. Steam power led to the concentration of work in factories, with their layout determined by the connection of the conveyer belts that snaked around the factories to one or two big steam engines. The roll-out of electrification in the early twentieth century allowed for individual machines with their own power sockets, but the manufacturing advantages of the kind of production lines pioneered by Henry Ford continued to be a powerful factor in workers congregating in factories. With public transport and cars providing the means to commute over longer distances, cities grew in size.

The location of manufacturing was determined by proximity to raw materials or to major railways or shipping centres; its decline after the Second World War saw the concomitant decline of many once great cities that had offered these advantages, as is evident in the rust belt of the US, in the Midlands and north of England, the Ruhr in Germany and the north of France. New office jobs were generated in the rapidly expanding civil service and in professional services such as banking, law, accountancy, media and consultancies. These jobs were located close to government, clients, service suppliers and major airports, and so are concentrated in a smaller number of cities. With increasing concentration came a growth in amenities and entertainment, further enhancing major cities.

In recent decades, the roll-out of high-speed broadband and growth of services jobs has allowed for more flexibility in where people can live. In the early 1970s, when miners' strikes in the UK led to energy shortages and the three-day week, both work and home were severely affected.[2] During the pandemic, not only were power, broadband and other vital services maintained but the fact that such a small part of the economy is now factory-based meant that a change to working at home was far less disruptive. Whereas at the time of the miners' strikes a quarter of British workers were employed in manufacturing, today this sector employs less than 8 per cent.[3]

Future of Offices

The idea of a future of blending remote work with an 'optional office' is gaining traction; this change will have wide-ranging consequences for where people live and for the future of cities. A survey of more than 10,000 workers in twelve countries showed that nine out of ten would like to continue to work from home after the pandemic, even though only one in twenty were permitted to work from home prior to the pandemic.[4] Most are keen to work from home three to four days a week and believe that this would increase both productivity and loyalty to their employers.

If home-based work is preferred by most people, why prior to the pandemic did barely 3 per cent of workers do it and why were office developments booming?[5] Offices were needed when people exchanged large amounts of paper and broadband and digital options were not available.[6] Although offices outgrew this function decades ago, inertia kept work in what economists term a 'bad equilibrium'. The pandemic has propelled us into a new, improved state. This required overcoming three obstacles.[7] The first was willingness, as many people expected to go to offices to work. The second was efficiency, as meetings, supplies and service delivery, and internal and external meetings, seemed to require being located in one place and near other businesses. The third is the sunk cost of investments – given all the spending on office systems and lack of investment in home systems, employers were reluctant to make the changes required. During the pandemic, out of necessity all three of these obstacles to remote work were addressed.

The pandemic attacked the dynamic ecosystems that make cities so attractive, notably the complex, dense and diverse mix of people, skills, networks and industries. Historically this has been a prime source of economic growth and innovation, and the reason why productivity in major cities is twice that found elsewhere. Cities have offered a constantly evolving but well-established network of suppliers and customers whose close proximity is not only efficient but also leads to continuous information exchange, often informal, and the accumulation of tacit knowledge. The broadening and deepening of contacts and information, including on opportunities and methods, together with new ideas provided by the constant flow of newcomers and migrants, fuels the dynamism.[8] It is this vibrancy that is threatened by the flight to the suburbs and by remote working.

The speed at which offices were abandoned is astounding. Before the pandemic struck, less than 3 per cent of people in the US worked from home regularly; now the majority have experienced working from home. The extent to which workers will return to offices is proving to be a complex question and one which is hanging over the $32 trillion commercial property market.[9] When lockdowns were eased, 84 per cent of French workers returned to their desks but less than 40 per cent of British workers.[10] In the UK, a large corporate survey found that three-quarters of company directors said that they would retain home-working after the pandemic, and over half said this would lead to a reduction in their need for offices.[11]

Companies that do not offer remote working options are

likely to lose talented staff to companies that offer more flexibility.[12] A survey of attitudes to remote working in the US, UK, France, Germany, Japan and Australia found that only 12 per cent of workers wanted to return to past office routines and that the overwhelming majority preferred to work remotely, as it improved their work–life balance, reduced stress and increased productivity.[13] In the US, about 90 per cent of US workers surveyed do not want to return to their offices full time and many companies have introduced more flexible arrangements, with this being particularly prevalent in the technology sector. Jack Dorsey, head of Twitter, has announced that his staff need never come back to the office.[14] Google, Salesforce and Twitter are among the tech companies that announced that they were extending remote working at least to the summer of 2021. Facebook has split its workforce into three categories of workers, with some able to remain permanently at home, others encouraged to come in a few days a week and the moderators who scan content for unsuitable material, most of whom are contractors working in offices outside the US, told to return to the office full time even during the pandemic due to security concerns regarding the material they access.

Google has announced that it will permanently adopt a three days in two days out of the office policy. This system seeks to balance flexibility with collaboration and creativity which Google believes requires time physically together with others at work. PwC, one of the big four accounting companies, has indicated that, in the UK, all of its 22,000 employees are expected to use the office to some degree.[15] Siemens, the Munich-based industrial group, has told about half its total global workforce, roughly 140,000 of its employees, that they can work from home for three days a week indefinitely and over half of German companies overall are adopting the same policies.[16] Standard Chartered bank, which has 85,000 global employees, has offered permanent 'flexi-working' arrangements to 90 per cent of its staff and is aiming to provide 'near home' workspaces to more than 90 per cent of its staff by 2023.[17] Larry Fink, the chief executive of BlackRock, expects that while two-thirds of its staff will return many will never do so.[18] Jes Staley, CEO of Barclays, believes that headquarters buildings will become 'a thing of the past', while leading international law firms envisage that their need for expensive offices will decline by as much as a half due to permanent increases in remote working.[19] In Japan, Fujitsu is halving its office space, giving its 80,000 employees unprecedented flexibility in a country that hitherto has been known for its extended office hours and crowded commutes.[20]

Following the pandemic, around the world the majority of workers will return to offices for three to four days a week, but not with the regularity that previously regimented workers and led to overcrowded roads and public transport. The implication, according to Nicolas Aubert of Willis Towers Watson, an advisory business, is that he 'would be very surprised if corporations in professional services kept more than 50 per cent of their real estate, and it might be significantly less . . . there is a serious risk that what was once a prime real-estate asset is now an overpriced half-empty building.'[21] A long-term decline in demand for office space of at least 10 per cent is forecast for major cities around the world.[22] In the US, demand for work in high-rise offices is projected to drop by 25 per cent following the pandemic.[23] Technology companies are likely to become even less office-bound, with the majority of businesses planning on cutting their commercial office space by 40 to 60 per cent, allowing staff to work from home for two to four days a week, and about 30 per cent of the companies planning to get rid of their offices entirely and go remote-first.[24] A key reason given is that they will be able to draw on the global talent pool, rather than having to be restricted to those who are prepared to live within a thirty-mile radius of the office.

Whereas there are some costs associated with setting up workers to operate from home, this option saves employers an average of $18,000 (£14,000) per worker per year in rent and overheads.[25] It is these savings that explain Pinterest's willingness to pay an $89 million penalty to cancel the contract on its new city-centre office building in San Francisco.[26]

Remaining office space will be reconfigured to encourage interaction with desk space reserved for those who choose or need to work in offices. The rows of desktop computers that have been a feature of many offices are likely to give way to both formal and informal spaces, with meeting and Zoom rooms, as well as lounge areas, easy chairs and sofas and, as was pioneered by the Silicon Valley tech companies, cafe-like areas with games. An additional feature is likely to be areas that can be used by external collaborators, with one law firm I interviewed providing space for clients to use, to build loyalty and to deepen interdisciplinary learning and enhance productivity.[27]

It's not only office spaces that will be reconfigured to be more suitable for occasional usage and conducive for meetings and social interactions. Homes need to be reconfigured too. Prior to the pandemic, property owners around the world were contributing to a home improvement boom as they sought to upgrade and extend their properties through loft conversions, more energy-efficient heating systems and investments in gardens and terraces. While the pandemic has meant greater demand for renovations, it has also led to changing priorities. For one, the fashion for open-plan spaces is being reversed as individuals sharing a home come to appreciate closed doors that insulate them from noise in the house. The need to secure privacy, spend more time childminding and be in the kitchen more is likely to lead to imaginative new designs.

Future of Shops
It is not only offices that emptied out during the pandemic. With their decline the ecosystems around them of dry-cleaners, hairdressers and barbers, sandwich shops, cafes and restaurants are also severely threatened. The dispersion of office functions left many city-centre offices with more empty offices and collapsing property values, while the rise of online services accelerated the

decline of high streets and big city shopping centres. The risk is that city centres become 'ghost towns'.[28]

The combination of remote working and online shopping led to record closures of high street shops, with the greatest impact being on city centres. In the UK, more than 11,000 chain outlets closed, with a significant share of these closures permanent.[29] One of the biggest landlords in London, Shaftesbury, reported that during the pandemic only 41 per cent of their rents were being paid, a fifth of their apartments could not be let and the majority of its 611 shops, restaurants, cafes and pubs were closed for a prolonged period.[30] The City of Westminster, at the heart of London, experienced a 63 per cent decline in its economic output in 2020, compared to the previous year.[31]

City-centre footfall during 2020 was 42 per cent down on the previous year.[32] Starbucks attributed over $2 billion in losses in 2020 to the desertion of central business districts in cities around the world.[33] In New York, the pandemic was estimated to have led to up to half of the city's 23,650 restaurants closing permanently, leading to the loss of 159,000 jobs and over $13 billion in revenues.[34]

In the US, the pandemic accelerated what has been described as a 'retail apocalypse' that began when bricks-and-mortar shops started closing following the 2008 crisis. In the first nine months of 2020, more than 14,000 shop chains closed, far surpassing the total of 9,879 in 2019. Many of the chains, such as Brooks Brothers, J. Crew, JCPenney, Kmart, Le Pain Quotidien, Lord & Taylor, Modell's Sports, Pizza Hut and Sears declared bankruptcy, while other retail chains such as Bloomingdale's, Gap, Macy's, Neiman Marcus, Nordstrom, Victoria's Secret, Walgreens and Zara closed hundreds of locations.[35] Shops that have remained in business are finding new ways to stay alive. Target, for example, began kerb-side collection in 2017 and during the pandemic saw demand for this service increase sevenfold, while Walmart's digital sales increased by 50 per cent in 2020.[36]

The pandemic propelled the UK, once characterised as a

nation of shopkeepers, to start doing about a third of its shopping online, up from a fifth at the start of 2020 and 7 per cent in 2010.[37] The result is that having spent the last three decades expanding their shops, there is now about a third more space available than retailers need.[38] As leases are relinquished and shops collapse, a growing overhang of space will depress prices, resulting in premises being occupied by tenants providing personal or leisure services, rather than the sale of goods that can be purchased online.

In the UK, the Arcadia group (known for Topshop, Miss Selfridge, Burton and other brands) and Debenhams chains closed down, Marks & Spencer furloughed a third of its total workforce and closed more than fifty shops as its clothing sales collapsed, and the Sainsbury supermarket chain announced 3,500 job cuts, closing its fresh fish and meat counters and 420 of its standalone Argos shops, while expanding its digital and neighbourhood outlets.[39] Local supermarkets within neighbourhoods concentrating on convenience foods did well, with Co-op opening fifty local supermarkets during the final four months of 2020.[40] In China, convenience stores saw a 120 per cent increase in their sales during the pandemic, with a growing range of these kinds of stores there and elsewhere teaming up with online delivery services. In the UK, the Deliveroo food delivery platform (part-owned by Amazon) started ferrying food and drink from supermarkets as well as restaurants and pop-up kitchens located in industrial estates and other low-cost locations.[41]

Many of the chains are key tenants in suburban shopping centres. In the US, the number of shopping centres has been declining since the 1990s, and a quarter of the 1,000 or so remaining are likely to close by 2025, with the pandemic accelerating this decline.[42] Those that remain will be primarily entertainment centres. At the new $5bn American Dream shopping centre in New Jersey, prior to the pandemic 45 per cent of its space was dedicated to retail; this is now under 30 per cent and more space has been given over to entertainment and leisure

facilities – it boasts a ski slope, Legoland and Ferris wheel.[43] The
hollowing out of shops and offices poses a dire threat to cities
not only because it removes a key reason for their existence,
but because it simultaneously reduces the income derived from
property and other local taxes. Allied to this is the question of
where workers who work remotely will pay local income taxes.
This could have profound implications for local finance, in the
US and other countries where this applies. So, for example,
Connecticut and New Jersey are challenging New York's ability to
tax the income of the hundreds of thousands of commuters who,
prior to the pandemic, worked in New York on the grounds that
their principal workplace is now in the states where they reside.
While the responsibilities of local authorities differ around the
world, in many countries local taxes fund the provision of vital
services, including fire, police and rubbish collection and roads
maintenance as well as libraries, sports and other community
facilities. The danger is that as the funding of these services
contracts, cities become less attractive and less secure, which
is what happened in Detroit, for example. This then further
undermines central business districts and accelerates the flight
from the city by those who can afford to leave.

Property Prices
City centres around the world have experienced a sharper
contraction in economic activity than the suburbs or smaller
town centres. In Manhattan activity declined by over a half, and
in London by over a third, with similar declines evident elsewhere.[44]

The economic collapse combined with the flight from the
office has led to a dramatic reversal of the fortunes of property
investors. Investments in commercial properties – offices, shops,
hotels, apartments and warehouses – quadrupled to $32 trillion
in the decade to 2020.[45] For long-term investors such as pension
funds, property consistently outperformed other asset classes,
offering seemingly stable returns in a world of declining interest

rates. Property developers were able to borrow at historically low interest rates built to meet the growing demand of investors and booming cities. Until the pandemic.

In the UK, commercial property values slumped by around 12 per cent in 2020, with this average masking wide variation.[46] Warehouses that could serve online purchases saw rising demand, while shopping centre valuations declined by an estimated 28 per cent and other retail and offices premises by 20 per cent.[47] A decline in these values not only hurts the investors in these properties, but also retired workers whose pension funds have been invested in property as returns on other long-term assets, such as bonds, decline with the collapse in interest rates.

Given the uncertainty, companies around the world are shying away from taking on longer-term leases, with year-on-year drops of 59 per cent in London, 66 per cent in New York and 77 per cent in Tokyo.[48] In the UK, less than half of office, shop and apartment tenants paid their rent on time during lockdown and hotels suffered a 90 per cent decline in occupancy.[49]

A study by my Future of Work research group at Oxford University found that if office workers spent two days a week at home it would take twenty-six years of strong growth in recruitment to fill the vacated space.[50] The full impact of the flight from offices will not be felt immediately as corporate leases typically last at least five years; however this has already led to a plummeting in the value of property funds as long-term investors, such as pension funds, size up the implications of excess supply, which inevitably will lead to falling rental incomes and valuations. In the longer term, remodelling of existing offices for other purposes, including for apartments, hotels and amusement arcades, is likely, as is the freezing of plans for new construction.

The race to suburbia and further afield saw a sharp fall in inner-city rentals in 2020, down 20 per cent or more in inner London areas, reflecting a 23 per cent year-on-year decline in people looking to rent in city locations.[51] New York City rents also dropped steeply, with a vacancy rate of 6 per cent for the first time in well over decades, while those in neighbouring Brooklyn, where tenants get more space for the same price, remained firmer.[52]

For those who can afford it, the attraction of second homes and rural idylls that can be easily accessed will last well beyond the pandemic. During 2020, in the US demand for rural properties increased by a third, and in the UK there was a 126 per cent year-on-year increase in people in cities looking for properties in rural village locations, with a greater desire to have gardens, more room and access to green space cited by half the respondents.[53] Hamptons estate agents recorded a 63 per cent increase in enquiries by Londoners seeking to move to commuter villages.[54] In the UK, over a fifth of all the house purchases in 2020 were driven by individuals keen to move out of cities to a home with more space, with detached house prices in the south-west of England increasing by around 7 per cent in 2020.[55]

The second half of 2020 saw an all-time record rise in demand for suburban properties due to families leaving inner cities and seeking more space.[56] About a quarter of commuters live more than fifteen miles (twenty-four kilometres) from their offices, and with less frequent commuting, these distances are likely to grow.[57] While daily commuters typically sought homes within an hour of their offices, less frequent commuters are prepared to venture much further afield – sales of properties two to three hours from London were up by over 20 per cent in 2020, compared to the previous year.[58]

The factors driving higher house prices are likely to be sustained. These are: record low interest rates, the lack of alternative investment options, lower expenditure on travel and other goods and services, more time being spent at home, growing recognition of the importance of nature and the environment, the need for offices and privacy for remote work, and the reduced need to be within easy commuting distance of work due to more flexible arrangements.

In the US, as in the UK, Europe and Australia, house prices have risen to record highs in recent years. Despite the pandemic, or rather because of it, in the US and UK average house prices increased by well over 5 per cent and in Germany during 2020 they were up 11 per cent.[59] Overall sales in the US in 2020 were 20 per cent up on the previous year, with the median price for a home hitting $311,800, up $40,000 on 2019.[60] This increase was almost entirely driven by purchases at the higher end of the market, with homes valued below $250,000 seeing only a 4 per cent increase in sales while sales of houses costing more than a million dollars more than doubled.[61] Most of the sales were to existing homeowners who were trading up to bigger houses.[62]

The decline in first-time buyers reflects and reinforces deep-rooted inequalities, as those with home equity can afford to trade up while a growing share of the population cannot reach the bottom rung of the home-ownership ladder. This will entrench the intergenerational divide between older workers who already own homes and younger people who cannot afford to buy them. In the UK, the share of young people who own a home or live in local authority council or housing association homes has halved since the 1990s, with more than half of 18- 29-year-olds now having to live with parents and private rentals accounting for the balance.[63] To the extent that the flight from the city reduces prices they may become more affordable, and in the UK a temporary exemption from the stamp duty tax on house purchases led to a short-lived rise in purchases by first-time buyers. But growing job insecurity and the unwillingness of lenders to issue home loans without greater security is undermining the potential for young people to own a home and reinforcing the divide between baby boomers and subsequent generations.

While those living in more affluent neighbourhoods can look forward to less commuting and to enjoying more nearby amenities, poorer individuals who cannot afford to live in the plush suburbs face the prospect of reverse or cross-town commuting. As poorer workers remain locked into their inner-city or less prosperous commuter neighbourhoods, and a growing share of jobs are in the homes and commercial centres located in wealthier suburbs, poorer workers will have to commute over longer distances. While demand for commuting into city centres will diminish, the often weak cross-town and orbital public transport links between suburbs will prove inad-equate and require massive investment, if workers are not to be forced to commute by first going into the city-centre hubs before transferring to buses and trains travelling to distant suburbs. The weakness and cost of these options is likely to result in rising car use, as the paucity of public transport options drives people to increasingly relying on private vehicles or minibus taxis, as has long been the case in developing countries where public transport is inadequate.

Far from remote working reducing the dependence on public transport of essential workers and others who cannot work from home, it will increase it. This is not only because their incomes have been eroded, but also because they will be commuting over long distances, as employment opportunities arise further from the city centres, in suburban shops, restaurants and other services that support widely geographically distributed remote workers. If there is one lesson to take from the desperate lives of those in the Midwest of the US chronicled by economist Angus Deaton and his co-author Anne Case, it is that when towns lose work, being able to get to areas where job opportunities are growing is the difference between hope and despair.[64] Getting a job and getting to a job are two very different things, with this disconnect explaining why areas of high unemployment persist despite jobs being available elsewhere.[65]

Public Transport
The pandemic revealed the extent to which cities depend on essential workers and in turn how dependent these workers are

on public transport. As commuters deserted buses and trains, and regulations imposed new restrictions and costs, the collapse in revenues for public transport systems turned what was a looming crisis into a financial catastrophe.

In the UK, Covid-19 proved the death knell for privatisation, leaving the government with no option but to bail out the railways with a £7.1 billion lifeline, more than twice as much in real terms as they cost before the privatisation three decades ago.[66] Transport for London, which runs the capital's underground and bus system, has also been forced to grovel to the government for emergency loans as it needs £5.7 billion to sustain public transport to the end of 2021.[67] The conditions imposed include raising fares, increasing congestion zone charges, and suspending plans for Crossrail 2, which would link north and south London.[68]

New York's Metropolitan Transportation Authority (MTA) lost $200 million a week during the pandemic as fares, tunnel and road tolls and subsidies all collapsed, while its costs increased, for reasons including nightly closure and the deep cleaning of carriages and platforms.[69] If it is unable to secure $12 billion of federal funding by the end of 2021, the MTA has anticipated reducing its services by 40 per cent in the city and by over a half in the suburbs, while also having to increase fares and delay maintenance and investment.[70]

The contraction of public transport systems is likely to spell more congestion in the longer term, as a 10 per cent reduction in public transport results in 30 per cent more road traffic.[71] During the pandemic, car dealerships reported increased purchases from city dwellers who were keen to avoid public transport.[72] In the UK, in the initial months of the pandemic long waiting lists developed for new cars, leading to record demand for used cars, the price of which increased sharply, with interest from young people aged 18–24 doubling compared to pre-pandemic levels.[73]

As public transport becomes more infrequent and cost savings on new equipment and maintenance lead to more erratic services, it will become more difficult to commute to work and to access nightlife and entertainment, placing further pressure on cities. Almost a third of New York households get by on under $30,000 a year.[74] It is these low-income families in cities and towns around the world, who rely on public transport and are particularly dependent on jobs in hospitality and other sectors and were particularly hard-hit by the pandemic, who would be most affected by cuts and rising costs in public transport, reinforcing inequalities.

Public transport was already in a precarious state before the pandemic. The pandemic revealed that while richer individuals have the luxury to ignore it, effective public transport systems matter not only for low-income people but also for the continued operation of the hospitals, shops and essential services on which we all rely. The pandemic has threatened a downward death spiral in public transport, and with it a further deterioration of transport options, erosion of low-paid workers' incomes and a deterioration in urban economies and services. Public transport links have defined the shape and vibrancy of cities. For cities to thrive and to provide affordable jobs requires a renewed commitment to public transport and its public funding.

Rescue Cities

Young digital nomads who can work from anywhere are attracted to the cosmopolitan life of big cities, preferring the cafes, clubs and streets of thriving cosmopolitan neighbourhoods. It is easier to find new friends and potential romantic partners in a dense city than in the suburbs or small towns. The result is that the demographic profile of dynamic cities will increasingly reflect an hourglass shape, with a large cohort of younger people, a smaller middle-aged group (as many families move out) and a large group of elderly who no longer have children and who are attracted to cultural amenities in cities, or are locked into poor neighbourhoods and cannot afford to leave.

The benefits of geographical proximity in terms of innovation and productivity grow with the increasing density of skilled and creative individuals, and for this reason people living in cities are on average 50 per cent more productive than those living in smaller towns.[75] They also are more innovative.[76] Part of the reason is that there are more opportunities for learning and serendipitous exchanges with other highly productive people.[77] For ideas to propagate requires physical rather than simply virtual contacts; the more people meet, for example, in coffee shops in Silicon Valley, the greater their ability to file new patents.[78]

Knowledge workers who share proximity spawn new ideas and businesses, with their benefits quickly reaching further. On average, every innovative and creative individual supports five other jobs, from lawyers to baristas.[79] There are other benefits to cities, too. People living in dense urban areas have a far lower carbon footprint than those living in larger homes and are less reliant on cars to get around or online delivery vehicles to bring them goods.

The political and economic dominance of some major cities is not healthy. The UK and France are among the most centralised countries, with the political and economic elite in London and Paris exercising a decisive influence over the country. Mayors, district councils and local authorities in the UK have less autonomy than in other high-income economies like Germany. This has not only compounded the difficulties associated with adapting local planning rules and regulations to the pandemic but also means that local professional facilities that service government are more centralised. In countries like Germany, Italy and the US, on the other hand, a smaller share of economic and political power is vested in the capital cities. In these countries, regional centres have legal and hospitality services that are already well established and able to benefit from and adapt to new demands from a growing number of home-working residents.

The decline of city centres, as offices and the myriad associated shops and services close, could benefit the surrounding suburbs and more distant towns and villages. As workers spend longer in their neighbourhoods, they will spend more locally, on everything from food and clothes to buying gifts and haircuts, and local recreation, entertainment and meals. They will also have more desire to improve their homes and gardens, employing local builders and other small businesses. With more time spent in their neighbourhoods, they are likely to become more involved in local civic activities and local politics. This could mean benefits to communities such as greater local volunteerism, engagement and expenditure, providing the basis for a reinvigoration of places that previously may have felt like dormitory towns or holiday villages.

Before the pandemic, the Mayor of Paris had been championing the idea of the 'fifteen-minute city' in which citizens would work and live near their homes, in much greener and cleaner environments where transport would be mainly on foot or bicycle. The pandemic has propelled ideas such as this to the forefront of discussions in numerous towns and cities, accelerating the creation of liveable clean cities in which urban redesign plays a central role in the post-Covid recovery.

The severity of Covid-19 in urban areas has been linked to air pollution and this together with the striking improvements in air quality during the lockdown has heightened awareness of the benefits of clean air and less traffic. Seeing the stars and hearing birds has been a tangible benefit of Covid-19 and one that will lead to lasting pressures for a cleaner environment. It will also accelerate the pressure on cities towards curbing traffic and noxious fumes. Already in city after city cycle shops are experiencing record purchases, mayors have announced new cycleways and the pandemic has accelerated the conversion of public spaces into more liveable and cleaner environments.

Holiday destinations and places of natural beauty have enjoyed growing demand, with seaside cottages and rural retreats receiving record bookings and a rapid escalation in property prices. The result is that there is not only a need to reorient transport to cater for the growth in employment opportunities in the suburbs, but also to take account of new patterns of domestic leisure travel. This increasing congestion on small countryside roads will lead to a resurgence in demand for rural rail services.

In the UK the demand for leisure travel and curtailment of commuting during the pandemic meant greater weekend than weekday demand on rail services, which was last experienced in the 1950s.[80] The need to rebalance the demand between commuter and leisure routes is likely to remain an enduring feature of the pandemic.

The need for workers to come together in offices has shaped the organisation of modern life and cities.[81] By weakening the office's hold on society, the pandemic has unleashed new opportunities for remote work, which has profound implications for where people live, work and play. However, the death of cities has been foretold before; they remain extraordinarily resilient. While Covid-19 will reshape cities, in many ways for the better, it will not lead to the decline of cities as primary sources of economic and cultural vibrancy. Much depends on how cities respond. Paris with its fifteen-minute human-scale city and the City of London with its determination to 'reimagine London in order to seize the moment' show that while it will not happen without decisive action, cities can, as before, become the focus of more sustainable and thriving societies. To ensure this also leads to more inclusive cities, the needs of disabled and elderly citizens must necessarily be taken into account.[82]

The decline of town centres has been decades in the making, but the coronavirus pandemic has pushed them to the brink, forcing a radical rethink regarding their future. Instead of chain stores providing the backbone of the high street, local and independent businesses that are committed to their towns and neighbourhoods should provide the foundation of a new revival.[83] These deliver a variety of services and enable communities to come together and connect. Reinventing high streets as

civic spaces fit for the twenty-first century should be supported
by local governments through a reduction in business rates.
Landlords who own the properties need to recognise that
whereas in the short term they cannot charge the rents that
previously were paid by the chains, in the long term the survival
of these retail areas depends on a new approach that facilitates
the growth of local and community-based enterprises. Funding
support from government should also facilitate the purchase
of property for community-managed businesses, breaking the
stranglehold that large property empires have over commercial
property.

Turning office buildings into affordable residential apartments and shuttered shops into start-up enterprise zones, shared
offices, pop-up theatres and performance spaces, food markets
and the home of other small local businesses is the first step
to ensuring that cities once again become the bustling, dynamic
meeting places and sources of friendship, entertainment, work
and prosperity that for thousands of years have defined their
existence. Stewardship that puts the needs of inhabitants first
and creates liveable, clean and secure environments will re-
energise cities.

Contrary to popular belief, in addition to the economic benefits, living in densely populated cities can offer many health
benefits, even in a pandemic. A study of 36 major world cities
and 913 metropolitan areas in the US found no association
between their population density and rates of Covid-19 infections.[84] In the longer term, life expectancy is higher in cities than
for those living in less dense areas, in part because city dwellers
are more likely to walk and exercise and less likely to suffer from
dietary and other chronic diseases, and far less likely to be
involved in a car accident.

The benefits associated with city life mean that globally rapid
urbanisation will remain the defining feature of the twenty-first
century. What the pandemic has revealed is not that cities are
fragile, but rather that community is a lifeblood that powers the

growth of jobs and opportunities. By accelerating the transformation of offices and shops, the pandemic forces cities to reinvent themselves to ensure that they provide clean, safe and prosperous communities and homes for the future. Rescuing cities and ensuring that they change to meet new challenges is essential if our economies and societies are to thrive.

CHAPTER 9

Improving Mental Health

As economist Noreena Hertz highlights in her book *The Lonely Century*, the pandemic has exacerbated loneliness and mental health problems. It has also brought these issues out of the shadows, creating the opportunity to confront and address this critical challenge.

During the pandemic, more than half of humanity were confined to their homes at one time or another.[1] When the 1918 Spanish Flu struck in the US, on average more than four family members shared a home, and less than 10 per cent of people lived alone.[2] Today the average family size is closer to two and over a quarter of people live alone. In Sweden, singles constitute the majority of households, and in big cities the share of people living alone is even higher. Over 60 per cent of the inhabitants of Stockholm live alone, as do 55 per cent of Londoners. This is primarily a problem in richer countries – in Pakistan only about 1 per cent of people live alone.

In the immediate aftermath of the pandemic, lockdowns led to a temporary increase in young people returning to the homes they last lived in as teenagers. Even before the pandemic, teenagers and young adults were among the loneliest people, despite being the most digitally connected.[3] The pandemic locked teenagers in with their families, ending their ability to roam and socialise with friends. Those forced to return to their childhood homes when they thought that they had left them experienced a reverse in their transition into an independent adult life. The stop-start repetition of lockdowns and uncertainties regarding when normal social life could continue added to their anxieties.

In the US, over half of young adults (aged eighteen to twenty-nine) lived with their parents in the summer of 2020, exceeding the previous record when the 1940 census revealed this figure to be 48 per cent during the Second World War.[4] By the 1960s, the number had fallen to 29 per cent, but subsequently it has been climbing and reached around 40 per cent in the past decade.[5] This 'boomerang' of young adults in their twenties and early thirties returning home is likely to become a permanent feature of post-pandemic society, as Covid-19 has also exacerbated the difficulties young people have faced in the job market. Their situation had already been undermined by the 2008 financial crisis, leading to a growing share of young people finding that they cannot afford to own or rent properties and that they need to postpone settling down with a partner to increasingly later ages. The undermining of independence and increased pressure on all generations has in itself increased stress and caused a surge in mental health difficulties.[6]

Stress

A national survey in the UK showed that 36 per cent of the population felt their job security was worse during the pandemic, 35 per cent were poorer, and 45 per cent said that their stress levels had increased, with 38 per cent saying they suffered increasing mental health issues.[7] Women and young people experienced the greatest difficulties, with 55 per cent of 18-to 24-year-olds saying they were lonely, compared to 31 per cent of those over the age of seventy.[8] With over half of the people claiming welfare benefits doing so for the first time, a feeling of guilt and failure has been widespread, particularly among those who never imagined that they would have to be dependent on charity and government benefits.[9]

The pandemic has thrown into sharp relief how important communities are as a form of safety net, but the rise of individualism has seen community structures and organisations wither in recent decades, and those that survived, such as pubs, were closed during the lockdown, often leaving the family as sole source of refuge and support. While for many there have been positive experiences, families experiencing difficulties suffered greatly from the stress of living in unbroken close proximity.

Incidences of domestic abuse increased by at least 20 per cent, with the UN describing the worldwide increase as a 'shadow pandemic'.[10] In Australia 2020 will be remembered as the worst ever year of domestic violence as the coronavirus restrictions, combined with unemployment and financial stress, have caused cases to spike across the country, with the deaths of more than thirty-three women.[11] In the UK, two-thirds of women in abusive relationships indicated that they suffered greater abuse during the pandemic and three-quarters indicated that the lockdown made it harder to escape their abuser. The desperate situation of individuals trapped at home with their abusers is revealed in England by the statistic that one call was made to police every thirty seconds during the first lockdown.[12] Another tragic outcome of the pandemic was an alarming rise in babies being killed or harmed. In the UK recorded infant deaths rose by a fifth compared to previous years, with this attributed to a 'toxic mix' of isolation, mental illness and health staff and social workers unable to conduct home visits during the pandemic.[13]

For many couples the pandemic has been a make-or-break experience. Whereas previously working couples may have spent a few hours a day together, it is rare in lockdown to spend more than a few hours apart. As in other dimensions of the pandemic, underlying fault lines have been revealed, and Covid-19 has precipitated a sharp rise in divorces, with many unhappy marriages finally ending and law firms in a wide range of countries reporting a 30 to 40 per cent increase in demand for their divorce services.[14]

For those seeking new relationships, the pandemic provided new challenges. In 1995 about one in five couples met their partners at work. Just prior to the pandemic this had fallen to one in ten, and the pandemic led to a further collapse in office romances.[15] However, lockdown did lead to a 30 per cent rise in online dating.[16] The difficulties of meeting encouraged the use of new features, such as video chat, which allowed for the virtual pursuit of online relationships, with the most rapid increase in demand coming from women under thirty years old. When online dating started about fifteen years ago it was mainly focused on short-term relationships. Then, less than 3 per cent of marriages were between people who met online, whereas today they account for well over 40 per cent of married couples, with centuries'-old traditions being rapidly overturned.[17] Overall, though, during the pandemic it became more difficult to meet people and find longer-term partners, which added to people's sense of loneliness and isolation.

Isolation

Over 2,000 years ago, Socrates observed that children 'love chatter in the place of exercise'.[18] Scholars studying cognitive development have found that adolescents in particular require social interaction and that isolation from their peers is particularly harmful to the formation of their personal identities. Younger children have suffered similarly from the lack of connection. A survey undertaken during the pandemic by Professor Cathy Creswell of Oxford University found an increase in feelings of unhappiness, anxiety and low mood among primary school children.[19]

Humans are by nature social animals and prolonged social deprivation has been shown to have a severely negative impact. Indeed, the United Nations considers solitary confinement exceeding fifteen days to be a form of torture and both the US Supreme Court and European Court of Human Rights have condemned it and noted that it leads to reduced mental and physical capabilities. It is not surprising therefore that prolonged isolation has led to an increase in loneliness, anxiety and depression. Even for those who are not physically isolated, social distancing measures have led to an absence of reassuring physical contact, which is known to reduce stress.

As the elderly were particularly vulnerable to Covid-19, most were confined to their homes for long periods. About half of the eight million Britons who live alone are over sixty-five. Their difficulties are compounded by the fact that only 44 per cent feel confident using the internet, compared to 95 per cent of young people, which serves to increase the anxieties felt by people in this age group who needed to rely on online shopping and video calls with family.[20]

Adding to their isolation was the sense of danger and loss that many have endured. In North America, Europe, South Africa and the UK care homes accounted for a third to a half of the excess deaths attributed to Covid-19.[21] The result was the suspension of communal meals and residents being confined to their rooms. Visits by family and friends typically were forbidden, even for the desperately sick. The absence of hugging and physical contact was particularly tough, not least for those with dementia who do not fully comprehend the reasons for their forced isolation. Family members around the world who were unable to say their goodbyes or even attend the funerals of loved ones may require professional help in addressing the resulting complicated grief.

Single people who lived alone were among the least at risk from the virus but were at the greatest risk of mental health difficulties. Over two-thirds of the 18 to 34-year-olds in the UK had difficulty in feeling positive, compared to half of those over fifty-five.[22] In the US over 45 per cent of adults reported that their mental health had been negatively impacted, in the UK 40 per cent and in China 35 per cent of adults experienced similarly negative consequences.[23] The longer they endured isolation, the greater the effect on mental health, with The Lancet finding that the impact of pandemics resembled that of people suffering from post-traumatic stress disorder (PTSD).[24]

Many people have additionally faced economic uncertainty

and job loss, which has compounded the risks of mood disorders and substance abuse. As occurred during the Spanish Flu of 1918 and SARS in 2003, the Covid-19 pandemic led to a rapid increase in calls to suicide prevention hotlines, and in suicides themselves.[25]

During the early stages of the lockdown in 2020, 57 per cent of the respondents reported symptoms of anxiety and a startling 64 per cent recorded common signs of depression.[26] Most worryingly, one survey suggests that in the US as many as 11 per cent of people had contemplated suicide during the lockdown (up from 4 per cent prior to the pandemic), this rising to over a quarter of 18-to-24-year-olds, which is deeply troubling.[27]

A striking feature of the surveys of public opinion is that a significant minority felt better, and even enjoyed lockdown, with the security and diminished 'fear of missing out' (FOMO) being among the reasons for reporting less anxiety. Much depends on personal circumstances and whether the individuals had secure jobs or educational prospects, were in a supportive home environment and had the broadband and space for working and for outdoor leisure activities.

A major study in the UK reported a 'chasm' between the mental health of children in richer and poorer households, with children in the 4- to 11-year-old primary school range from poor households most negatively affected.[28] The Mental Health Foundation in the UK has highlighted that pre-existing psychological conditions have been exacerbated and that economic difficulties are deepening the negative impact, observing that 'we are all in the same storm, but we are not all in the same boat.'[29] The underlying inequalities in income and opportunity in society have been compounded by the increased stress and mental health difficulties faced by low-income and young people. The scarring from the pandemic could well make the affected individuals more vulnerable in the future, with this requiring timely counselling and other interventions. In addition, the development of a more community-based approach to social relations is required; the solidarity shown towards elder people during the pandemic needs to be permanently extended more widely to create more inclusive and caring communities that, among the other benefits they offer, will reduce the risk of isolation and mental illnesses.

Global Mental Health Pandemic

Like the pandemic, the rise in mental ill health has spread globally. In India, the already high rates rose further still, with a sharp increase in suicide among the 6.6 million middle-class professionals who lost their jobs during the pandemic.[30] Similarly to what has been reported in other countries, in India the 15–25 age group were most vulnerable to self-harm, with more than one student an hour reported to have committed suicide during the pandemic.[31] African countries were spared the worst of Covid-19, but have suffered most from the economic consequences and so are vulnerable to the mental health repercussions. In Malawi, for example, the 57 per cent rise in suicides in 2020, the highest level since records began, has been attributed to desperation of former breadwinners not being able to support families.[32]

While many countries have adopted remote consultations to overcome disruptions to in-person mental health services, within countries there are large disparities by income and education levels in access to these services. There are even bigger differences in access between countries, with over 80 per cent of high-income countries using remote counselling and services to try to address mental health issues, whereas under a half of developing countries have such facilities.[33] The poorer the country and the household the less likely they are to have accessed remote health or other online services.[34] Those sharing accommodation found it particularly difficult during lockdown to find the privacy needed to engage in confidential consultations. A therapist with children at home whom I interviewed told me of her difficulty in finding sufficient privacy to meet confidentially with clients without children interrupting her, while a number of her clients were finding it impossible to get away from their partners and families to engage in confidential conversations.

Remote counselling and hotlines were busier than ever during the pandemic but for many these could not replace the comfort of physical consultations and were not always accessible. Over 70 per cent of 130 countries surveyed by the WHO reported that their mental health services had been disrupted by the pandemic.[35] In two-thirds of countries, disruptions were reported to critical harm response services and about half of addiction treatment centres were not functioning normally, while around a third of patients were unable to access their medications for mental illness.[36]

In the US, the pandemic worsened opioid and other addictions, with the number of people needing treatment considerably higher, while the provision of detox and treatment services was reduced due to absences of staff, the requisitioning of wards for the pandemic, strict rules on physical distancing, and crippling financial losses. Mental health organisations reported the loss of a quarter of their revenues, and over a third were forced to close by the end of 2020.[37] This led the CEO of a leading US mental health industry association to warn that 'without immediate action, we can expect a secondary and devastating public health crisis.'[38]

The lasting impact of the pandemic on mental health will continue to take its toll over the decades to come. In the US, a shocking one in five patients with Covid-19 reported that they were suffering from mental health issues within three months of the pandemic starting, with anxiety disorders and insomnia being the most prevalent problems and the use of anti-depressants in the US and UK at an all-time high.[39] We should be prepared for a large increase in post-traumatic stress disorder, notably among those who were hospitalised or unable to visit loved ones due to restrictions.

Delays Deadly

The pandemic has greatly increased serious mental health problems as well as compounding chronic and other health issues, which were largely neglected when overstretched health systems had to focus on the immediate response to Covid-19. There was also considerable misdiagnosis, as I discovered when an elderly relative who had pulmonary oedema was hospitalised and immediately – wrongly – put in a Covid-19 ward, where she was exposed to the virus.

In many countries the risks posed by the neglect of chronic diseases and illnesses other than Covid-19 may well have led to more deaths than the pandemic itself. The dramatic decline in A&E admissions during lockdowns and the postponement of all but the most critical treatments led to a sharp rise in heart failure, stroke and other deaths at home, impacting particularly negatively on elderly people, who are the most vulnerable.

The Royal College of Surgeons in the UK described a 'tsunami' of cancelled operations.[40] By November 2020, more than two million people had waited for longer than eighteen weeks for routine operations, such as hip replacements, and more than 163,000 for longer than a year, 100 times more than the 1,600 patients who were waiting for operations before the pandemic.[41] As hospitals postponed admissions and individuals avoided seeing their doctors or going to A&E for fear of contagion, deaths at home during the pandemic in the UK were about a third higher than previous years.[42] Deaths at home from heart diseases among men were up by a quarter and among women, deaths at home from Alzheimer's and dementia rose by three-quarters.[43] The twenty-month backlog in cancer consultations and treatments similarly will continue to raise avoidable deaths for years to come.[44]

In developing countries, the impact has been even worse, as vital vaccinations and public health programmes to reduce malaria and the other biggest killers were neglected while resources were directed to addressing the pandemic and lockdowns curtailed public health programmes. These secondary impacts on chronic diseases together with the impact on mental health will continue to take a toll on societies around the world long after the pandemic has disappeared.

Rescue from Loneliness and Mental Ill Health

Although money cannot buy happiness, it can reduce uncertainty and a wide range of anxieties.[45] The pandemic, by creating immense economic hardship and compounding insecurity, undermined the physical and mental health of millions of people. To ensure a future of improved mental well-being requires addressing the twin challenges of overcoming inequality and providing decent work for all. It also requires that we address the climate emergency, which, particularly among young people, is becoming a major source of anxiety.[46]

There has been a well-documented and much decried lack of services for mental health for many years. This neglect derives in part from the fact that mental ill-health tends to be measured less and is easier to ignore than many other types of health problems. This contributes to underestimation and underfunding, with far too few resources and little attention paid to these issues.

Covid-19 has compounded mental health illnesses and loneliness, yet by enabling a more open discussion and removing some of the stigma it could help address these challenges. This requires interventions and funding on a much greater scale. Although governments pay lip service to mental health, budgets have been declining while the needs have risen. Whereas physical ailments are widely recognised, mental health, which can be equally debilitating, is often hidden and is neglected. Greater funding of psychiatric and social services is required, including by paying mental health professionals salaries that accord with their qualifications, experience and the stress they face. Access to free and prompt counselling should be available in every general medical

practice; coverage is currently sporadic and uneven, with many
in need not receiving treatment or being put on lengthy waiting
lists.

Isolation is unhealthy, and people without strong social
connections have a 50 per cent higher chance of dying early,
equivalent to smoking fifteen cigarettes a day.[47] Relationships
with friends and family have also been shown to reduce the risk
of dementia and a wide range of mental illnesses.[48] Combatting
loneliness is achievable through fostering strong social connections, prioritising access to internet connectivity by vulnerable
groups and the development of community-based activities.
These have been severely undermined through the pervasive
growth of the culture of individualism and the rollback of social
and community services in recent decades. Addressing mental
health and loneliness requires that it is an integral part of the
broader design of more cohesive and collaborative societies. The
pandemic has lifted the veil on these issues and prompted a
broader consideration of what sort of society we want to live
in and how governments, cities, businesses and communities can
contribute to overcoming these challenges.

In the aftermath of the coronavirus pandemic many people
who have not been able to see their loved ones prior to their
death are likely to suffer complex grief and post-traumatic stress
disorder. Qualified professionals and support groups will be
needed to be readily available to assist and reach out to those
in need. After the world wars, and many other wars including
those in Vietnam, Iraq and Afghanistan, soldiers returned with
PTSD, then called 'shell shock'. In most cases their conditions
were hidden, with devastating consequences for families, as
those affected were distant and detached and subject to nightmares and violent episodes. These days it is (generally) no
longer considered 'unmanly' or shameful to admit to these
symptoms and there are a variety of therapies that can help
people suffering, both physically and mentally, from the effects
of traumatic experiences.

We are yet to see what the long-term effects of the Covid-19 pandemic will be on mental health, but much depends on whether mental illness is adequately addressed in a timely manner. The same traumatic event can be experienced very differently depending on the level of care and support provided. As has been evidenced by people who have suffered from other traumas, we can assume that people who have been traumatised by the experiences of the pandemic, either having had Covid-19 and fearing that they would die, or having close family or friends hospitalised, as well as the backdrop of insecurity, lost employment, fear and dread, will fare better if they have had the opportunity to share these experiences and fears with supportive family, friends or health professionals. This applies equally to the doctors, nurses and other essential workers who are on the frontline, who, in addition to being exhausted, are being severely emotionally challenged, with nearly half of NHS critical care staff reporting that they suffered from PTSD, depression or anxiety.[49]

In New York, the response of more than 6,000 volunteer counsellors to Governor Cuomo's plea for help was a timely response, but not a substitute for systematic, nationwide responses that pay and support counselling and other mental health services, ensuring that these are available for those most in need.[50]

After the Second World War institutions in the UK such as the Tavistock Institute and Portman Clinic became part of the new National Health Service, as the government recognised the need for interdisciplinary approaches across all professional groups and for all ages to overcome the trauma of the war and its long-term consequences. Today there is a similar urgent need to look afresh and invest in the institutions and holistic support necessary to improve the mental well-being of our societies. To bounce back to the system of mental health that existed before the pandemic would be disastrous, as it would fail to recognise the urgent needs arising from the pandemic, and the grossly inadequate system that existed previously, which the pandemic has revealed and exacerbated.

PART THREE

COOPERATION: WHY WORKING TOGETHER BRINGS SHARED PROSPERITY

CHAPTER 10

Politics and Power Shifts

The spread of the pandemic itself, as has been the case with pandemics through the ages, was through the arteries of trade and integration. During the Roman Empire, trade and its links facilitated rapid progress, but in the second century CE the same links led to the spread of what is likely to have been smallpox. A century later another plague disrupted trade and led to a permanent decline in the empire as well as the relative fortunes of southern Europe to those of the northern part of the continent, which was less severely affected.[1] Similarly, Covid-19 is likely not only to lead to a new phase of globalisation but also in the fullness of time to be seen to be a watershed dividing the era of US domination from that of a resurgent China.

As journalist Martin Wolf of the *Financial Times* has pointed out, the rivalry today between the US and China echoes that between England and Germany in the early twentieth century, which culminated in the First World War and the collapse of the first great phase of globalisation.[2] Containing the growing tensions between the US and China is vital if we are to create a safer and more inclusive world. Conflict leads to development in reverse. From 1913 it took sixty years, until the 1970s, before trade regained the significance it had as a share of global economic activity. Geopolitical conflict also risks escalating all potential global threats: to prevent future pandemics, limit climate change, nuclear threats and any of the other existential dangers we face requires the US, China and the European Union to work together as an essential foundation of global peace and security.

Pandemic Accelerates Political Shifts

Although the rise of Asia and relative decline of the US has been ongoing for decades, the pandemic compounded the failures of President Trump and reinforced America's retreat, while China and its neighbours' relative success in managing the pandemic has accelerated the rise of East Asia relative to other regions. Globally, after a long decline, the prestige of the US collapsed precipitously during 2020, with its claim to be number one tragically reflected in its having the highest number of fatalities of any country.

The US's domestic failures were mirrored by its alienation of the international community. The US under President Trump actively undermined the international order it had assiduously built over seven decades. At a time when global cooperation and leadership was desperately needed, the US turned its back on the world. President Biden and his experienced cabinet could not be more different from that of Trump, offering the prospect of a partial restoration in the US's reputation both domestically and in foreign policy. This could make an immense difference to the achievement of shared goals. It will take time for the US's reputation to be restored internationally. Meanwhile, China's influence will continue to grow. The US will never again be able to shape world affairs unilaterally. As Covid-19 has impacted far more severely on the US economy than the Chinese, which has rebounded rapidly, China is now expected to overtake the US economically before 2028, five years ahead of previous predictions. Politically, the pandemic has already permanently punctured the idea of American superiority, and with it the view that it represents a meritocratic or democratic ideal to which other countries should aspire. How the US comes to terms with its loss of dominant economic and military power will determine whether we are entering a more splintered world centred around competing US and Chinese spheres of power, or whether the US and China will be able to bridge their differences and work together to reduce global risks and create a future of shared prosperity. In this, the European Union's role is pivotal.

The European Union has been invigorated by the shock of the withdrawal of Britain. Under the leadership of its President, Ursula von der Leyen, it has made significant progress in addressing the health and economic threats posed by the pandemic while committing to a new green deal to reduce carbon emissions. Its ability to project power on the international stage is however constrained by the need for consensus among its twenty-seven constituent countries, with Poland and Hungary in particular undermining its ability to provide strong leadership for the multilateral system.

Meanwhile, the UK has lost the political leverage it once exercised through its influence on European policy and faces a perfect storm of crises, dealing with the severe economic fallout of Brexit and its mishandling of the pandemic. The transatlantic 'special relationship' with the UK will be far less important to the US than that with the European Union. Britain's hosting of the COP26 climate summit and G7 meeting in 2021 will be the first meeting of these groups with the new US Biden administration, offering an opportunity to accelerate actions on climate change and to create a new global compact to place developing countries back on track to achieve the globally agreed Sustainable Development Goals, which include the elimination of extreme poverty and hunger worldwide. The UK's severe cut to its aid budget and fraught relations with both the European Union and China need to be overcome if Britain is to step up to this historic opportunity.

The refusal of President Trump to concede the election and his unsubstantiated allegations of voter irregularities, which culminated in the occupation of the Capitol by an insurrectionary mob, have undermined the US's already weak position as a role model for democracy. Joe Biden's presidency will go some

way to restore respect for the US on the world stage, and rein-
state elements of the US's international role, including through
its prompt recommitment to the Paris Climate Agreement, to
membership of the WHO and to paying its arrears and a more
constructive role at the UN.

Domestically, the umbilical relationship between political
power and finance, and internationally the US's relentless pursuit
of economic and strategic interests above democratic and human
rights concerns, including by supporting autocrats and anti-
democratic coups, have for over a century undermined its moral
authority. However, given his voter base, the pursuit of democracy and human rights is likely to feature on President Biden's
foreign policy agenda, and we may expect a more robust response
to autocrats such as President Putin.

Rising frictions between the US and China were apparent
before the pandemic, as was the weakening of the growth in
trade flows. However, the pandemic turned countries inwards
as they focused on their own emergencies, and as President
Trump sought to blame the 'Chinese virus' for the US's ills,
relations between the US and China deteriorated further.

During the pandemic, China seized the opportunity to step
into the global leadership vacuum left by Trump's US. President
Trump's withdrawal from the WHO provided the opportunity
for President Xi to give the opening keynote speech at its May
2020 assembly. China's already hyperactive diplomatic service
has gone into a yet higher gear, responding to the emergency
by being among the first to ship vital medical equipment to Italy,
the US and more than 150 countries. By leveraging its strength
in manufacturing it was able to produce over 200 billion masks,
2 billion protective suits and 800 million testing kits, which,
together with its rapid roll-out of vaccines, served to cement
dependence on Chinese suppliers and, in poor countries, Chinese
donations.[3]

While in high-income countries, the image of China has been
tarnished by it being blamed as the origin of the pandemic, in

much of Africa and Latin America the pandemic is generally believed to have originated in Europe and the US. In middle- and low-income countries the soft power of liberal democracies is being allowed to wither and that of authoritarian powers, especially China and Russia, is being aggressively promoted. Austerity and a declining interest in world affairs in the US, UK and Europe has led to an underinvestment in diplomacy just as China and Russia are stepping up their diplomatic efforts. This is reflected in sharp increases in the number of their diplomats deployed overseas and the funding of external media and cultural exchanges.

Over the past decade, China has opened 200 Confucius Institutes around the world, while in the UK the BBC World Service, British Council and Foreign Office have all seen their budgets slashed, and the budgets of the US State Department and Voice of America have been similarly reduced.[4] Meanwhile China's Belt and Road Initiative has engaged more than 100 countries with a combination of grants, loans and technical assistance, which has rapidly expanded its presence globally. Russia has no qualms in projecting its hard power. Its cyber-attacks, deadly attacks on opposition figures, meddling with elections and support for fake news intensified during the pandemic, including through undermining public support for lockdowns and supporting anti-vaccination movements, serving to spread mistrust in governments.

Despite these wide-ranging actions, during the Trump Presidency it was neither China nor Russia that posed the biggest threat to the multilateral system, but rather the very custodian of the system itself: the US.

The pandemic starkly revealed that whereas the US had been the global gamekeeper in the entire post-Second World War period, during the Trump Presidency it had become its most dangerous poacher. Its active fracturing of geopolitics facilitated the collapse of geo-economics. During all previous post-Second World War crises it was the US that convened the global response. When global finance collapsed in 2008, President George W. Bush called world leaders and successfully convinced China to play a central role in the global response. During the pandemic, the growing attacks and scapegoating of China by President Trump reinforced trade tensions and crippled the prospects for resolute global action to address the health and economic emergencies.

Political Cooperation

The disarray in global politics that resulted from the failure of US leadership preceded the pandemic. While it did not cause the pandemic, it amplified its global impact as throughout 2020 frictions between the US and China, as well as between the US and European Union, undermined a coordinated global economic or health response to the pandemic. Prior to the pandemic, benign neglect had already led to the withering of the WHO and the chronic underfunding of the global network of scientists and organisations dedicated to stopping pandemics. Not only was the pandemic aggravated by the vacuum in global political leadership. This is also the reason for the too-timid response to the climate emergency and the failure to address global threats, such as escalating armed conflicts and the threat posed by Russia.

The world desperately needs effective multilateral institutions to manage our shared threats, but these should not be modelled on those which have decayed and are totally unfit for twenty-first-century purpose. A radical reform of the global institutional architecture is necessary.

Pandemics, climate change, cyber-attacks, antibiotic resistance and global financial meltdowns – to name a few – are no longer abstract spectres, they are the defining challenges of our time. Now, more than ever, we inhabit a global village. Yet we lack competent village elders, or the tools needed for the solving of our shared problems. The alphabet soup of regional and global organisations that has evolved over the past eighty years is unfit to meet the rapidly evolving twenty-first-century challenges. The radical reform of global governance is urgently required.

Such change does not imply the end of national sovereignty or a radical challenge to local autonomy and legitimacy. For local problems that can be confined and dealt with inside national borders, the intervention of global entities is unwarranted and unwelcome. But there are an increasing number of threats that have no regard for national boundaries. Such challenges require coordination and agreements that invariably mean giving up some national sovereignty and subscribing to rules that bind different countries together. Piecemeal national efforts without coordination have been and will continue to be impotent in the face of systemic threats that transcend sovereign borders.

The stakes for getting this right have never been so high. But the omens are not good. If past decades provide a guide, new problems will simply be thrown at old institutions, created for other purposes. The WHO, UN, IMF, World Bank and others are overloaded and cannot deliver on their mushrooming mandates. We need to redesign global governance, ensuring that well-defined manageable mandates are applied to existing organisations, that new institutions are established when old ones cannot cope, and that coordination across governing bodies from local to regional or global is both constant and effective. The establishment of a shared system of rules to promote inclusive and sustainable globalisation is urgently needed.

Yesterday's structures are not equipped to deal with today's problems, but thankfully it is not too late. Aggressive action must be taken, and such action would be effective if it incorporates five core principles that I have developed together with my Oxford colleague, Ngaire Woods. First, global action is only required on global problems. Local jurisdictions matter and should continue to address local and national problems on their own terms. Second, while not everyone must be included in global negotiations, inclusion of key actors is essential. For example, if the biggest polluters are not bound by climate change agreements, the agreement cannot be effective – and this principle must be central to any reform efforts. The key actors are not always countries – companies, cities and communities are vital to the solving of problems too, as I explain below. Third, efficiency is essential. Unwieldy bodies that include everyone are worse than nimble bodies that involve the key players who can make a major difference to resolving the issue. For example, the small island nation of the Maldives, which is in danger of being enveloped by rising oceans, but is an insignificant producer of greenhouse gases, need not be included in questions about how to stop climate change. But it would need to be represented in negotiations about how to address the impacts of global warming. Fourth, legitimacy is required for effective global governance. A system must be in place wherein countries may disagree with certain rules of the game but accept the referees. Fifth, enforceability is paramount. None of these principles matter if they cannot be enforced.

Stopping future pandemics is the ultimate political challenge; pandemics are the only global threat that require *all* countries to cooperate, as they can spread from and to anywhere in the world. Other threats can be resolved by a much smaller group of actors. For example, nine countries have the capability to generate a global nuclear war and a similarly small number of countries are systemically important in finance and could bring about a global financial collapse. The top ten emitters account for over two-thirds of the greenhouse gas emissions that need to be stopped to slow climate change. In fact, just three countries – the US, China and India – and the European Union account for more than two-thirds of global carbon emissions. Insisting we reach global consensus on these hugely important issues can lead to gridlock, as the more participants there are in global negotiations the harder it is to reach consensus. Most problems can be resolved by much smaller groups, including coalitions of a critical mass of countries, cities, companies and communities.

To address twenty-first-century challenges requires new approaches to a system that to date has almost exclusively relied on governments. This is not surprising, given the system emerged after the Second World War when a small number of countries held all the power and civil society, cities and businesses played a less significant role politically than they do today.

For example, to stop the next financial crisis a dozen or so banks and financial companies need to be tightly regulated – the responsibility of a handful of countries that host the headquarters of these businesses, working together with a global regulatory authority that can monitor and control their activities. To slow climate change it is particularly important that the three countries and the countries of the European Union, which together account for well over two-thirds of global carbon emissions, take urgent action. The same principle applies to other threats such as those posed by cyber-attacks, antibiotic resistance, nuclear threats, armed conflict and terrorism: a small number of countries working with a critical mass of non-state actors such as cities and companies can make an outsize contribution to solving the problem.

Not so with pandemics, which are unique in that they can come from anywhere. The response of many governments has been to turn inwards, sealing national borders and engaging in a competitive race to source equipment and vaccines. This nationalism threatens to undermine efforts to distribute vaccines globally, efforts that are vital to contain Covid-19. It also makes it more difficult to address the economic fallout and to stop the next pandemic, which could be even more deadly. Clearly, political cooperation is required to manage catastrophes now and in the future; without it we fall prey to a growing number of crises that could threaten global stability.

Historically, the push to reform global governance has been born in the wake of tragedy – just as the UN and the Bretton Woods Institutions rose phoenix-like from the ashes of the Second World War. The pandemic has created another such moment, and it is vital that it is not wasted. Global governance is *the* challenge of our time. Our arsenal of outdated institutions cannot cope with existing threats to health, peace, stability and prosperity. Whether we like it or not, we are all in this together. It is time for us to start acting like it.

Pandemics and Populism

The pandemic accentuated inequalities within countries and between them. There is a danger that this growing inequality will lead to increasing disillusionment with mainstream politicians who are perceived to be insensitive to the needs of those who feel marginalised. As happened following the financial crisis, this is likely to engender support for populist leaders who blame the elite and foreigners for their economic failures.

The pandemic has further polarised opinions, by intensifying the inequalities and by placing at the centre of politics questions of individual freedom. In the US, the growth of libertarian protests reflects this and was fanned by President Trump and social media, with fake and parallel news universes playing a growing role in fuelling anti-establishment anger. A growing number of minds have been dangerously infected by conspiracy theories propagated on social media, including those that claim that the pandemic is a hoax and that vaccines are designed to insert microchips to control behaviour. The pandemic revealed the urgent need for the extension of the rules governing the spreading of lies in print to be extended to social media platforms, particularly in instances where this may cause danger to the lives of innocent people, as is the case with undermining efforts to stop contagion of deadly infectious diseases.

The political consequences of millions of people around the world suddenly finding themselves worse off through no fault of their own are unpredictable. When this happened after the financial crisis of 2008 the result was rising public anger and populism. The decade since has seen citizens paying a heavy price for this in inexperienced leaders who care more about soundbites than expertise. Populists who have pushed for small governments and lower taxes have undermined the effectiveness of national and international institutions.

Within the US and UK and in many European countries, the undermining of government capacity and the failure of leaders to control the pandemic has led to a deepening of the still raw wounds inflicted by austerity and protectionism. Globally, it has further strained relations between these democracies and China, with even countries that are highly dependent on China for exports and for their student and tourist revenues, such as Australia, now estranged.

The sharp swing in public opinion against China, which many blame for the pandemic, has been compounded by growing concern about the treatment of the Uighurs and the suppression of democracy in Hong Kong. The widening gulf between the self-confidence of China arising from its quick and robust recovery from the pandemic, and how it is perceived in Europe and the US, needs to be bridged if a new Cold War is to be avoided. Despite the pandemic, in 2020 China's economy grew by 2 per cent, while all other major economies contracted.

Democracies rest on political consent and competence. New Zealand Prime Minister Jacinda Ardern and German Chancellor Angela Merkel won strong public support for harsh measures limiting citizens' freedom through their competence and straight talking. Presidents Trump, Bolsonaro, Erdogan, Obrador and Putin were among those who suggested the health concerns were overblown, promoted fake science and publicly contradicted their own and international health authorities. It is not by coincidence that three populist leaders who fiercely promote individualism over societal values and regularly flouted expert advice – Trump, Bolsonaro and Johnson – were among the first leaders who caught coronavirus. By overriding scientific advice and delaying lockdowns they allowed the virus to spread more rapidly than has been the case in countries where leaders assiduously followed the WHO guidelines.

By exposing the weaknesses of populist politicians in countries including the US, UK, Brazil, Israel and India the pandemic has given citizens evidence they are likely to act on when their next opportunity to vote for their leaders arises. However, the depth of support for populist leaders should not be underestimated. They channel the anger of citizens resentful of the failure of generations of mainstream politicians to represent their views. In the US Presidential election in November 2020, the catastrophic pandemic and associated collapse of the economy cost President Trump a second term. Nevertheless, the fact that he still secured more than 74 million votes, and 11 million more than when he was elected President in 2016, is indicative of the impact of rising inequality, unemployment and the depth of anger with the political establishment that President Biden represents.

The pandemic in many countries bolstered support for mainstream politicians, who typically are trusted more in times of crisis. A YouGov poll undertaken in twenty-six countries showed a steep decline in support for populist ideas during 2020, including in all eight European countries surveyed.[5] The failures of populists in power in the US, Russia and Turkey to protect citizens from the dire health and economic consequences of Covid-19 did not help their cause. In Europe, the pandemic reversed the rise of populist parties of the far right. Support collapsed for Austria's Freedom Party, Germany's Alternative for Germany (AfD), Italy's Northern League, and UKIP in the UK. The disarray in the mainstream parties nevertheless allowed Rassemblement National under Marine le Pen in France and Vox in Spain to maintain their strong presence. This, together with the increased support for President Trump, despite his failures, and the growing militancy as evident in the occupation of the Capitol, as well as the resurgence of populist leaders in Latin America, points to the fact that weakening of populist challenges elsewhere is likely to be only a temporary phenomenon.

All generations suffer during crises, but they have a particularly lasting impact on poorer and younger people. When the 2020 pandemic struck, southern Europe had not yet recovered from the financial crisis of 2008 and youth unemployment in Spain and Italy was still stuck above 30 per cent. As *The Economist* observed: 'Economic misery has a tendency to compound. Low wages now beget low wages later, and meagre pensions after that . . . For older generations, a recession is an unfortunate pothole, which most will drive over without even blowing a tyre. But for southern Europe's younger people, it is an enormous sinkhole from which it will be hard to clamber out.'[6] The millennial generation born in the 1980s and 90s were promised the rewards of an era that was meant to overcome the conflicts of the Cold War and allow citizens everywhere to harvest the benefits of globalisation. Their hopes have been dashed, first by the financial crisis and then by the pandemic.

Political attitudes tend to crystalize when people are in their mid- to late twenties, so the two crises already experienced by young people are likely to have lasting political consequences. In northern Europe, unemployment among young people never exceeded 11 per cent during the financial crisis, and had declined to below 5 per cent before Covid-19 struck.[7] Young people in northern Europe were, as a result, far less worried about their incomes and job prospects and their political concerns were more focused on 'post-material' issues related to the environment, human rights, gender, equality and questions of values and culture.

In the 2019 European election this was reflected in the number of Green Party MEPs doubling in northern Europe and the prominence given to questions related to the cultural assimilation of migrants and refugees into societies. In southern Europe, conversely, jobs and incomes were centre stage and the Green Party failed to make inroads, with the youth expressing their anger at their plight by supporting parties that advocated radical economic alternatives. Two-thirds of Spanish young people now declare themselves to be dissatisfied with democracy, providing fertile ground for populist parties, such as Vox on the right and

Podemos on the radical left. In Italy, almost half of voters aged twenty-five to thirty-four supported the far-right Northern League or the populist left Five Star Movement.[8] The Brothers of Italy (FDI), a nationalist hard-right party, has been the biggest beneficiary of the pandemic, rising from 5 to 16 per cent support in polls, as it has been more effective than the League in articulating an anti-establishment pro-traditionalist set of values and promising to improve the lives of the millions of people whose livelihoods have been destroyed by Covid-19.

Those born after 1980 are becoming a bigger part of the voting-age population, and this is likely to alter the shape of politics for generations. Having experienced the economic fallout from the pandemic, and for those in their thirties also the financial crisis of 2008, the under-forties are on average considerably poorer than older generations were at their age. Their real take-home pay is still below the level it was before the financial crisis. In the UK, 34-year-olds now have a quarter less wealth than those born ten years before had at their age.[9] They also face worse job prospects, greater debt, rising taxes and an out-of-reach property market. A survey of students in the UK found that more than half had become more politicised as a result of the pandemic.[10] It would be surprising if this does not translate into support for political parties who offer the prospects of a fresh approach to politics and the real prospect of more radical reform.

The Call for Radical Reform

The pandemic marks the end of the era of individualism, characterised by Maggie Thatcher's claim that 'there's no such thing as society . . . it is our duty to look after ourselves' and Ronald Reagan's claim that 'government is not the solution to our problem; government is the problem.'[11] The pandemic has pushed the ideological pendulum to the left, with politicians and pundits talking about the importance of government and community.

The best predictor of how people vote is not, as Bill Clinton had it, 'the economy, stupid', but rather their subjective sense of well-being, which depends on much more, including health and anxieties regarding the future.[12] If establishment politicians cannot protect people from growing anxiety, they are likely to be punished at the ballot box. The financial crisis gave us Trump, Brexit and populism, but it remains to be seen whether perceptions regarding the incompetence of populists in office is going to lead voters in Europe and elsewhere to revert to the tried and tested mainstream as the majority have in the US, even if a very sizeable minority still cling to demagogues.

The frictions that divided societies (not least in Britain over Brexit) were briefly overcome as families, neighbours and communities came together to address the common threat posed by the pandemic. Health, community and family became more important. But the pandemic also revealed new fault lines in our communities, most notably in the US, where the Presidential election took place at the height of the pandemic; there were over 100,000 infections on election day, and yet many of President Trump's supporters defied experts and refused to wear masks.

The rise of militant libertarianism and support for white supremacist views during the pandemic startled even the FBI, which identified far-right militia as the most significant extremist threat on US soil.[13] Tensions between the federal government and various states escalated during the pandemic, with these mirroring the underlying polarisation of attitudes. This was reflected most strongly in more than 17 million guns being sold in the first nine months of 2020, breaking the record for any previous full year and leading to shortages of popular models.[14]

In many countries, the pandemic led both poor and middle-class people to suffer a sharp reversal of expectations of their futures, due to both growing inequality and a contraction of the overall size of the economic pie. The heightening of economic uncertainties in a number of countries has combined with rising concern regarding threats to democracy, adding to the anger of citizens whose nerves have been frayed and emotions stretched by the crisis. Despite their exhaustion and the pandemic dangers, people took to the streets in 2020 in increasing numbers. In the US, protests took place in most cities, as they did in the UK and across Europe. In Latin America, there were waves of protests against the government in Brazil, Bolivia, Chile, Colombia, Ecuador, Peru and Venezuela.[15] Similarly, protests were evident in Belarus, Kyrgyzstan, Kazakhstan, Hong Kong, Thailand, Indonesia and in South Africa, Malawi, Côte d'Ivoire and Nigeria.

The Black Lives Matter protests, which started as spontaneous uprisings against the killing by a policeman of a black man, George Floyd in the US on 25 May 2020, within a week sparked protests in over a hundred countries globally with demonstrators repeating his dying final words, 'I can't breathe'. Fewer than ten years before, the words 'I can't breathe' had been uttered by another police victim, Eric Garner, without sparking global protests.[16] But this time it touched a nerve. The combination of a shared sense of community and rising inequality gave rise to growing civic action and over 8,500 civil rights demonstrations in the US during 2020.[17] The profound changes in our personal priorities occasioned by Covid-19, as well as the rapid global spread on social and other media of images and information that touched a growing number of citizens, provided the basis for mass demonstrations. The injustices faced by black, Asian and minority ethnic groups are not new, but the pandemic intensified and revealed the inequalities; people from minority backgrounds were considerably more likely to die or be seriously ill, or to lose their jobs and incomes, than white people. Covid-19 heightened awareness and underlined the importance of putting an end to entrenched inequalities.

Populist anger such as is described in Eric Lonergan and Mark Blyth's book *Angrynomics* is the result of a failure to ensure that the benefits of globalisation and growth are shared. The authors highlight that between 1981 and 2017 the UK's GDP doubled and yet the use of food banks increased by 1,000 per cent.[18] The moral outrage, they argue, lies behind the justified anger with the elites and explains support for Brexit and populist politicians. To the extent that Covid-19 has increased these inequalities, the anger will surely get worse.

The widening disconnect between Main Street and Wall Street will have profound political ramifications, amplifying the shocks to the system that arose from the 2008 financial crisis. It was that crisis which created the climate for President Trump's election, for Brexit in Britain and for the triumph of populist politicians in Italy, Spain, Greece, the Philippines, Brazil, Mexico, India and many other countries.

By increasing our awareness of the importance of community and of growing inequality, Covid-19 could very well trigger a shift towards a politics of greater inclusion and lower tolerance for inequality. Parties of the extreme right will compete with those of the radical left and centre to claim to represent ordinary people. In times of crisis, citizens are more willing to rally around a flag and embrace radical change. The question is what flag and what change?

Pandemic Attacks Civil Liberties
When hopes of rising prospects are dashed, anger grows and politics becomes more unpredictable. So too do the authoritarian instincts of governments, with rising attacks on protestors and civil liberties. The pandemic gave politicians everywhere a means to increase their power.

In Hungary, Viktor Orbán wasted no time in seizing the opportunity to enact on 30 March 2020 a 'coronavirus law' that gave him unlimited power to rule by decree, with no expiry date.[19] Within a month, eighty-four countries had given themselves emergency powers, typically including restricting the right of movement, allowing censorship of the media, banning public gatherings and, in many cases, suspending parliament. In Belarus, President Lukashenko, Europe's longest-serving ruler, sought to prevent a populist uprising when his re-election was brought into doubt, while his protector Vladimir Putin similarly used the pandemic to further suppress his political opposition. In Azerbaijan the silencing of the opposition was justified as a 'historical necessity' as the virus was used as an expedient for what Human Rights Watch has described as a 'vicious crackdown on dissenting voices', enhancing the authority of the President who launched attacks against the Armenian enclaves of Nagorno-Karabakh.[20]

Governments have used the emergency as an opportunity to restrict opposition and dissenting voices and introduce more authoritarian measures.[21] Attacks on minorities and civil society have become more common, as have attempts to paint peaceful protestors as radicals or 'rioters'.[22] Democracy and human rights deteriorated during 2020 in over eighty countries, with the pandemic associated with by far the most rapid reversion since the end of the Cold War thirty years ago.[23]

When people feel anxious, as they do during pandemics, they are more likely to become xenophobic and less likely to support immigrants and groups they consider outsiders. Blaming others for your ills becomes easier. In India, Prime Minister Modi sought to blame Muslims for being 'super-spreaders'.[24] In Bulgaria, Romany neighbourhoods suffered from harsher lockdowns. Turkey's religious authorities blamed gay people. Malaysian officials blamed migrant workers. In the US President Trump blamed the Chinese. And in the UK the Home Affairs Minister Priti Patel used the pandemic as an opportunity to redouble her attacks on migrants and refugees, suggesting that asylum seekers be sent to a remote island in the South Atlantic and branding lawyers who supported them unpatriotic.[25]

Even in previously robust democracies the health emergency altered the balance between privacy, surveillance and safety. The global use of emergency powers designed for war to introduce lockdowns was not widely challenged, other than in the US by mainly libertarian extremists and in Europe by small groups of demonstrators. The acceptance of greater state surveillance is evident in the widespread adoption of health apps that cross previously inviolable privacy red lines, including sharing the location, contacts and messages of citizens.

Governments have dominated the response to Covid-19. Citizens everywhere are looking to political rather than business leaders to address their urgent health and economic needs. The lockdown has demonstrated the absolute authority of governments, with national interest overriding all commercial and individual interests.

Trust and Political Systems

The jury is out on whether autocratic or democratic governments have better handled the pandemic, as both have recorded spectacular failures but also modest successes. Among the worst performers have been autocracies like Russia and democracies like the US, UK, Spain and Brazil. Those that have done well include autocratic governments such as China and Vietnam and democracies such as Taiwan, South Korea, New Zealand and Greece. Among the democratic governments, those with the most social cohesion and support for early lockdowns and contact tracing have done best, as have countries with female leaders, notably New Zealand, Taiwan, Norway, Finland, Iceland, Denmark and Germany.[26]

The pandemic has stretched trust to breaking point in many societies, while in others it has restored it. The advanced economies had been suffering from a collapse in trust long before the pandemic struck; rising inequality and the chasm between the pain felt by most citizens and the booming stock market has increased public distrust.

In 2008, there was a collapse in trust in the officials and experts who allowed the financial crisis to happen. This time, experts were spared and in countries where the pandemic was most severe it was the politicians who were blamed. The exception was Sweden, where the politicians stepped back and allowed the state epidemiologist Anders Tegnell to dictate policies, providing an easy target when those policies resulted in worse health outcomes.

Conspiracy theories that attribute the pandemic to malevolent governments or individuals abound. In the US, 30 per cent of people believed the pandemic was manufactured in a laboratory and 35 per cent said that they would refuse a vaccine.[27] Dealing with any of the great threats we face, including stopping future pandemics, nuclear war, climate change or cyber-attacks, requires that we listen to the experts and that they become more effective at communicating the facts.

Trust between politicians is vital, too. It was challenging in 2020 to meet nationally, let alone internationally. Meeting over Zoom is no way to foster new connections and establish a rapport and build trust. Zoom cannot provide those crucial 'the room where it happens' moments that have turned the tide of history, when previous adversaries come together over a shared purpose and are able to socialise and connect over coffee breaks and meals.

At the seventy-fifth anniversary of the United Nations in September 2020, and the G20 meetings in November 2020, the virtual platforms allowed for wider participation as there were no space or security constraints, and participation was costless and convenient. However, the absence of corridor and coffee shop conversations meant that very little was achieved that was not already scripted.[28] Media coverage of both events was also less than a third of what it had been in previous years, in part because the meetings were not accompanied by the media circuses that normally accompany major global meetings and provide opportunities for journalists to socialise with participants.

The strongest bonds and friendships developed at home or at work are built from time spent together informally over meals or relaxing. This also is the case with the politicians and diplomats on whom we rely to find solutions to global problems, and the journalists who seek to inform and influence us. Remote connections could lead to a more remote and fragmented world, at a time when what we need are closer connections.

Rescue Politics

In Looney Tunes cartoons, Wile E. Coyote of Road Runner fame runs off the edge of a cliff and keeps going for a short while before realising his plight and plummeting to earth. So it is with the leaders of our countries, who kept trust with the electorate by conjuring up $12 trillion to keep companies and workers from collapsing, holding off the inevitable as long as the health emergency was at its worst. But as soon as the cash injection of adrenalin ended, unemployment and bankruptcies soared. The political reckoning is inevitable.

Covid-19, as economist Diane Coyle observed, took an X-ray of our societies and exposed the fractures and pathologies of inequalities, underfunded services, corporate scandals, institutional weaknesses and inadequacies of our experts and leaders in defining and resolving these issues.[29]

Competence shines through during crises. Populists who rely on slogans proved their ineptitude. As a result, the pandemic planted political time bombs in countries that handled it badly.[30] Trust in government collapsed, with 78 per cent of French, 71 per cent of Italians and an even greater share of the British not trusting their national leaders.[31]

This resulted in a growing appetite for change. Almost 90 per cent of people want corporations to 'stop using overseas tax havens' and to 'guarantee fair wages for all workers' and large majorities, especially in Europe, back a green new deal.[32] In the US, a poll of young people found that 82 per cent supported the Black Lives Matter protests.[33]

Despite the appetite for change, two-thirds of people in the US, UK and Europe think it is unlikely to happen, believing that entrenched powers will preserve the status quo.[34] This certainly is the case if we bounce back to business as usual. But if ever there was a moment for real change, it is now.

To achieve lasting change, we need to ensure that the politicians who decide our fate are not in the pockets of business. In the US, the November 2020 Presidential election cost over $14 billion and each seat in Congress requires at least $10 million to be spent on advertising and other revenues, so by the time politicians enter office they are deeply indebted to a wide range of paymasters and lobbies. Corruption is a cancer that spreads insidiously through societies and must be stopped if our governments are to represent the needs of ordinary citizens. In countries where we are fortunate enough to be able to vote for our leaders we generally get the governments we choose, even though wide-ranging impediments, such as the electoral college system in the US and the gerrymandering manipulation of the boundaries of electoral constituencies, frequently distort outcomes.

The pandemic has allowed us to think more deeply about the individuals who wish to lead us and whether what their parties are fighting for is aligned with our interests. In so doing, we need to take care to ensure that our short-term interests, such as wanting to pay lower taxes, are not prioritised over much more important longer-term requirements to safeguard our lives and the well-being of others.

In politics the urgent crowds out the important. Short-term demands are attended to while longer-term slower-moving threats are left to fester. During crises the preoccupation with the moment can be all-consuming. This focus on crisis management can undermine the potential for long-term change as politicians, civil servants and CEOs put aside their longer-term policy ambitions, due to overstretched agendas and a public craving a return to normalcy.

As politicians strive to normalise societies and return to a pre-pandemic world there is a danger that their prior commitments to reform will be forgotten or set aside as they deal with the aftermath of the pandemic. This is especially the case when it comes to the global pursuit of human rights, stopping climate change and addressing other major threats. As the media have become consumed by stories related to the coronavirus and its immediate aftermath, so too have politicians, whose actions tend to be informed by the headlines, and increasingly by the constant barrage of social media. In the days when a small number of printed newspapers and national broadcasters informed views about the world on an intermittent 24-hour cycle, the politicians together with the media barons could set their agendas and shape public acceptance to a much greater extent than today, when they are too often engaged in continually responsive political spin.

History teaches us that devastating wars, famines and pandemics are more often than not the trigger for profound social and economic change. If we as citizens aspire to change, the media and politicians will follow.

The terrible aftermath of the First World War and failure through too-timid responses to stop the Great Depression from turning into a catastrophic collapse showed the politicians of the 1940s the need to act fast and aim high if they were to overcome deep-rooted challenges and achieve long-term goals. The ambitions of Churchill and Roosevelt created a lasting global peace and set the stage for a new world order. The deep scarring of the Depression, which in parts of the US and UK left well over half the workforce unemployed, explains the New Deal in the US and the record electoral swing that in 1945 gave Clement Attlee the mandate for radical reform. By the 1970s, the sense of purpose behind the reforms had dissipated and the lessons of the 1930s and 40s were forgotten. Governments increasingly were depicted as the source of the problems that societies encountered, which allowed for the dismantling of industrial policies to promote growth, and the decline of taxes and redistributive welfare systems. In the UK, while initially pursued by conservative governments, such views were sustained under Tony Blair's 'New Labour' government, as they were in the US by the failure of Democratic governments under Clinton and Obama to reverse the Reagan- and Bush-era tax cuts.

The narrowing of the vision and capabilities of the state also meant that when new crises arose the responses were inadequate, leading to a downward spiral in national and collective crisis management. The timid and delayed response to the oil price shock of the 1970s meant that it triggered a global economic crisis (when Britain and dozens of other countries had to be bailed out by the IMF), and similar failures to act fast and decisively have amplified the impact of the Asian crisis of the 1990s, the global financial crisis of 2008, the Euro crisis of 2010 and the coronavirus pandemic of 2020.

Governments and international institutions responded to the financial crisis and then again to the pandemic by belatedly recognising their need for more economic firepower. The dramatic increases in money supply and government support for businesses during the pandemic reflect this learning. But what has not been learnt is that this cannot simply be confined to the short-term actions of an emergency response to address the health and economic crisis while it is raging. Without addressing the underlying causes, crises are bound to escalate; much longer-term systemic changes are required. In democracies, governments that ignore short-term needs are likely to lose power. Businesses that ignore short-term pressures similarly are likely to become bankrupt. A focus on the short term is therefore necessary, but if this is a preoccupation that comes at the expense of the longer-term needs, societies, like companies, wither and decline. To address urgent needs while also engaging in vital structural reforms, national and corporate leaders need to be able to juggle both the short- and long-term balls. If either is dropped, they fail.

The ability of Churchill and Roosevelt to plan for the longer term during the gravest years of the Second World War makes their achievements all the more impressive. Although terrible short-term sacrifices were made, with so many dying and suffering, in focusing on long-term ambitions they enabled those who survived to look forward to better things. Catastrophic crises create a widespread yearning for a safer and more stable world. Solidarity can overcome selfishness. It was this that gave rise to the United Nations, the Bretton Woods Institutions and the welfare state. The scale of the Marshall Plan dwarfed that of any previous and all subsequent aid packages. Over five years the US sent 1 per cent of its GDP a year to Europe, which today would amount to around $210 billion per year, mainly in the form of flexible grants designed to meet local needs and disbursed to local institutions, which later contributed to the cancellation of German government and corporate debts.

As Harvard Professor Amartya Sen has pointed out, despite the enormous hardships in the UK during the Second World War, growing solidarity led to a reduction in inequality. Nutrition and health improved for those who had previously been deprived, through rationing and distribution according to need. And children born during the war decade of the 1940s enjoyed an average improvement of life expectancy of over 6.5 years, due to improvements in nutrition among the underfed and the introduction of free health services.[35] With the creation of the welfare state these were sustained and improved upon in the years that followed.

Solidarity did not end after the war. On the contrary, the determination of voters to enshrine these principles in law propelled the Labour Party, which made the welfare state the centrepiece of its campaign, into office in 1945. Attlee lost to Churchill in the 1951 general election, but despite Labour not returning to power for the next thirteen years, the priorities established in the immediate post-war period continued to define British politics for the next three decades. It was not until Margaret Thatcher became Prime Minister in 1979 that the welfare state was undermined. The primary means by which this happened was by shrivelling the size of government and redistribution by a cut in the tax rate for the highest earners from 83 to 40 per cent. Similarly, in the US Roosevelt's successors continued with policies that prioritised the post-war consensus and a commitment to full employment. The top tax rate in the US was kept above 70 per cent until 1981, when Reagan dropped

it to 28 per cent, with a similar commitment to neoliberal policies that aimed to reduce the size of government, cut back on
welfare and redistribution and minimise the regulation of the
private sector.

In the same way that post-Second World War Keynesian
consensus lasted for over three decades, and the subsequent
neoliberal counter-revolution has dominated politics in the US,
UK and many European countries for four decades, the consequences of our current crisis will shape politics for decades to
come. Whether it leads to permanent improvements depends
on our will to achieve these lasting changes.[36] The lesson of the
Second World War is that collective sacrifice requires a new
social contract that benefits everyone. During 2020, this sacrifice
was apparent everywhere, but a new social contract has not yet
been forged. It is this absence which makes the calls from leaders
invoking the wartime spirit ring so hollow.

The remarkable solidarity witnessed in many countries needs
to be harnessed to reduce inequalities and to create a new social
contract that allows for shared flourishing within countries.
Covid-19 has shown that governments can find the money, and
that we have the capacity to change our behaviour.

While the pandemic has united us, it also has widened the
economic gulfs in our societies. This could inflame populism
and anger, or it could be overcome through a new social contract
that seeks to heal the wounds of our society. To achieve this
requires rescuing politics from populist politicians whose expertise is in seductive soundbites and ensuring our societies are led
by those who can deliver on policies that will prioritise the urgent
needs of people and our planet.

The priorities in each country will be different, as will the
means, but everywhere a new social contract is likely to involve
higher levels of taxation and the creation of a more robust safety
net. To be effective, this should include a guarantee of a
minimum basic income for all adults in all high-income countries,
as these countries can afford it. The modernisation of education

and health systems requires higher levels of government investment. Governments also need to more actively incentivise the
transition to a carbon-free economy. This requires higher taxes
for carbon and other pollutants, and governments investing
alongside the private sector in new electrical grid and battery
capacity to enable private investment to overcome the intermit-
tency constraint of fully renewable powered energy systems.
The provision of technical education should be given higher
status and more funding to ensure that the necessary skills are
developed to meet the needs of the energy transition and to
overcome shortages in care and health services. To cope with
the wrenching adjustment to labour markets that is arising from
the automation of jobs, governments need to ensure that housing
and transport systems allow people to get to these new jobs,
which are typically in different locations from the old jobs.

It is time to stop blaming foreigners and globalisation for the
problems that citizens face. We need to address challenges
head-on by enacting policies that create more inclusive societies
and work with others internationally to contain shared threats
and manage globalisation.

CHAPTER II

Inclusive Globalisation

The pandemic struck at the end of a particularly rapid and wide-reaching phase in globalisation. In 2019, international travel, migration and financial and digital flows across national borders had reached record levels, and although trade in goods had begun to decline, trade in services was rising.

In the three decades prior to the pandemic, exports rose rom 15 to 25 per cent of the global economy, which was especially beneficial for developing countries, which on average grew at around 4 per cent.[1] The financial crisis of 2008 had slowed the growth in trade globally.[2] In the years preceding the pandemic, growing protectionism threw grit into the wheels of trade, further slowing its growth and causing uncertainty. The pandemic reinforced these protectionist trends.

Globalisation is a slippery concept, with an extraordinarily wide range of definitions and dimensions. Economists have tended to focus on trade and investment flows as a share of global GDP, and as these ratios have declined since their peak before the financial crisis, some argue that globalisation is slowing down. But this is too narrow a way to think of it. As incomes grow, we should expect some flows to decline as countries have built the bulk of their towns and roads and need less cement, steel and other commodities. There is also a limit to how many shoes, cars, fridges or microwaves any individual is likely to purchase. As incomes rise, we tend to buy higher-quality goods, rather than just accumulating more and more things.

The higher the incomes of individuals, and of countries, the greater the share of expenditure will be on services, like entertainment or meals, much of which is not imported. Services that are imported, such as purchasing music or films from abroad or paying for subscriptions, are classed as intangible flows, and many of these are digital services.

The pandemic led to manufacturing trade declining by a fifth, foreign investment contracting by a third, and the amount migrants sent home declining by a fifth in 2020 compared to 2019.[3] As these flows recover, they will also transform. Supply chains will be restructured to diversify sources and reduce the risks associated with single points of failure. A widening range of manufacturing and services industries are becoming automated. Robots are building cars and replacing people in online delivery warehouses. As this process advances, the production processes increasingly will move back to the largest markets, as the cost of machines is cheaper and skilled operators and spare parts are more available in high-income countries. Consumers want rapid delivery, and this is best achieved by locating automated process near to major markets. In services, call centre staff are increasingly being replaced by chatbots. Similarly, individuals undertaking administrative tasks are being replaced by digital systems, located in the computer cloud. This accelerating move from physical to intangible and digital services is massively disrupting job markets. It also poses new statistical challenges, including in attributing outputs to any one country. Unless explicitly prohibited by local laws, the data can be stored in servers anywhere and, equally, those operating the system could do so from any country. While digital systems transcend national borders, the laws governing them do not. Countries urgently need to understand and agree an international system of determining where profits and taxes are due, under which jurisdiction data privacy is assured, and under which conditions the staff are employed.

As automation advances, and immediacy of delivery becomes

more important to producers, trade in physical goods is likely to become more regional. For example, in East Asia China's Belt and Road Initiative and the new Regional Comprehensive Economic Partnership (RCEP) trade agreement between Asian and Pacific countries (notably excluding the US) aims to strengthen trade between countries of the region.

Existing production systems that involve the construction of expensive facilities and the availability of highly trained workers and specialised suppliers, as is the case with sophisticated electronics. However, as robots are used more in complex production processes, moving factories will become easier. Production involving less capital investment and more widely available skills, such as garment manufacture, is less rooted and so following the pandemic we should anticipate greater changes in suppliers and a greater regionalisation of trade patterns for these labour-intensive processes, which can relocate to alternative cheaper labour locations within the developing world.

McKinsey consultants have estimated that up to a quarter of global supply chains, and half of pharmaceutical and apparel manufacture, could be restructured by 2025, with Covid-19 accelerating companies' decisions to adjust production in response to changing patterns of costs and the growing commercial and political pressure to become more resilient.[4] However, we should not expect sharp shifts in the US sourcing of manufactured products in response to political concerns, as President Biden is likely to play a less interventionist role than President Trump. In addition, it would take considerable time for a US parent company to relocate one of its complex manufacturing plants from one foreign location to another, should that be desired. For example, given that a biopharmaceutical manufacturing plant costs over $2 billion and takes five to ten years to build, pharmaceutical companies are locked into existing locations.[5]

Despite the dire warnings, supply chains held up remarkably well during the peak of the pandemic. The occasional shortages of toilet paper or soap were due to unanticipated bursts in demand, hoarding and distributional changes, with for example toilet paper that previously would have been bought by offices being redirected to suburban supermarkets, or flour that previously would have been sold in big bags to restaurants being repackaged for smaller domestic purchases.

The fact that the big grocery shops were able to keep their extraordinary range of products, including out-of-season fruit and vegetables shipped or airfreighted over great distance throughout the pandemic, is testimony to the resilience of the supply chains. Large grocery shops have almost double the amount of variety that they had in 1990, at the dawn of the recent wave of globalisation. Prior to the pandemic, growing awareness of the environmental and human rights dimensions of production systems was leading to a reconsideration and rationalisation of suppliers, but this has now been fast-tracked as businesses seek to improve their resilience against disruptions.[6] As a result, we should anticipate a reduction in the bewildering array of choices consumers face of almost identical products as suppliers rationalise their sources to reduce the carbon footprint, packaging and reliance on suppliers that do not meet rising standards. This is already beginning to happen in metropolitan youthful and high-income neighbourhoods, where grocery shops are reducing packaging and sourcing a growing share of their produce from certified suppliers who meet their environmental, social and governance requirements.

Far from the pandemic leading to deglobalisation, in this area as in others it will hasten changes already under way. The forced acceleration of previously slow and hesitant trends is best reflected in digital globalisation. Overnight, video conferencing replaced physical meetings. Nine-year-old Zoom is now valued at over $42 billion, more than any airline. During the pandemic, in addition to my university lectures and tutorials, I have participated in Zoom birthday parties, Zoom weddings and, sadly, Zoom funerals; with remote meetings, other than time zone considerations the location of the event becomes almost irrelevant. This heightened connectivity reflects a dramatic acceleration of digital globalisation.

Financial globalisation is likely to speed up alongside cross-border mergers and acquisitions, as the pandemic leads to a radical repricing of assets and investors pick over the carcasses of collapsed businesses. As they seek to raise returns, global investors will increase their investments in Southeast Asia to take advantage of its early rapid rebound.

Cross-border private financial flows will proliferate and transform, but so too will flows from governments and international agencies. More than a hundred countries have had their financial foundations ripped away by the economic tsunami that has accompanied the pandemic. Their bailout by the IMF, World Bank and others is inevitable, as is the restructuring of their private debt. Whereas in earlier crises it would mainly be Washington-based institutions and US and UK banks that needed to be involved in the restructuring, this now requires a far wider group of public and private creditors, including those based in China.

Globalisation with Chinese Characteristics

China's growing presence on the cultural and political stage will be a defining feature of the next phase of globalisation, reinforced by its growing political power and economic heft. It and other East Asian economies have emerged first from the pandemic, allowing the East Asian region to significantly increase its share of the global economic pie. By the end of 2021, the Chinese economy is forecast to be 10 per cent bigger than it was before the pandemic, while Europe and the US will be about 5 per cent smaller and the UK could have contracted by as much as a tenth from pre-pandemic levels.[7] Foreign businesses need to increase their investments in China, as it is the largest and fastest-growing market, and will do so despite the political pressures they may be under to reduce their involvement due to concerns about the violation of human rights, or geopolitical rivalry.

Far from the pandemic leading to a decoupling of the US and China, it has, in certain respects, strengthened the bonds. This reality flies in the face of President Trump's attempts to isolate China and is testimony to the effectiveness of China's wooing of US investors and its growing significance as one of the few remaining growth markets. With the Chinese market expected to grow from $24 trillion in 2018 to $41 trillion in 2023, the market is by far the biggest opportunity for any globally ambitious company.[8] Attracted by its size and positive economic outlook, in the year to June 2020 over $200 billion flowed into Chinese capital markets from abroad, and foreign holdings of Chinese stocks increased by 50 per cent and bonds by 28 per cent.[9] In 2020, encouraged by the lifting of restrictions in China on foreign ownership in the financial sector, two pillars of the US financial establishment, Goldman Sachs and Morgan Stanley, took majority stakes in their Chinese ventures; Citi, the biggest US bank, gained approval to undertake institutional investment in China; BlackRock, the largest global asset manager, started selling its mutual funds in China; and Vanguard, the biggest global provider of mutual funds with $7.2 trillion under management, shifted its Asian headquarters to Shanghai.[10] US payments companies such as Mastercard and PayPal and ratings agencies including S&P and Moody's also geared up their Chinese operations in 2020. Despite the trade wars, over the eighteen months to June 2020 the value of foreign mergers and acquisitions was higher than at any time in the preceding ten years.

With the ten-year yield on Chinese government bonds at 3.18 per cent compared to 0.8 per cent in the US, financial returns have overcome political concerns. The poor outlook of the US and robust recovery in China means this flow of funds into China is likely to increase.[11] During 2020, the quantity of Chinese onshore bonds held by foreign investors rose 20 per cent above prior year levels to exceed $421 billion.[12] In October 2020, when China sold dollar debt to US buyers for the first time, demand was over four times the amount on offer, providing a clear indication that the appetite of US pension funds and other investors in China was, in the words of a banker, not affected 'at all' by rising political frictions during the Trump Presidency.[13] And under a Biden Presidency is it likely to prove even less likely to be affected.

Attempts by the US government to reduce investment in China by private businesses, in order to slow its growth, have had very little impact. The Trump administration's prohibition on US government pension funds investing in China was immaterial for China, while undermining the opportunity for US pensioners to diversify their assets and benefit from the high returns on offer. The US banning of Huawei digital equipment and pressure placed on its suppliers and US allies to follow suit slowed the company's growth in the short term, but in the medium term is likely to increase the capabilities of the Chinese technology sector. In this, as in other areas, the pandemic has accelerated rather than diminished China's place as the new centre of gravity of globalisation. As one reflection of this, in 2020 North Atlantic container traffic is just one-third of the volume flowing on the US–Asia and Europe–Asia routes.[14]

China's share of global exports hit an all-time high in 2020.[15] It is already the largest trade partner for 124 countries, with the US trailing a distant second as the biggest supplier to 56 countries.[16] China produces an estimated 28 per cent of the world's manufactured goods, which is nearly as much as the US, Germany and Japan combined.[17] As over 87 per cent of the value of Chinese goods are made domestically, and as its 1.4 billion consumers are enjoying rising incomes, it is less vulnerable to US sanctions or pandemic disruptions to global trade than the other major economies, where domestic demand is stagnating and exports are a more important driver of growth.[18] Whereas in 2006 36 per cent of China's economy depended on exports, barely 17 per cent does now.[19] For this reason, even though the trade war launched by President Trump in 2018 has meant that tariffs on Chinese goods entering the US are six times higher than previously, the impact on China has been less than on the US, where it is contributing to higher prices, rather than choking demand.[20] During the pandemic, it was Chinese exporters that benefited from the surge in demand for masks and other urgently needed medical supplies, as well as for computers and other items for home use.

In many respects, the US depends more on China than China does on the US. China's early post-Covid-19 revival of its economy has allowed its exporters to gain market share, increasing its share to 30 per cent of all imports into Japan and a quarter of all imports into Europe in 2020 – the highest levels to date.[21] Meanwhile, US agricultural exporters are increasingly dependent on the Chinese market, with grain exporters during the height of the lockdown enjoying record sales to China.

The pandemic and rising anti-Chinese sentiment did not lead to lower trade with China. It did, however, reinforce underlying structural factors that are likely to lead to a transformation of trade, notably automation and changing cost structures. Chinese labour costs have been increasing recently due to a combination of its rapid economic growth, the associated rising demand for workers, and its exceptionally low fertility rates, which means there are about four million fewer Chinese workers each year. The migration of more than 700 million people over the past four decades from the Chinese countryside to the city for urban jobs has provided an ample supply of workers, but rural areas are now also short of workers and so this flow can no longer compensate for the declining number of people entering the workforce.

Higher labour costs have driven exporters to build new capacity in lower-cost locations, such as Vietnam, Cambodia, Ethiopia and even Mexico.[22] Tensions between US and China and concerns regarding dependence on one supplier will accelerate this process, which is already well under way. But as the rest of the world demands more Chinese products, and the relative significance of the US as an importer declines, actions by the US are unlikely to threaten China's dominant share of world trade.

Shifts in trade patterns around the world towards more locally- and regionally-sourced goods will reinforce these trends. Many companies embrace what some term 'China +1' strategies, which are to continue to use their Chinese suppliers but to be less dependent on them and diversify to additional sources. In many respects, manufacturing companies are catching up with those in the food industry, who have long sought to source from diverse suppliers to hedge against the notoriously unpredictable and weather-related fluctuations that affect many food products.[23]

Resilience and Supply Chains

Within days of the outbreak being identified, global markets were destabilised. Seemingly unconnected lives were connected as coffee farmers in Central American and Ethiopian villages discovered that the price of their coffee had plunged by over 20 per cent, as Starbucks closed more than half of its 4,300 Chinese outlets and other coffee chains responded similarly.[24] Copper and cocoa were almost as badly impacted, as Chinese demand contracted and other countries soon followed suit. Oil prices collapsed due to lower demand, given the response to the virus in many countries involved a cessation of transport and then fresh plans to accelerate the transition to renewables. Meanwhile citrus farmers in South Africa and elsewhere benefited from people around the world buying more oranges, in their desire to consume more Vitamin C for their health.

The quick recovery of China from the virus has helped in the return to a stabilisation of prices and demand, but the restoration of global growth requires the global trading system to avoid fragmenting into nationalist or even regional blocks. In a world of trading blocks in the Americas, Europe and Asia, Africa is likely to be the greatest loser as it lacks the high-income hub around which trade in other regions revolves.

The development of reliable and reasonably priced medical

supplies and medicines in response to the pandemic also requires a global trading system. The World Trade Organization has a particularly vital role to play in ensuring open borders and monitoring adherence to the regulations that govern global trade. Ensuring that authentic and approved medical supplies are available to all is essential, as is the need to limit the use of export bans that seek to stop manufacturers selling their products to other countries.

Many around the world believe that globalisation has gone too far, and that the relentless search for higher profits has led to outsourcing to lower-cost locations, causing vulnerability. The pandemic, by revealing the extent of interdependencies between nations, has exacerbated these concerns.

These fears, however, are not evidence-based. For 99 per cent of all EU supplies, for example, the top four suppliers are businesses in other EU countries.[25] None of the top four suppliers of products urgently needed to combat Covid-19 came from outside the EU.[26] In practice, supplies from outside the EU supplement the internal supplies. A recent analysis of the EU's trade finds that 'imports from the rest of the world make every EU state more resilient by diversifying its sources of supply'.[27] After analysing more than 9,000 products and supply risks, it concludes that forcing companies to source all their supplies in the European Union would 'increase costs and hit citizens in the poorest countries hardest' while also reducing diversification and resilience, and the ability of the EU to face future health and other crises.[28]

Protectionism by countries that have the capacity to manufacture vaccines, masks or other equipment greatly limits the potential for those that cannot do so to address their needs.[29] Preventing vaccine nationalism is especially important if the health risks posed by Covid-19 and the devastating economic consequences are to be overcome.

As trade increasingly becomes less about *where* and more about *how* products are produced, in terms of the standards and regulations, and as the US, EU and China adopt very different standards, satisfying them all may become increasingly difficult, if not impossible. The race to the top in standards, including data protection, environmental safeguards and human rights, could provide benefits for all. This is the benefit of a more globalised world. If the world fragments into different trading blocks, locking countries into spheres of influence, this opportunity to lift global standards will be lost.

The global food system has demonstrated its resilience, with most consumers not seeing any significant shortages in their supermarkets, and prices for most staples falling despite the pandemic and despite the fact that 80 per cent of the world's population relies on imports for at least part of its diet.[30] Most countries are more dependent on imports today than they were at the start of the century, but this has not been at the cost of resilience in the system. In part this is because the price of bulk shipping has gone down, as has the price of oil and fertilisers. Where hunger has increased it is not because food is not available, but because incomes have collapsed or, as Nobel laureate Amartya Sen has shown, because the politically powerful prevent access to affordable food for those in need.[31]

Refrigerated and container shipping of food products is one of the reasons for the resilience of food systems. Global container shipping, surprisingly, made profits during the pandemic as the three companies that control 85 per cent of the key routes cut their fleets and held their rates high while fuel prices went down.[32] *The Economist* observed that 'Covid-19 put wind in shipping companies' sails.'[33] Prior to the pandemic this $180 billion industry had been suffering from overcapacity, as the slowdown in trade over the past decade and glut of new ships had taken its toll.[34] Having revolutionised shipping in the 70s, container traffic has grown a hundredfold in the past fifty years and has come to be seen as a bellwether of globalisation.

In defiance of President Trump's call to reduce the US's dependence on Chinese products, demand soared, as was reflected in the cost of sending a container from China to the US, doubling in the second half of 2020 to record highs.[35] During the pandemic California's Long Beach port reported its busiest period ever, with China sending a record $52 billion across the Pacific to North America in November 2020 and 20 container vessels from China each day unloaded in Los Angeles' port.[36] Container traffic between Europe and China has similarly reached record levels, with the cost of shipping a 40-foot container from Shanghai to Rotterdam in late 2020 costing six times more than in 2019.[37] This surprising resilience, together with the new European Union-China and Asia-Pacific trade and investment deals, points to yet more evidence that those who see the pandemic as sounding the death knell for globalisation have failed to understand its resilience and ability to transform itself. One measure of this is that DHL's connectedness index of globalisation, which measures the dense web of physical and digital flows between countries, has remained well above the levels it plumbed following the 2008 financial crisis.[38]

While global travel and tourism will be depressed for a long time, countries that managed to suppress the pandemic restarted first domestic tourism and then foreign tourism. Tourism within China and the East Asian region benefited from citizens avoiding the rest of the world, and particularly the US, where the crisis was deeper and longer and where Asians felt increasingly unwelcome. Unlike personal travel, which is likely to rebound, business travel will be permanently affected, with future growth set on a lower and slower growth trajectory than prior to the pandemic. This will precipitate seismic movement in the $1.4 trillion business travel sector.[39] The reconfiguration of passenger jets into cargo planes has provided a much-needed lifeline to some airlines, with courier delivery companies reporting record demand; this is likely to increase further, as they play a key role in the distribution of vaccines and delivery of online orders.

Regulation Required

The benefits that globalisation brings are often diffuse and few politicians are prepared to defend open borders and freer trade. What is more obvious is that globalisation does appear to have increased the power of the global elite. It is also evident that globalisation has led to higher risk. The risks are often concentrated in specific localities, where, for example, workers are more vulnerable to losing their job to a lower-cost location. But risks can also be systemic, as has been demonstrated by the pandemic, by the financial crisis and by a failure to manage the unintended consequences of global growth, evident with climate change and rising inequality. These risks are the underbelly of globalisation. The failure to manage them is leading to a growing pushback against globalisation.

By accelerating a shift in globalisation, the pandemic has simultaneously moved the tectonic plates of national and geopolitics in ways that reverberate and reshape globalisation. What is now at stake is whether this leads to a more divided world, returning to the world of Cold War trading blocs, or whether it will lead to rising shared standards and more cooperation.

The end of the neoliberal era in the US, UK and Europe heralds a return to more active governments. In the US, there now is bipartisan support for government to intervene more actively in business. In Europe, since Covid-19, rules preventing government aid for business have been suspended, and in the UK the Conservative government is similarly planning to increase support for business. Ironically, it is communist China that now has the strongest interest in maintaining a free-trade system, in order to facilitate its exports. The Biden administration provides the opportunity for a return to the rules-based system of the World Trade Organization, as well as working with China and the EU to bolster the WHO and actions on climate change.

As well as Covid-19 in many respects accelerating rather than killing globalisation, it has also hastened its transformation to a system that is increasingly digital, depending on automated production processes. With China playing an increasing role, both economically and politically, the pandemic has hastened the arrival of a new phase of globalisation that, while still dominated by the old rules of the game established under US and European leadership, will increasingly reflect Chinese characteristics.

Rescue Globalisation

Globalisation can be a source of immense progress, but also of immense harm. The answer is not to stop globalisation but to harness it. Its rules need rewriting to ensure that the positive aspects can be harvested and the negative consequences mitigated.

Pascal Lamy, the former head of the World Trade Organization, has observed that by increasing the sensitivity to risk, the pandemic is likely to turn governments from protectionism to 'precautionism'. This will entail a greater focus on consumer protection, food standards, and the harms that suppliers may cause, whether it be through their use of child or forced labour or their damage to the environment. This could provide a back door to protectionism but could also encourage a global improvement in standards. Almost inevitably it will lead to the introduction of new tariffs or taxes that aim to stop carbon-intensive production being exported to other countries, as many countries have done. To calculate our carbon footprints, we need to count not only our domestic emissions, but also those arising from our imported products. In the case of the UK, this would double current emissions, which are calculated from domestic emissions alone.[40] The climate impact of a particular production process is the same irrespective of in which country the emissions occur, and producers should not get away with exporting their climate footprint or other polluting products such as nuclear waste or plastics to another country.

The regulation of digital flows, including those related to fake news and cybercrime, needs much greater attention. So too does the creation of clear, common and equivalent rules with transparency in personal and corporate tax for individuals and companies. Global citizens have responsibilities to all the jurisdictions from which they derive their wealth and in which they live.

The pandemic has highlighted the extent to which, as the writer William Gibson observed, 'The future is already here – it's just not evenly distributed.'[41] Those working in the digital world have barely been touched by the pandemic, while others have found themselves defenceless in the face of the health and economic emergencies. Addressing growing inequality within and between countries requires the pragmatic management of globalisation.

The pandemic has shown that to rescue globalisation we need to invigorate global governance to ensure that it is fit for twenty-first-century purpose. To create a more equitable and sustainable world requires that we see globalisation as a means to spread ideas such as literacy, gender and racial equality and respect for human rights.

For globalisation to contribute to poverty reduction, developing countries need to benefit from investment from abroad, and have market access for their exports. It is vital to overcome digital and health divides. A key dimension of globalisation is providing aid to help finance the poorest countries to build the educational, health, infrastructure and other foundations for growth. In these ways, globalisation can be a force for progress globally. But these flows are not entirely benign; in fact they can be extremely dangerous, which is why they urgently require better management.

Covid-19 has tested globalisation by highlighting the extent to which it contributes to contagion, as the virus has spread due to our networked world. But overcoming the threats we face and creating a less unequal world cannot be achieved by deglobalising. As the United Nations Secretary General has warned, 'When countries go in their own direction, the virus goes in every direction.'[42] The pandemic cannot be stopped by countries acting alone. Already, we have seen how the vaccine has been developed through an unprecedentedly intense global scientific collaboration. And, for the global economy to recover, the vaccine has to be distributed everywhere. If the pandemic has taught us anything, it is that no country is an island and that a coordinated response to global challenges is required.

CHAPTER 12

Responding to the Climate Emergency

With the world in stasis for the first time in centuries, the pandemic revealed the potential for addressing the climate emergency. Within days, our behaviours and lifestyles were altered. Flying and commuting were drastically reduced and we not only cut back carbon emissions but also came to appreciate the benefits of cleaner air and less noise pollution. Governments, too, demonstrated they have almost unlimited regulatory and economic power and the potential to rebuild economies by fast-tracking spending on renewable energy to create clean and sustainable jobs. Globally, high-income countries need to live up to their pledge in the 2015 Paris Climate Agreement to channel $100 billion a year in funding to developing countries to reduce their dependence on fossil fuels and adapt to the worsening impacts of climate change.[1] The devastating impact of the pandemic on poor countries makes increased aid, which can create jobs while addressing a critical global need to reduce carbon emissions, even more vital.

Covid-19 has demonstrated the importance of the umbilical relationship between human and planetary health. The threat posed by human encroachment into the natural habitats of bats and other animals, conduits for disease and potential pandemics, is well documented. So too is the growing evidence of the impact of rising greenhouse gases on climate. While the threat from the pandemic is temporary, the threat from climate change is permanent. Already, climate and the associated changes have led scientific commentators to worry that we are in the midst of a mass extinction.[2]

The increased frequency with which viruses have jumped from animals to humans in recent decades reflects the extent to which humans are increasingly invading and destroying the natural habitat of our animal neighbours. As we encroach on the habitats of wild animals and more animals are reared in intensely crowded conditions and transported to abattoirs and urban markets, transmission from animals to humans is more likely. As bats harbour a wide range of viruses and increasingly are compelled to look for food on farms, they infect livestock that humans then come into close contact with and consume.

Our demand for meat is another reason for higher risk, with more than 80 billion animals being slaughtered every year to feed our insatiable appetite.[3] With more than 99 per cent of livestock in the US now factory farmed, the risks are growing not only of animals harbouring diseases, but also of growing antibiotic resistance, as more antibiotics are given to animals to try to contain their rising propensity to disease as they are increasingly confined and crowded.[4] The grave risk posed was highlighted by the dangerous mutation of Covid-19 in mink farms in Denmark, which threatened the efficacy of vaccines, leading to the recommended slaughter of the entire mink population of 17 million.[5] In addition to the drastic improvements we would see to human health and in animal welfare, stopping factory farming and reducing meat consumption would have a beneficial effect on deforestation and climate change.[6]

Pandemic Reveals Possibilities

The pandemic has brought many of us into closer proximity with nature. More time at home and a growing acknowledgement of the precariousness of our lives has led to a deepening appreciation of the natural world. Some commentators have gone so far as to suggest that the pandemic may even be exercising a healing effect on our planet's atmosphere, eco-systems and biodiversity.

Covid-19 did temporarily reduce air pollution and greenhouse gas emissions – especially carbon dioxide, nitrogen dioxide and particulate matter.[7] By June 2020, as a result of the five-month spread of Covid-19 across Asia, Europe and North America and the subsequent lockdowns curtailing movement, global carbon dioxide emissions fell by 17 per cent compared with average levels in 2019.[8] For 2020 as a whole, emissions fell about 8 per cent, to levels last achieved a decade before.[9] A big reason for this reduction was the drop in manufacturing, power generation, flying and congestion. Steep downturns in traffic contributed to a sharp decline in the nitrogen dioxide hovering above the world's sprawling metropolises.[10] Remote working is estimated to reduce commuters' energy use by two-thirds compared to working from the office, mainly as a result of driving less.[11]

These improvements are temporary and without decisive action will be reversed. Indeed, as industrial activity and energy use reverted to pre-pandemic levels in China and elsewhere, they continued their upward trajectory. Whether greenhouse-gas emissions will be permanently reduced depends on what national, state and municipal governments do next.

Three out of every four individuals polled expect their govern-ments to make environmental protection a priority when planning the post-pandemic recovery.[12] Throughout the world, people believe that governments should give greater attention to climate change and that this poses at least as great a threat as the pandemic, with support for this view ranging from close to 87 per cent in China to 60 per cent of US citizens. These differences perhaps reflect the extent of the impact of the pandemic as much as concerns about climate change.[13]

Covid-19 is creating the potential for more investment in emissions reduction and 'building back cleaner'. Before the pandemic, climate action had already risen on the agenda, fuelled in part by widespread protest movements such as Fridays for the Future and Extinction Rebellion. A growing share of the population is reluctant to go back to the 'old normal'. This desire for change creates an opportunity to push forward plans for a greener economy.

The old arguments that governments cannot afford higher levels of expenditure have been rendered redundant by the massive boost to spending that the pandemic precipitated. And the belief that people cannot change their behaviour in the interests of others has been refuted by the extraordinarily rapid changes to individual lifestyles, encouraged by new guidelines and regulations.

Enlightened city leaders understand that greener cities are healthier cities. The pandemic has led to more than two dozen major cities around the world cutting back the use of cars, building bicycle lanes, pedestrianising streets, and starting ride-sharing initiatives. The United Nations has even established a World Bicycle Day to spread awareness about how bikes can help power a greener post-pandemic future.[14]

Heightened environmental awareness is also leading to actions to reduce waste and create more circular economies. China's war against food waste in August 2020 led to portion sizes in restaurants being reduced. Meanwhile consumer awareness over the environmental impact of fashion has increased. In response to the growing interest in the environmental impact of consumption, Selfridges, a British department store, has announced Project Earth, a five-year sustainability plan that includes offering customers second-hand Selfridges clothes and a rental service, including for luxury items such as Louis Vuitton handbags (a £1,000 handbag would set you back £128 for four days).[15]

President Xi in September 2020 scored a diplomatic coup by pledging that China would be carbon neutral by 2060 and ensuring that its carbon emissions, which currently account for almost a quarter of global emissions, would peak no later than 2030. Given that China is the biggest global importer of oil and coal, this highly significant move will hasten the transition to a zero-carbon economy and add to the pressure on fossil fuel producers.

The pandemic marks the beginning of the end of oil and fossil fuels. With oil trading at prices below $55 a barrel (a barrel contains 35 imperial gallons or 159 litres), the majority of producers cannot make a profit and new investment in fossil fuels is too risky. In previous crises when demand fell, the lower prices would have reduced production, which, aided by the Organization of the Petroleum Exporting Countries (OPEC), the legal cartel for oil, over time would have caused prices to rise as demand once again exceeded supply. Yet this time things were different and downward pressure on oil prices will be maintained.

Demand for oil is now past its peak. Consumption will continue to fall even more quickly than production can be cut back, as record levels of inventories add to the supplies and the US moves to exporting energy due to the growth in gas from fracking and rapidly rising renewable energy. To add to this pressure, government subsidies for oil are finally being reduced in many countries. The cartel maintained by OPEC will fall apart as oil producers race to pump as much as possible, before demand collapses completely and consumers switch to fossil-free energy sources.

The prospect of achieving the ambitions of the Paris Agreement to limit global warming to below two degrees Celsius compared to pre-industrial levels, which in 2019 appeared impossibly optimistic, a year later appeared achievable. China has committed to radically reducing its use of fossil fuels and both President Biden and the European Union have committed to achieving net-zero carbon emissions by 2050. The US aims to spend $2 trillion over four years, and the European Union plans on investing €350 ($430) billion per year for the next decade to achieve its targets. Adding to the encouraging commitments of key governments are the signals from business. During 2020, the value of renewable energy businesses doubled, while that of fossil fuel businesses went down by more than a quarter.

The pandemic heralded the end of the era of powerful petro-states, which need over $70 a barrel to balance their budgets, with their oil revenue in 2020 plummeting to around half of what it was in 2019.[16] For more than a hundred years, the insatiable demand for oil has been intimately tied up with US foreign policy, with the growing dependence of the US on imports of oil to fuel its economy leading it to ensure it had friendly petro-state suppliers, whose exports of oil then financed their development. The renewables revolution together with rising US domestic shale oil production has severed this dependence on Middle East supplies, and will mean that the US is no longer likely to consider political, economic and military support and interventions in the region to secure its energy sources as a strategic necessity.

Breaking the link between energy and oil has profound geopolitical implications that will reverberate far beyond the nations whose wealth and power have been built on fossil fuels. Covid-19 has accelerated this transition and provided a glimpse into what is at stake in this historic transition. With the decline of petro-states will come the rise of electro-states, able to produce solar, wind and other renewable power cheaply. They will become the key exporters of the new power generators of the future. As China is already the biggest producer of solar and wind power and biggest exporter of solar panels, the move to renewable energy will benefit it.

During the pandemic, renewable energy use grew more rapidly than in any previous period in the US. Almost 90 per cent of new electricity generation in 2020 was from renewable sources, with just 10 per cent from gas and coal.[17] Globally, there has been a fivefold increase in renewable energy capacity in the decade to 2020, with solar power growing fifteenfold over the past decade, establishing itself as the cheapest source of power in history.[18] As a result of these trends, renewables are now anticipated to displace coal as the largest source of power by 2025.[19]

In the US, renewables in 2020 accounted for over 55 per cent of new energy generation with, somewhat surprisingly, the Republican-controlled states in the US making the most rapid conversion to renewable energy.[20] Texas, Kansas and Oklahoma rely more on wind and solar than the Democratic-dominated north-eastern states as they have more sun and space for solar panels and wind farms, and the 'not in my backyard' restrictions that delay investments in heavily populated and wealthier areas are less prevalent. In the US, 'wind-turbine technicians' and 'solar-panel installers' are now among the most rapidly growing job categories. In Texas alone more than 35,000 jobs have been created in renewable energy, encouraging politicians eager to find jobs that can withstand the combined Covid-19 and collapsing oil price to look beyond fossil fuels to renewable energy opportunities.[21]

In the UK, the combination of the reduction in demand for electricity in offices and in manufacturing and a warm and windy summer meant the country was able to record the most days without fossil fuel use since electricity was first generated in 1882.[22] Pressure from companies is adding to the impetus to move towards renewables even in some recalcitrant countries. So, for example, Sony has warned the Japanese government that it may have to shift its manufacturing to another country unless renewable energy supplies are increased, as Apple, Facebook and other companies are demanding that their equipment suppliers only use renewable power. Japanese electronics companies such as Ricoh are similarly affected, while consumer pressure is also leading the Kao cosmetic business to pressure the Japanese government to wean itself off fossil fuels.[23]

Distraction and Delay

While the pandemic accelerated progress towards renewable fuels in some parts of the world, elsewhere it delayed initiatives towards a greener future. In Brazil, President Bolsonaro relaxed regulations that restricted deforestation and slackened the enforcement of those laws that remained. This meant that emissions from the burning of the Amazon in 2020 rose by an estimated 20 per cent above prior years.[24] Land grabs have increased, as has the encroachment on indigenous rights. Furthermore, because of the trade war that President Trump initiated with China, China has reduced its imports of soya from the US and instead increased imports from Brazil. This additional demand led to further encroachment into the Amazon, as cattle farmers pushed further into virgin forest as their land was turned over to soya.

Other negative signs around the world include the potential for stimulus packages to speed the return to dependence on fossil fuels. The last time that carbon dioxide emissions fell was during the financial crisis. Within a year, carbon emissions had rebounded, aided by the stimulus packages introduced by governments, which greatly increased construction and infrastructure spending. Then, lower oil prices also undermined efforts to substitute renewable for fossil fuels.

Stimulus packages that could similarly lead to higher carbon emissions are once again in evidence, as are low prices for fossil fuels. In Canada, a bailout for the oil and gas industry will encourage further production, airlines everywhere are being bailed out, and numerous countries have announced an infrastructure spending spree – China is dedicating $3.5 trillion to infrastructure spending.[25] Already by May 2020 emission levels in China had exceeded pre-pandemic levels. Friends in Beijing confirmed the return of the brown-grey fog of pollution that makes the mountains surrounding the city invisible.[26]

Although the signals from the US, Europe and China point in a positive direction, it is essential that governments in their response to the pandemic and associated economic emergency do not undermine their longer-term commitments to achieving zero net emissions by taking actions that in the short term will increase emissions. More than $500 billion in subsidies is going into airlines and other carbon-emitting sectors, and $151 billion of the Covid-19 recovery funds was allocated to fossil fuel energy companies. With a few noteworthy exceptions, such as France making a condition of its bailout for Air France that it reduces its carbon emissions, governments have missed an opportunity to tie their support to improvements in business behaviour.[27] Barely 1 per cent of the $12 trillion stimulus package announced by rich countries is devoted to the energy transition; in the US, under 1 per cent of President Trump's 2020 package of stimulus measures went to green investments.[28] All told, in eighteen major economies government expenditure to counter the economic impact of the pandemic did more harm than good to the environment and undermined efforts to reduce carbon emissions.[29]

To ensure that Covid-19 leads to accelerated actions on climate change, the mistakes of the financial crisis need to be avoided and stimulus packages need to be dedicated to a green new deal that creates jobs, growth and reduced carbon emissions. The European Union has been at the forefront of these efforts, with a third of its €750 billion (£677 billion) stimulus package allocated to environmental improvements. President Biden similarly has indicated that his $2 trillion green stimulus aims to provide a massive boost to the economy, while simultaneously accelerating the reduction in carbon emissions.

Covid-19 delayed much-needed action to address the world's climate crisis. The COP26 Climate Change Conference scheduled for November 2020 was postponed by a year, which delayed the strengthening of the Paris international agreement to hold temperature rises below two degrees Celsius. Diplomatic progress to protect biological diversity and the oceans has similarly stalled, with the Nature Pledge signed at the UN General Assembly meetings in September 2020 attracting less than a third of global nations and missing the two biggest polluters,

COP26

China and the US. The pandemic likewise distracted attention from unprecedented environmental calamities, including rampant forest fires, the accelerated deforestation of the Amazon and record melting of the polar ice.[30] The pandemic has also increased plastic pollution, including through microplastics entering waterways due to rising production of disposable gloves, surgical masks and other non-recyclable products.[31] Already by September 2020, plastic gloves and face masks were found discarded on a third of British beaches and two-thirds of inland pathways.[32]

The costs of current inaction are becoming increasingly clear. The fires in the US in 2020 alone are estimated to have cost over $20 billion and burned more than three million hectares, while in Australia more than 18 million hectares were burned, at an estimated cost of $79 billion.[33] In Europe, the WHO estimates air pollution costs $1.6 trillion a year in diseases and deaths.[34] Poor people are worst affected everywhere, and poor countries are the most vulnerable to the impact of climate change. The rise of oceans poses an existential threat to as many as half of Bangladesh's 161 million inhabitants, as it does to citizens of other low-lying countries and island states.[35] Fragile lands, such as those across the Sahel region of Africa, are being rendered unhabitable, with this threatening widespread famine and rapidly rising numbers of refugees.

Globally, outdoor air pollution causes more than 4.2 million deaths every year and leads to chronic health problems for millions more.[36] During the pandemic, the temporary reductions in pollution due to reduced burning of coal and oil as traffic and industrial activity fell resulted in a 40 per cent reduction in nitrogen dioxide and 10 per cent reduction in particulate pollution, with this estimated to have saved more than 11,000 lives in Europe in just one month of lockdown.[37] In addition, in Europe during the pandemic lower pollution is calculated to have led to 1.3 million fewer days of sick leave from work, and 6,000 fewer asthma attacks in children.[38]

Rescue the Environment

The environmental dividends of the pandemic did not solve any of the existing, chronic challenges. A temporary rescue will only have a minor impact. But what the pandemic did teach us is that action to address climate change is not only necessary, it is possible. We can change our behaviour. Governments can act. A massive green new deal that weans our societies off fossil fuels and creates jobs and a clean environment is now not only necessary, it is economically and politically feasible.

Covid-19 did not heal the Earth, even though this is a seductive idea. Photos of wild boar in the heart of Barcelona, goats taking over Welsh towns, clear views of the Himalayas from the state of Punjab and aquamarine canals in Venice provided much-needed hopeful images in 2020. These suggested that nature's capacity for regeneration had been activated.

While it is true that air, noise and water pollution as well as greenhouse gas emissions declined in 2020, this will not be sustained in the post-pandemic era if radical measures are not taken to decarbonize the global economy and alter consumption habits. Without a radical reduction in the eating of meat, flying and air cargo flights (which the growing demand for online delivery is increasing), it will be impossible to reduce sufficiently the greenhouse gas emissions that cause climate change.

Stimulus packages that place the environment and job creation at their centre could provide a massive boost to employment creation and a clean economy. It is this, rather than the return to dirty old jobs, that needs to be the focus of economic regeneration.

The pandemic could rescue the Paris Agreement if a significant part of the $12 trillion rich countries have allocated to protect their economies is devoted to fast-tracking their transition to the green economy. Nothing short of dramatically increased investments and actions is required, costing around $1.4 trillion per year for the next five years, which would be much less than what was committed in 2020 by rich countries to address the coronavirus economic emergency.[39] A rapid step-up in investments in clean energy and step-down in fossil fuel use over the coming five years provides the only hope of sticking to the Paris target of restricting temperature rises to within 1.5 °C. If it is left longer or investments are not of a sufficiently large scale now, this window of possibility will be permanently lost.[40]

The pandemic threw new light on our everyday relationship with our environment and revealed the need to learn to live with, not against, nature. It has increased our awareness of local environments, and the domestic sourcing of food and other essentials. Yet, the pandemic increased the power of giant suppliers and hastened the decline of small companies. Boosting demand for local products and services could help to offset this hegemony by supporting small local businesses. Covid-19 increased local travel and leisure at the expense of foreign trips, providing a boom for small businesses catering for staycations and visits to nearby leisure spots as well as reducing airline emissions. This embryonic growth now needs to be sustained. At the same time, as public transport systems come under increasing strain and many individuals have relocated further from their offices, surveys in many countries point to a real danger that the use of private vehicles will exceed pre-pandemic levels in 2021.[41] Moving to a fully electric public transport fleet, drawing on renewable energy and investing in public transport systems is thus more urgent than ever. So too is the elimination of petrol and diesel vehicles, with the UK government's announcement that new cars and vans powered wholly by petrol or diesel will not be sold in the UK from 2030 a welcome step in this direction.

Greater investment in local solutions to meet food and energy needs is required, including in neighbourhood renewable solar and wind power grids, as well as local intensive production of vegetables and other plants. The conversion of unused car parks, warehouses and offices into hydroponic urban farms solely dependent on green energy would be a productive way to invest in local jobs and to reduce carbon footprints. So, too, would be a massive roll-out of investments in home insulation and solar panel installation, which could create jobs immediately.

The digital economy is not necessarily a cleaner economy. The internet alone is estimated to account for about the same quantity of carbon emissions as the global aviation industry, and the digital economy overall contributes up to 10 per cent of emissions.[42] While remote work has the advantage of being a substitute for commuting and flying, the growing energy demand of computing networks means that it is the most rapidly growing source of carbon emissions in many advanced economies. Switching to solar, wind and hydro-powered computer power and the development of more energy-efficient technologies is vital if humanity is to reverse the climate emergency.

The only way to truly heal the planet, and to save ourselves, is to take this opportunity to build radically greener economies, invest in renewable energy, increasingly consume plant-based diets, phase out fossil fuels, create decent and sustainable jobs and permanently shift to green mobility solutions. By showing that governments can find the money to address planetary emergencies, and that we can change our behaviour, the pandemic has demonstrated the feasibility of radical reductions in climate emissions.

There are many signs that a growing number of leaders understand the depth of the climate emergency and are exploring how the post-pandemic stimulus could meet climate objectives, as has been evident in the commitments of Presidents Biden, Xi, von der Leyen of the European Union and many others. It is also encouraging that most governments have deferred to scientists on the pandemic, and we should expect them to do the same on climate.

In 2020, the European Union announced its €1 trillion green transition plan and South Korea announced a $133 billion new green deal, China committed to reducing its carbon emissions by 55 per cent by 2030 and President Biden has promised a $2 trillion green new deal – all of these initiatives are explicitly designed to reach decarbonisation targets while reviving economies and creating jobs.[43] Launching the Korean New Deal, President Moon called it a 'blueprint for South Korea's next hundred years' and a means to create two million jobs in the next few years, while establishing a comprehensive social safety net and facilitating the transition to a digital and a zero-carbon economy.[44] In the UK the Prime Minister has talked in ambitious terms about turning the UK into a renewable powerhouse, while the opposition Labour Party has called for the creation of a 'zero-carbon army of young people'.[45] Moving from bold statements to concrete actions is now necessary to rescue the environment.

CHAPTER 13

Stopping Global Crises

In January 2020, as Covid-19 was already spreading, a global pandemic did not make it into the top ten of the most likely risks identified by the World Economic Forum's *Global Risks Report 2020* unveiled in Davos. In fact, a pandemic was ranked as having the lowest potential impact of the top ten risks facing the world. This inability to identify looming disasters was similarly evident in 2007, when a global financial crisis was missing from the *Global Risks Report*'s top ten list. Yet, within a year the worst such crisis on record had overwhelmed the world economy.[1]

The failure of the World Economic Forum to predict crises reflects a much wider problem – none of the global organisations that produce risk rankings saw pandemics as a likely threat. In October 2019 a global risk survey of 1,726 experts from 58 countries by Axa and Eurasia Group, the President of which is the renowned analyst Ian Bremmer, placed pandemics in a lowly eighth place out of their ranking of the top ten threats we face, with cybersecurity, social discontent, natural resource management, artificial intelligence and pollution among others scoring higher.[2] How did the thousands of experts and the many organisations that claim to have insights into risk get it so wrong? Is it possible to predict future pandemics and other major crises, and by so doing stop them?

Risk experts typically reflect prevailing views rather than provide fresh insights, despite elaborate models and presentations that display traffic-light warning colours for levels of danger.

The low ranking they accorded to pandemics mirrored the low level of concern among the public, with a spike in 2009 following SARS having dissipated quickly as the threat of pandemics was thought to have declined to negligible levels. The only divergence in views between the experts and the public over the past decade was on inequality, which the public have been increasingly worried about, while experts were less concerned, and cyber-security, which experts worried more about than the public.

The widely held view that the 2020 coronavirus pandemic was a 'once-in-a-century' event reflects the failure to recognise that the nature of risk has changed in fundamental ways, and that just because the last global pandemic was the Spanish Flu of 1918, a century ago, it does not mean that it is likely the next will be in a hundred years' time. Unfortunately, pandemics are becoming much more frequent and more likely, as are other risks. This inability to understand the changing nature of risk reflects the fact that the risk management profession is backward-looking and has failed to incorporate the fundamental changes that globalisation, technological change and increased population density have caused to the nature of future risks. It is informed by the last big risk event and past headlines.

Risk managers tend to be captured by groupthink as they draw on surveys that distil the views of other risk managers, rather than of experts on pandemics, cyber-attacks, climate disasters or other dangerous threats. Given the prestige of the institutions such as the World Economic Forum or major management consultancies who provide the surveys, it is difficult for maverick thinkers to tell their boards or bosses anything different and so consensus views prevail. In recent decades, globalisation has led to revolutionary changes that have outstripped the slower evolution of institutions, causing a widening gap between our increasingly complex systems and our methods for managing their risks.

The failure of the risk professionals to identify the danger posed by pandemics stands in stark contrast to pandemic specialists and many others, who have attempted to sound the alarm bell. In my book *The Butterfly Defect: Why Globalization Creates Systemic Risks, and What to Do About It*, back in in 2014, I indicated that not only was a pandemic inevitable but that it would lead to a global economic collapse. In each subsequent year I repeated this, and in 2017 in *Age of Discovery: Navigating the Storms of Our Second Renaissance* I compared the spreading of risks during the Renaissance period of 500 years ago to today, highlighting how early globalisation through the voyages of discovery led to the spreading of diseases that killed most of the native American population and brought back diseases that killed millions of Europeans. Increasing connectivity coupled with rising population density and higher levels of encroachment on natural systems, I wrote, made future pandemics inevitable and these would cause an economic collapse. The only uncertainty was when it would happen.

Pandemics will recur, alongside other more frequent and consequential threats unless we act decisively to stop them. The reason is that we live in an increasingly unstable and complex hyperconnected system. An infected passenger flies from Wuhan to Milan, causing a pandemic; a computer virus reaches an internet connection and infects computers globally; housing loan defaults in the Midwest of the US trigger a global economic crisis.[3] The super-spreaders of the goods of globalisation – airport hubs, fibre-optic cables, global financial centres – are also the super-spreaders of the bads. This is what I have termed the *'butterfly defect'* of globalisation: the systemic risk endemic in our hyperconnected world, in which small actions in one place can spread rapidly to have global effects. It draws on the renowned physicist Edward Lorenz's observation that when a butterfly flaps its wings above Brazil it can be the cause of a tornado in Texas, which became known as the butterfly effect, a term that defines the instability inherent in complex interconnected systems.

Globalisation creates systemic risks. But stopping globalisation will not stop global threats. Rather, it would amplify them. There is no wall high enough to keep out climate change, pandemics and other catastrophic future risks. But high walls undermine the potential for cooperation required to manage our shared risks. Protectionism reduces investment, trade, migration and technological advances, all of which create jobs and higher incomes. Deglobalisation would result in falling incomes and a lower capacity of countries to build resilience. The solution is in working together to make globalisation safe and sustainable, not in working against each other.

Leadership is required to manage the negative dimensions of globalisation and harvest the positive, to ensure progress is not overwhelmed by common threats. Resilient systems are only as strong as their weakest links. Stopping the next pandemic, which could be even worse than Covid-19, must be a priority. This requires reinforcing and reforming the WHO to give it the governance, staff and capacity it needs to become the world's rapid response fighting force on global health.

The coronavirus pandemic has demonstrated that a crisis that starts elsewhere soon becomes a crisis at home. As pandemics can arise anywhere and numerous infectious diseases that threaten world health arise in developing countries, a much greater effort is required to stop these diseases at source, including through supporting the building of local knowledge and scientific and medical capacity. Along with the WHO, Gates Foundation and others, the US Centers for Disease Control and Prevention has been at the heart of building such capacity, including in China and Africa. But austerity cuts to its budget and the politicisation of its governance have in recent years undermined the effectiveness of its global activities. Stopping the next pandemic, and overcoming malaria, tuberculosis and other big killers, requires that rich countries allocate more funds to these international collaborative efforts. The focus should be on both the prevention of deadly diseases and on their cure. Investing in the long term in this area, as in investing in renewable energy to address climate change, and in creating decent jobs to overcome inequality, is the best way to secure our future.

Networked Problems Require Networked Solutions

Addressing networked threats such as pandemics, cybercrime, cascading financial crises, antibiotic resistance and climate change requires transformation in all parts of the system. Actions need to begin with us as individuals changing our behaviour – for example by wearing masks to prevent the spread of infectious diseases, avoiding fast fashion and reducing our consumption of plastics, as well as weaning ourselves off fossil fuel usage and red meat.

Resilience cannot be delegated to others. It is everyone's responsibility. The extent of social trust and shared knowledge in societies, or what economists call 'social capital', has a powerful influence on resilience. Being able to rely on family, friends, communities and colleagues makes a marked difference to the resilience of individuals, and the same is true for neighbourhoods, cities and businesses.

Resilience needs to be built deliberately into business. Companies should maintain a prudent level of spare finance as a valuable investment in resilience, not just as excess fat to be trimmed to maximise leverage. The short-term profit-maximising focus on leanness, which involves reducing spare capacity or spare cash and the pursuit of 'just-in-time' management systems, can undermine longer-term resilience. Governments and companies should note the lessons from the Eyjafjallajökull volcano, the Tohoku tsunami, Hurricanes Katrina to Maria, and now coronavirus – that widespread leanness can compound into systemic fragility. Our financial, digital, trade and other systems are intertwined through complex networks. The intersecting nodes and hubs are concentrated in specific locations, such as global financial centres and major ports and airports. This concentration of logistical or other nodes in one location makes them vulner-able, as does the concentration of key personnel and information in headquarters buildings. Resilience can be enhanced by greater geographical diversification, even though the benefits of this have not yet found their way into compe-tition policy or risk management strategies.

A growing number of shareholders and managers of forward-looking businesses have expressed their desire to improve the hardiness of business in the face of systemic shocks. Politicians too, are keen to improve the resilience of the public sector. This requires a deeper analysis, including to determine exact cause and effect: resilience to what, for example, and how much resilience? Unfortunately, even the wealthiest governments, busi-nesses or individuals cannot be resilient against all possible shocks.

Resilience can also be improved by decentralisation, so indi-viduals, businesses, countries, regions and cities are empowered to make their own decisions. The principle of subsidiarity, by which whatever can be delegated to lower levels of authority should be, should complement rather than be a substitute for oversight by higher levels of authority. Businesses need to be responsible for their own risk management, but within a frame-work set by governments.

Global systemic risks require that individual countries also yield some autonomy to supranational institutions. Those coun-tries that have assiduously followed the guidelines of the WHO have done best, whether they are relatively poor, like Vietnam or Mongolia, or richer, like Finland and New Zealand. Stark differences between countries in the management of Covid-19 have demonstrated the importance of operating at multiple levels to contain risk and that a combination of robust international, national, subnational and local actions are required.

Multilateral international institutions ought to be at the apex of this layered approach. Yet there remains a set of 'orphan' issues that have no institutional home. A number of international bodies provide analysis and information on climate change, such as the International Panel on Climate Change (IPCC). But there is no global institution with decision-making and enforcement power to coordinate responses. There is also no major global organisation working on cybercrime, despite the fact that a single computer virus like WannaCry or NotPetya – whether produced by organised state agencies or 'lone wolf' individuals – can spread globally and cause billions of dollars' worth of damage and mayhem within days. This threat, like that of extremist ideologies and the subversion of democracy or vaccination campaigns through fake news, is spread opportunistically through the digital networks of globalisation. While these threats transcend national borders, as do the threats posed by climate change, pandemics or terrorism, current responses are predominantly national and therefore inadequate.

Significant progress can still be made using the Pareto principle, which states that for many outcomes about 80 per cent derive from about 20 per cent of the causes, giving rise to the 80/20 rule by which a vital small set of actors can usually resolve a large part of any problem. Those who contribute the greatest share of the problem have the greatest responsibility to resolve it. A small number of countries and companies account for well over two-thirds of carbon emissions. New York State accounts for more carbon emissions than forty-five African countries. It also consumes more antibiotics than all of these nations combined. As the Oxford Martin Commission for Future Generations report *Now for the Long Term* argued, a C20-C30-C40 partnership of the twenty largest countries, thirty companies and forty cities would include enough of the key players to make a significant difference in addressing climate change. The success of coalitions that emerged to tackle ozone depletion or reverse the tide on HIV/AIDS provide inspirational insights on the ability of coalitions of committed citizens, companies and countries to make a difference, bolstering the efforts of the UN and multilateral institutions.

Stopping Pandemics

After the catastrophes of 2020, the WHO has identified five priority actions to prevent and prepare for pandemics in the future.[4] These are to reduce human exposure to the virus, strengthen early warning systems, intensify rapid containment operations, build coping capacity and coordinate global research.[5] These specific actions relate to all pandemics and it is tragic that they were not learnt in time to prepare us for Covid-19. Epidemiologist Larry Brilliant, who was at the fore-front of global efforts to eradicate smallpox, has summarised the two simple principles involved: 'early detection, early response'.[6] Early detection of global threats, whether they are viruses that could become a pandemic, or nuclear centrifuges that could produce atomic weapons, requires that countries share information and trust each other. When geopolitics is poisoned, early detection is stymied. In the case of Covid-19, heightened tensions between the US and China contributed to delays in the sharing of information regarding the outbreak and to the delayed global response to the pandemic. This undermined the global economic response and distribution of vaccines.

Globalisation increases the systemic risk of pandemics, yet can also be the source of prevention. To address this escalating risk to all our health global agreement is needed. Early detection is essential. The difficulty associated with managing infectious diseases and viruses grows exponentially with the number of people affected. The key is to locate the pathogen at its source, then isolate and contain it. As Dr Brilliant has stressed, 'You can't cure or prevent what you don't know is there.'[7] The internet provides global search engines that could be set up to browse millions of internet-based activities across different languages in order to detect infectious disease outbreaks, by tracking the demand for tissues or cough medicine, for example. These could both intuitively and empirically bear results much faster than institutions such as the WHO, which relies on reporting by individuals with long lag times as it takes time to gather data and for this to be collated and analysed.

During the SARS outbreak, the WHO itself was alerted to the problem by the online operation of the Global Public Health Intelligence Network (GPHIN).[8] Engaging civil society to support these activities and establishing the necessary technologies, including evolving bio-pathogen sensors linked to mobile phones to identify novel viruses and transmit their GPS location to distant specialists, provides the global ability to identify and contain pandemics at their source. So, too, does providing the necessary skills, laboratories and other capacity in all regions of the world to adequately monitor and identify potential pandemics.

Adding these capabilities afforded by new technologies is not a substitute for more effective coordination between countries. The unprecedented global scientific sharing of genomic contagion and treatment information during 2020 needs to be sustained and widened to other infectious diseases. So too does information on drug discovery, to allow for the widest possible application of vaccinations and drugs that can save lives and stop the spread of infectious diseases.

Once dangerous infectious diseases are detected, mechanisms for an early isolation of the disease must be immediately available and enacted. The establishment of national, regional or global capabilities in this regard is vital. The medical equivalent of special weapons and tactics (SWAT) teams with the capacity to get to anywhere rapidly without lengthy authorisation procedures is vital. By the time a highly contagious virus has skipped from the countryside to a megacity or from a megacity to a major airport, there is no bringing it back. Although the immediate response should be medical, the broader implications also need thinking through. For example, if the emergency requires the culling of all the poultry or pigs on which people depend for their livelihoods and nutrition, alternative mechanisms to support and compensate the affected population need to be put in place immediately. Systemic risks require systemic responses. The international scientific collaboration on HIV/AIDS, SARS, Ebola and Covid-19 highlights the vital role of research, coordination and global action.

Pandemics have no respect for national borders. Given that the incubation period of a potential pandemic may mean that it has escaped national jurisdictions before it is identified, it is fanciful to imagine that the threat can always be contained at a national border. Any pathogen that is carried through a major airport hub will be global within three days at the most. It was no coincidence that the coronavirus first made an impact outside China in the vicinity of major airport hubs – Milan, London and New York.

The permissive use of antibiotics needs to end if we are to ensure their continued efficacy. The distribution of over-the-counter antibiotics that do not require prescriptions and their use in non-human applications need to be restricted. With more than half of the antibiotics made allocated to animal husbandry to increase the profitability of factory farming and the growing use of antibiotics in other applications (such as being added to paints applied to ships' hulls to reduce the growth of barnacles), we are increasing the risk that when the point comes where we desperately need antibiotics for our survival, they will have become ineffective.

To achieve this ambitious public health and pandemic prevention agenda requires the urgent reform, upskilling, resourcing and empowerment of the WHO, so that it has the necessary mandate, authority, expertise and equipment to achieve the tasks identified above. This would not be costly, amounting to less than 1 per cent of the cost of the Covid-19 pandemic. What is required, more than money, is political will to ensure that the multilateral system for addressing the threats to our health and our planet is fit for purpose. Prevention of pandemics, like all other threats, costs a tiny fraction of the failure to act.

International Governance in the Twenty-First Century

Multilateral institutions that manage the problems that transcend national borders can only be as effective as their shareholders allow. [9] In response to the Covid-19 crisis, the IMF has streamlined its processes and provided unprecedented support for its members. But not all institutions have been able to rise to the challenge, and developing countries remain in dire need of additional multilateral support. The WHO should be the world's rapid response force on global health but was undermined by the US just when it was needed most. And while global trade desperately needed a shot in the arm, the effectiveness of the World Trade Organization was paralysed by trade wars and the blocking of much-needed appointments and reforms.

China-centred institutions are becoming increasingly important, including the Asian Infrastructure Investment Bank and the constellation of bilateral agreements forming the Belt and Road Initiative. Working with these institutions, rather than against them, is essential, as solving global problems requires more firepower and coordination. No global problem can be resolved without China's participation. More diverse personnel also bring greater effectiveness and legitimacy, with broader engagement providing a source of strength rather than anxiety.

In addition to the rise of new powers and the inclusion of more diverse government views, the growing role of private companies needs to be factored into the global architecture. Amazon Web Services and Google Cloud are now systemically important financial infrastructure, while Amazon Marketplace is critical for commerce, Alibaba for personal protective equipment, while Apple and Google have led on app-based contact tracing in many countries. Meanwhile, Facebook has emerged as a dominant distribution system for public health information – as well as a primary source of fake anti-vaccination stories, which highlights the need for much stricter regulation and reform of social media.

Insurance also has a vital role to play and within the business community the reinsurance companies such as Swiss Re, Munich Re and the large insurance companies and markets led by Lloyd's of London are constantly assessing, pricing and providing risk cover. This can help those who can afford it to mitigate losses, but many who most are in need are least able to get cover. The All England Lawn Tennis Club, for example, received a £174 million insurance payout that exceeded the losses it suffered from the pandemic-induced cancellation of the 2020 Wimbledon tournament.[10] Just this one payout far exceeded the combined total of £99 million available to 150 developing countries under the World Bank's pandemic insurance scheme. Establishing an effective and affordable insurance market that can help build resilience in poor countries and poor communities should be a vital part of a global risk management agenda.

As always, the next crisis will not conform to our old mental maps; establishing partnerships with those who understand the new landscape is vital to prepare for it. But the private sector is not always benign, and we require independent regulators who are able to control the rising power of superstar firms. A constant renewal of technical expertise is also required to ensure that the experience of the financial crisis, when experts and regulators failed to understand credit derivatives, is not repeated with newly emergent threats.

Four Meta-Horsemen

What are the biggest barriers to reform of global institutions to make them fit for the purpose of managing our shared threats? We can fight pestilence, war, famine and death – and have done in the past – but to do so we must confront the four meta-horsemen: short-termism, nationalism, cost and capture.

Covid-19 shows that where there is a will, all four meta-horsemen can be overcome. Politicians have a limited attention span, but electorates shaken by Covid-19 are likely to demand long-term solutions. Leaders in the US, UK, Sweden, Brazil and beyond faced growing criticism over their responses to the pandemic; voters will not forgive governments caught unprepared a second time. Nor will history forgive a generation of leaders who fail to prevent catastrophic climate change. As the inspirational leaders who created a new world order while fighting the Second World War taught us, it is possible to focus on both short-term and longer-term challenges simultaneously. The shareholders of global institutions, and of private companies, need to do the same thing.

The Covid-19 health and economic emergencies demonstrate that coordinated global efforts are required. To stop boomerang infections, we need international cooperation on vaccines. The extent to which this has been the case in addressing the coronavirus pandemic was evident in the first vaccine to be approved being developed by Turkish immigrants in Germany, funded by US company Pfizer, and manufactured in Belgium. But this vaccine is unaffordable to most countries and requires storage at −70 Celsius, which is not widely available. Fortunately, other vaccines such as the one developed by Oxford University and AstraZeneca, which can be stored in a fridge and costs one-twentieth of the Pfizer vaccine, are available. A massive global initiative is required to ensure that these can be distributed globally.

To overcome chronic shortages of doctors and nurses to address infectious and chronic diseases, we need immigrants and the free movement of skilled people around the world. And to address climate change, stop future financial crises and overcome poverty, we need to harvest the benefits of globalisation while resolutely remedying the weaknesses, not least the *butterfly defect* of systemic risk that means that if it is not stopped, our connectivity can lead to dangerous contagion.

Resources *are* available in high-income countries – governments and electorates simply need to reorder their priorities. Perhaps because war was the last potentially catastrophic shock that many countries experienced, governments around the world allocate an average of 6 per cent of their expenditures to the military but far less than one-hundredth of this amount to preventing pandemics, even though the future threat to the population from pandemics is now much greater than the threat from war. At the international level, the budget of the WHO is less than that of a single major hospital in the US or Europe.

As the response to the Covid-19 crisis has shown, when the national interest is at stake the resources can be found. These lessons need to be carried forward. Prevention is always cheaper than cure. Globally much more attention needs to be paid to interventions that could reduce the risks of malaria, HIV/AIDS, tuberculosis and other diseases. Interventions that would improve diets and would reduce chronic diseases, such as heart failure and diabetes, are required as these are the leading cause of death and disability in many countries.

The pandemic has created new possibilities and could change healthcare forever. It has brought to the fore the importance of data and the potential for remote medicine. Together, these developments could fundamentally change access to treatment and lower costs, allowing for consultations by a much wider set of health specialists. To ensure that the pandemic does indeed lead to better long-term outcomes existing institutions must be reformed, placing the long-term needs of society at the centre of policymakers' concerns.

The financial crisis highlighted the risks arising from group-think and the capture of regulatory agencies by lobbies. Ensuring that gamekeepers, whose responsibility it is to police the financial system, have the knowledge and independence to stay ahead and control the well-resourced financial poachers who are constantly seeking ways to evade the rules is essential for resilient systems. Inertia bedevils institutional reform. Overcoming the capture and domination of organisations by vested interests is vital to ensure that their governance, staff and activities reflect the needs of the future rather than those of the past. The institutional landscape is littered with well-intentioned reforms that have not been implemented.

Progress is possible, as is evident in the radical changes that many leaders have inspired. President Kennedy's successful 'moonshot' initiative provides a much-studied example of how this may be achieved through the alignment of ambition with funding and skills. Institutions also are capable of radical reform. From a limited technical organisation, the European Coal and Steel Community grew into the European Union, which has taken on a wide range of national responsibilities. Crisis can be a catalyst. As we have seen, the United Nations, IMF, World Bank, Marshall Plan and British welfare state were all forged in the fires of the Second World War. In the space of a few months during the pandemic the IMF approved a record number of loans in record time, with fewer conditions attached, while working remotely. National governments have torn up the old rule books to provide direct support to workers and businesses. What seemed impossible has been achieved.

Rescue from the Risk Precipice

There are many reasons to believe that we are living through the most profound period of rapid change ever. The philosopher Derek Parfit has argued that the growth in humanity's technical power now means that for the first time we have the power to transform not only our lives, but also our environment and the prospects for all future generations.[11]

The idea that we are at a hinge or inflection point is one that for many years has been persuasively argued by the UK's astronomer royal, Martin Rees. As a cosmologist Lord Rees is used to dealing in time spans of billions of years, yet he notes that in our short lifetimes we have the power to irreversibly degrade the biosphere or cause a catastrophic setback to civilisation. There is no shortage of threats, including worse pandemics, nuclear war, antimicrobial resistance and climate change, which many believe is the greatest risk to our survival.

If we can learn how to stop pandemics, we would learn to cooperate and be able to deal with other challenges, too. One thing is certain: our choices have the power to shape the lives of billions of people as well as those of other living creatures for generations to come.

Never before has all humanity experienced the same immediate threat. Digital connectivity meant that everyone everywhere learnt of our common danger and put hope in science to save us. That it took a virus 10,000 times smaller than a grain of sand to unite us reflects just how atomised our individual lives had become.

Globalisation provided the means for the virus to spread everywhere. But it also for the first time made us aware of our shared threat. No matter where we were, for the first time in history we experienced the same anxieties and desire for a better and safer world. Our interdependence was starkly evident not only in fears regarding contagion but also in our concerns for loved ones and friends. It was evident in the global passage of the virus and the cascading collapse of our economies. And it was revealed in our hopes of new vaccines developed in distant laboratories. Globalisation spread the virus but it also allowed scientists to find the cure.

Pandemics, like wars, have left profound political and economic legacies, changing the course of history. The 'Black Death' bubonic plague that killed over a third of the population of Europe in the fourteenth century created labour shortages that hastened the end of feudalism and serfdom. A yellow fever epidemic in 1802 ravaged Napoleon's troops, allowing the rebellious Haitian slaves – who had immunity – under Toussaint Louverture's inspirational leadership to force Napoleon to retreat. The very significant consequence was Napoleon abandoning French power in the New World and agreeing with Thomas Jefferson to the Louisiana Purchase, which doubled the size of the US.[12]

The coronavirus pandemic is likely to have a similarly seismic impact. But whereas in the past the causes and implications of pandemics were unknown and societies stumbled into the future, we now have a clearer understanding of the causes of diseases and how to prevent them to shape our futures for the better, as we do for climate change and the other great threats that we face. Countries that effectively contained the pandemic demonstrate that these threats can be addressed. Similarly, some countries have already stopped using fossil fuels, informed by evidence and a determination to confront our challenges.

We have it within our power to change our ways and shape the course of history. Not acting is equivalent to deciding to live above an active volcano. The failure of the Romans to take heed of the rumblings of Mount Vesuvius meant that when in CE 79 the volcanic eruption buried the cities of Pompeii and Herculaneum in molten lava they could claim it was the work of an angry god. Today the threats we face are understood and we have no such excuse.

The accumulation of knowledge places a new responsibility on societies. We can no longer claim we do not know or understand the consequences of our actions. We have gone from the innocence of adolescence to the maturity of adults, which brings with it new powers and obligations. The rapid growth in the evidence and insights offered by scientists and experts demonstrates with increasing clarity the causes and effects of human actions. We can draw on our collective wisdom to work out what to do and how to address our shared threats. It is overly optimistic to believe that the pandemic has created a eureka moment, or that knowledge inevitably motivates action, given the prevalence of fake news that undermines the evidence and the fact that short-term interests regularly trump longer-term needs. Nevertheless, societies do change their views, and often surprisingly quickly, as has been the case in recent decades in many countries on climate change, on attitudes to same-sex marriage and to the prevention of sexual harassment.

I left the country of my birth, South Africa, to go into exile and thought I would never return, as it was becoming enveloped in a bloody internal struggle. Yet, in 1994 the brutal apartheid regime peacefully gave way to a non-racial democracy. I realised then that with enough organisation and support good ideas can triumph and progress can prevail. As President Mandela, who had endured twenty-seven years in prison, said, 'It always seems impossible until it's done.'[13]

While there can be no doubt that Covid-19 has changed the world, how it does this depends on us. The pandemic has shown that for our own survival we need to think and behave as social beings, part of an interdependent society. What happens within our countries cannot be divorced from what is happening elsewhere. Similarly, all our lives are affecting and being affected by individuals elsewhere. The consequences of this growing entanglement of our lives with the rest of humanity cannot be resolved by market forces.

Our power to shape our environment and future has grown exponentially in recent decades. The number of human brains has doubled with the doubling of the world population over the past fifty years, and along with this so has human creativity. Our capacity to understand and to act has grown even more rapidly, along with massive advances in literacy and the accumulation and sharing of knowledge, as education and connectivity have increased much more quickly than population growth. Along with this new-found knowledge and power comes the potential for enormous destruction as well as an unprecedented potential to find and share solutions.

Our collective responsibility to manage risks has lagged behind our individual and societal understanding of personal risk management. We wear seat belts and follow the rules of the road to reduce our risk of accident and injury, accepting that regulations have evolved to ensure we not only protect ourselves, but others too. Similarly, we invest in alarms and fire protection and adhere to strict building codes to limit hazards in our homes. We also willingly pay for accident, health, burglary, and other insurance even though we hope we never have to use it. Our governments spend massively and we contribute our taxes to pay for the military to guard against war, however remote the risk. And yet the logic of investing to reduce risks does not seem to apply when we consider broader threats, such as those posed by pandemics or the climate emergency. By investing relatively small amounts we can safeguard the future and build resilience. This is essential if we are to avoid the next pandemic and overcome the challenge posed by climate change and other grave threats that inevitably would be the source of future global crises.

If the pandemic provides the catalyst for managing systemic risks it will have served to improve all our chances of living healthier, longer and more fulfilled lives. This time is different because the future of humanity is in our hands. We could wreck it or rescue it.

Rescue – From Global Crisis to a Better World

Despite the tragic deaths, suffering and sadness that it has caused, the pandemic could go down in history as the event that rescued humanity. It has created a once-in-a-generation opportunity to reset our lives and societies onto a sustainable path. Global surveys and protests have demonstrated the appetite for fresh thinking and a desire not to return to the pre-pandemic world.

The coronavirus rupture has shown that citizens are prepared to change their behaviour when required to do so and that governments are able to break out of their economic straight-jackets. Old excuses for inaction are no longer credible. The task now is to turn the reactive response to the health and economic emergencies into a proactive set of policies and actions to create an inclusive and sustainable world of shared prosperity. Before the pandemic this may have seemed unattainable, even idealistic. Changes that would have taken a decade or more to emerge have taken place almost overnight.

Among the positive changes have been a deeper recognition of the importance of nature, the role of essential workers, the contributions of science and experts, and having supportive family, friends and colleagues. But the pandemic has also exacerbated health and economic inequalities within countries and between them, devastating the lives and livelihoods of many and greatly increasing isolation and mental illness. A world that functions largely online is more atomised and may lead to a hardening of social and political silos. Unless the negative consequences of the pandemic are urgently addressed, they will cast a long, dark shadow.

The devastating consequences of Covid-19 have led to a deepening recognition that business as usual is highly destabilising and the source of our darkest fears. In so doing it has also revealed our capacity, desire and need for change. Covid-19 has shattered the mental mirrors that have prevented us from breaking from the past and embracing new horizons.

The idea that there is no such thing as society, only selfish individuals, can now be relegated to the dustbin of history. We have witnessed an outpouring of solidarity, not least of the young for the old and of essential workers for others. The young sacrificed their social lives, education and jobs and took on enormous debts to help the elderly get through Covid-19. Essential workers placed themselves at daily risk to staff our care homes and hospitals and ensure that food was delivered, rubbish collected and that lights stayed on. Many sacrificed their own health for others.

The intolerable costs of austerity and a culture that celebrated individualism and undermined the state has been starkly revealed. In the UK, funding for government health and safety inspections declined by two-thirds in the pre-pandemic decade and over a third of front-line workers feared that not enough was done to protect them from catching Covid-19.[1] Around the world, thousands of health workers died due to the absence of effective personal protection equipment.[2]

Society owes everyone who has made sacrifices a better future. Solidarity needs to be translated into political agendas that focus on inclusive long-term objectives. Prime Minister Lloyd George's 1918 rallying cry after the armistice that ended the First World War was that a 'fit country for heroes to live in' be created. We need to learn from the failure of this apt ambition to be realised.[3]

The world wars forever changed global politics and economics; Maynard Keynes argued that it was necessary to 'snatch from the exigencies of war positive social improvements'.[4] During one of my Zoom lectures, an elderly participant recalled the sense of optimism that the post-Second World War period engendered. He felt that everything he subsequently achieved was due to the post-war commitment to a welfare state, within a mixed economy in which government played a decisive role, providing him with an education, free healthcare, job security, a pension and an affordable home, none of which would have been available to him before the war.

The pandemic too will change everything, from our personal priorities to global power. Already it has brought profound changes in our work and home lives. It marks the end of the neoliberal era of individualism and its primacy of markets and prices, and heralds a swing of the political pendulum back to state intervention. As Nobel Laureate economist Angus Deaton has argued 'we now face a set of challenges which we cannot duck' which threaten the fabric of society, providing a 'once-in-a-generation opportunity to tackle the disadvantages faced by many that this pandemic has so devastatingly exposed'.[5]

Globalisation has caused this universal health and economic emergency. And yet, to address it we need more globalisation, not less. We cannot stop a global pandemic without more global politics. Nor can we stop climate change or any of the other great threats by political deglobalisation. Economic deglobalisation would condemn to continuing poverty the billions of people in the world who are yet to benefit from the jobs, ideas and opportunities that globalisation brings. It would mean that citizens of poor countries would not have access to the international vaccines, solar power panels, investment, exports, tourism and ideas that are urgently needed to rebuild countries and create a future of shared prosperity. The tragic outcome of this is evident in the deprivation in North Korea since its isolation.

If isolating ourselves and stopping globalisation could insulate us from risk it may be a price worth paying. But far from reducing risk, it will only increase it.

The greatest threat to our lives has historically come from internal or external conflicts. Now the threat comes from forces that are beyond the control of any one country and which require international cooperation, rather than assertions of supremacy. It is in every country's self-interest to cooperate to contain global threats. Similarly, it is in each of our own self-interest to contribute to the creation of more cohesive and stable societies.

If we learn to work together to stop pandemics, we will have learnt to cooperate. We will have learnt that our lives are intertwined with the lives of people across the world, including those in the poorest countries. Covid-19 has tested us. By passing the test we will have proved we can also conquer climate and other threats.

Nothing should be taken for granted. The virus is not only changing our possibilities and actions, but also the way we think, our dreams and our imaginations. There is a growing feeling, a zeitgeist that change is overdue. The author Kim Stanley Robinson has written, 'What felt impossible has become thinkable. We're getting a different sense of our place in history. We know we're entering a new world, a new era . . . In many ways, we have been overdue for such a shift. In our feelings, we've been lagging behind the times we live in . . . burning our ecological capital as if it were disposable income, wrecking our one and only home in ways that soon will be beyond our descendants' ability to repair.'[6]

Every crisis creates an opportunity, and it behoves us to explore the silver linings.[7] By highlighting the significance of systemic risks, the pandemic has raised awareness of other threats, including those posed by future pandemics and climate change, and has given us the means to rescue our lives and the future.

Rescue Values

The pandemic has changed everything; the way we work, the way we play, socialise and communicate, the way we learn and teach. Most of all, it has changed the way we think and what we care about most. It has changed our values. By rescuing us from individualism and placing a value on societal well-being – on us rather than me – it has reoriented us towards a more inclusive and caring world.[8] The idea that any individual's life and liberty can only be sustained by others has been an enduring tenet of all the world's major religions. And yet it has taken the pandemic to bring home the realisation that we sink or swim together.

During the pandemic, many families were unable to say their goodbyes to loved ones locked into care homes or hospitals. Doctors, nurses, carers and many others have exposed themselves to danger in the work they undertake on our behalf.

The willingness of individuals to put themselves at risk for strangers reflects courage that contradicts any characterisation of us as selfish individuals. At the same time the low value that employers and some governments place on human life was revealed in the failure to provide protective equipment not only for medical staff but also essential workers who are expected to take risks on society's behalf.

Citizens around the world spontaneously clapped for care workers, but this appreciation was not translated into higher pay or improved working conditions. Rescuing essential workers from hazardous and poorly paid situations requires that we offer them a better deal; it is time we applied the same standards to the front-line workers who take risks on behalf of society as we do to other professions such as the military in which individuals endanger themselves for the good of all.

The status (but not pay) of health workers has increased, while others have been tarnished by their association with what increasingly will be regarded as the sins of the past, such as financing fossil fuel industries and facilitating tax avoidance.

Scientists and experts have had their status restored and, after for some time being the object of political disdain are being taken seriously again and are informing policies, albeit at the risk of being manipulated and blamed when things go wrong.

Around the world, the pandemic has forced societies to reconsider their values, prompting deep reflection on the trade-off of lives for livelihoods, and young versus old. Nowhere has this been more evident than in the US, which under former President Trump suffered a crisis in values, including in upholding democracy and human rights as he embraced authoritarian dictators and autocrats around the world. He also demonstrated a disdain for the constitution and government institutions, eviscerating the FBI, Justice Department and other institutions designed to uphold societal values, as well as undermining those designed to fight the pandemic.

As is evident in the outpouring of anger regarding police brutality and the value attached to every human life that was at the centre of the Black Lives Matter protests, what was acceptable is no longer tolerated. The emotions evident here are indicative of the birthing pangs of a new world order that has values at its centre. So too was the election of President Biden in November 2020, which showed that the majority of US voters supported values associated with greater social cohesion.

Mark Carney, former Governor of the Bank of England, has pointed to how the pandemic has changed the way that people think about governments, economics and values.[9] 'After decades of risk being downloaded onto individuals, the bill has arrived and people don't know how to pay it.'[10] There is widespread anxiety regarding incomes and healthcare, which has undermined confidence in an economic model that relies on consumer borrowing, self-employed gig jobs and a booming housing market. The failure of this model to protect a growing share of citizens from hardship points to the potential for the pandemic to reassert the primacy of public values above values that are expressed simply through prices and profits.[11]

The philosopher Michael Sandel has warned against the dangers of moving from a market economy where goods and services are traded to a market society in which social values are also thought of as having a price and are tradeable.[12] With a growing number of people seeing the current dominant economic model, based on forty years of neoliberalism, as generating growing inequality, extreme poverty and ecological breakdown, the time has come to consider what system would generate better outcomes.

Entrenched differences in how people in different countries value human rights and democracy are unlikely to be overcome. These differences should be acknowledged and discussed, without negating areas of disagreement. Nevertheless, the pandemic could lead to us reasserting our common values on key areas where interests are aligned.

The pandemic has taught us that to defeat a virus we need to act collectively, and has highlighted what Amartya Sen has explored in his many books: that for individuals to flourish they require key capabilities – nutrition, health, education, freedom of expression, and jobs and income.   *policy*

Covid-19 has shown the extent to which policy matters. The same virus had a very different impact in different countries. Countries with higher levels of social cohesion and trust, good public institutions and a respect for expertise and regulations did better. Containing the virus has required the combination of effective and trustworthy leadership and competent and committed public sector employees, from doctors and nurses to the civil servants managing regulations and test, track and trace as well as those ensuring vital supplies and distributing welfare benefits.   *interdisciplinary*

The global health and economic crisis has highlighted the need for interdisciplinary expertise, with the roles of behavioural and economic sciences being as vital as that of medical expertise in weighing the costs and benefits of different measures. This collaboration is necessary for ensuring that the recovery creates

a healthier and more balanced economy and that we are simultaneously able to address the many great challenges we face.
The most successful policy interventions have drawn on a wide
range of social sciences, humanities and arts to gain insights
from social, historical, cultural, behavioural and economic
perspectives to complement those from medical, biological, engineering and other physical and life sciences.[13]

Disruptive times call for innovative solutions and new ways
of working to enhance creativity to build a better world. This
has been abundantly evident in science; 2020 is likely to go down
in history as a watershed year in scientific advancement.
Advances in biosciences have clearly been at the forefront, while
breakthroughs in AI allowed DeepMind to crack the 50-year-old
problem of protein folding, marking a major discovery in the
understanding of diseases and in drug discovery, which *Nature*
magazine predicted 'will change everything'.[14] The genomic
advances behind the Pfizer BioNTech and Moderna vaccines
offer the potential to usher in a new era of medicine that could
address heart diseases, cancer and other hitherto intractable
challenges. Unprecedented open-source collaboration, which
resulted in over 100,000 research papers being shared globally,
and the genomic sequence for Covid-19 being shared internationally over 200,000 times, lies behind the Oxford vaccine as
well as the rapid evolution of track, trace and test systems.[15]

None of this would have been possible without the extraordinary potential unleashed by computing power and the digital
economy. But the pace of progress of artificial intelligence and
robotics requires that for societies to thrive we humans focus
our energies on what machines cannot do: creativity. Attempts
to create cultural homogeneity stifle innovation and creativity,
whereas nurturing cultural diversity in which a thousand
flowers can bloom is essential for knowledge economies to
thrive. To this end, the President of the European Union, Ursula
von der Leyen, called for the establishment of a 'new European
Bauhaus' in response to the pandemic in which architects,

artists, students, engineers and others work together to create a more holistic and inclusive society. The European Green Deal for recovery from the pandemic explicitly includes cultural dimensions and new forms of collaboration designed to improve effectiveness and widen community engagement with diverse groups before and during programme design, not as an afterthought.

The global crisis has brought to the fore an apolitical communitarianism, evident in the growth of mutual-aid groups and a widespread desire to help and volunteer. Around the world, communities have displayed their admiration and support for health workers by clapping. Unlike with previous disasters, when we were led by celebrities like Bob Geldof and Bono, this time the mass demonstrations of solidarity arose from a spontaneous desire within us, reflecting a growing sense of community and fairness. This shared identity was also evident in the rapid global spread of the Black Lives Matter protests, which erupted spontaneously following the killing of George Floyd.

The pandemic is the most memorable shared experience of our lifetimes. In the US, more people have died from Covid-19 than all its twenty-first-century wars, and unemployment statistics exceeded the numbers seen during the Great Depression. Our societies will emerge severely scarred, whether by the loss of friends and family members, of education and job prospects, or formerly secure jobs and incomes. We have all suffered. The priority must now turn to healing the wounds.

This is a slow process. Wounds incurred centuries ago can linger long into the future. In many Asian societies people still avoid shaking hands or touching strangers and prefer to bow, having learnt the lessons of otherwise long-forgotten pandemics. East Asian individuals with colds or other respiratory infections have long been accustomed to wearing face masks to protect others. Societies that previously appeared impervious to these habits will now be sensitised.

Faced with collective disaster and previously unimaginable

changes, everyone is rethinking their priorities. A greater premium has been placed on proximity. The term 'nearest and dearest' was given expression during the pandemic in carefully calibrated decisions on where to be and who to call each day. Bonds forged in the pandemic will define relationships in the coming years, whereas those which have been lost will take conscious effort to restore.

Attracting expatriates to work abroad is likely to prove more difficult as those left stranded far from loved ones during the pandemic question their long-term plans. Countries like New Zealand and Ireland have seen the reversal of emigration trends, with more people returning than leaving and embassies and relocation agents experiencing sharp rises in demand for repatriation.[16] This has coincided with some environments, such as Hong Kong, becoming less attractive to expats while others, such as the UK and US, increased their barriers to entry.

By bringing to the fore questions regarding work–life balance, mental health and loneliness, the pandemic highlighted key dimensions of our lives that for too long were buried by a relentless search for individual meaning in more and more work, and more and more material possessions. The need for constant conspicuous consumption and the spiral of acquisition, achievement and envy has been broken by enforced lockdowns. By bringing into sharp relief the precariousness of our situations Covid-19 prompted an overdue examination and reordering of our priorities. To find greater satisfaction and meaning in our own lives and to save our communities and future generations from future crises will require that we establish different routines and think more deeply about what changes we can or wish to make in our own lives.

Re-evaluating our lives requires going beyond the unhealthy addiction to economic growth as the only or best measure of progress.[17] No one can flourish without a livelihood, which is why creating meaningful work and incomes for all who seek it, and overcoming poverty, is a necessary foundation for a healthy society. But new holistic measures of well-being need to be found, to allow governments to be guided and compared on a dashboard that goes beyond narrow economic measures. For governments, focusing on well-being also makes political sense as it is a better predictor of what voters prioritise and whether incumbent governments are likely to be re-elected.[18] New Zealand in 2019 adopted a 'well-being budget' and Bhutan in 2008 enshrined Gross National Happiness (GNH) in its constitution as the goal of its government, with this including the improvement of psychological well-being and ecological diversity. Initiatives to establish broader objectives are also under way in France, the UK and UAE, and China for the first time in 2020 scrapped its annual GDP target as a centrepiece of its five-year plan. *Community.*

A study by Harvard University that has tracked adults for over eighty years found that the best predictor of happiness is not income or life expectancy, but the number of people one can count on in crisis and the extent to which one is part of a community.[19] The pandemic has highlighted the extent to which a blinkered economic approach to setting government priorities can lead to a neglect of physical and mental health, with tragic consequences. It has also led to a neglect of the climate emergency and the rising dangers posed by growing inequality, poverty and systemic risks. The pandemic has revealed what is most valuable in our lives. The task now is to ensure this is reflected in our personal priorities and in the actions of our governments.

The Human Development Index, pioneered by the United Nations Development Programme over the past thirty years, has long championed a broader set of measures to guide policymaking. In 2020, the environmental impact of countries was for the first time given significant weight in the index, leading to a marked downgrading of the overall ranking of many rich countries. Norway, for example, was dropped from being ranked first to fifteenth, due to its dependence on oil exports, and Luxembourg fell 131 places, as its dependence on commuters who travel into the country each day greatly increases its carbon footprint.

Rescue Our Future

If this book has convinced you of anything, I hope it is that we should not return to business as usual. Preventing the next pandemic and creating a future of shared prosperity is within our grasp. But to reach it requires a step-change in direction, not incremental shuffles that are leading us over a precipice.

As Churchill once said, never let a good crisis go to waste. Tragically, the increasing frequency and intensity of cascading financial, cyber, environmental and health crises in recent decades has failed to provide the much-needed changes to reduce systemic risks. Now, the greatest danger is that as effective vaccines become available and life returns to normal we once again will be lulled into a false confidence, as happened after previous pandemic scares and also following the financial crisis. If this crisis finally creates the political will and necessary investments to stop future pandemics and other systemic crises, it will not have been in vain.

The failure of global leadership and the too-timid and too-late health and economic response compounded the Covid-19 health and economic emergency. A coordinated economic stimulus and global distribution of vaccines is essential for the recovery.[20] Such a stimulus should be focused on the transition to a fossil-free world, as not only would that reduce the risks associated with escalating climate change but it offers fast, labour-intensive employment, notably for individuals in trades requiring technical, practical skills, who have been especially disadvantaged by lockdowns and economic collapse.

By allocating a fifth of what has already been committed as part of the global stimulus, leaders around the world could turn the economic disaster into an opportunity not only to jump-start the transition to a green economy, but also to nurture a wide range of new business, reduce inequities and assist developing countries in their recovery while supplying energy to two billion people who have no reliable sources of cheap renewable power.[21]

The eminent historian Margaret MacMillan sees the pandemic of 2020 as a juncture when 'the rivers of history change direction' and political currents and social preferences become muddied and reconstituted as societies reject their past failures and try to take a new direction.[22] As was the case with wars and revolutions, the epic suffering of Covid-19 creates the prospect for rupture and opportunity for fundamental change.[23] But expectations are more often than not destroyed on the altar of pragmatism and incremental change.

In democracies change is slow and must await the next election cycle. If big ideas require big thinkers, where are the Keyneses, Roosevelts and Churchills of today? What happens, I asked Margaret MacMillan, if we don't have the leaders we need at these critical times? She explained that great leaders cannot act independently of the collective will of societies, although they are able to channel it. It was the determination not to repeat the cycle of world wars that led to the creation of a new world order in 1942. And when Churchill gave only tepid support for the creation of the welfare state, which Britons saw as a central pillar of the new order, he was replaced by the unknown Labour leader Clement Attlee, known as 'citizen Clem', in a landslide election, due to his ability to tap into the widespread demand for improvements in our quality of life.[24] Now, once again the provision of universal basic services and job guarantees for all who can work should be at the centre of a new social contract.

To prevent a bounce back to the same old reality we need a decisive break. A rupture is required, one that will lead to radical reforms. If this sounds scary, it is less so than the pandemics, escalating climate change, growing inequality, joblessness and instability that would inevitably flow from business as usual. Radical reform would not only lead to a more predictable and stable world, but is also less disruptive than 2020, which saw a rift in every aspect of our lives.

Many ideas that would have been regarded as revolutionary in January 2020 have already become the orthodoxy. And many of the ideas that we now regard as revolutionary were mainstream in previous periods. For example, until the 1970s, in Europe, the US and UK there were marginal tax rates of over 90 per cent and state ownership of banks and transport and energy utilities, and community and workers' organisations were not only a feature of most neighbourhoods, they also played a key role in government deliberations. Indeed, in many European countries, including Germany, such consultation remains the norm.

Until the pandemic, the idea that central banks could print money to finance governments' deficits was heresy. But within weeks of it starting, their actions to do so were being criticised as too timid. Ideas that previously were advocated by mavericks suddenly took centre stage.[25] This creates the opportunity for bold initiatives to rekindle growth while addressing the urgent need to create jobs, overcome inequality and accelerate the transition to a non-carbon economy. The need to overcome social isolation and provide the basis for community-based development, which meets people's needs and is environmentally sustainable, requires that strategies for the future go beyond traditional measures of growth to incorporate a wide set of considerations regarding well-being.

The *Financial Times*, which describes itself as the 'the world's leading global business publication', has insisted that 'Radical reforms are required to forge a world that will work for all.'[26] It welcomed the 'Dawn break(s) on a new age of economic thinking' as the IMF, the Vatican of economic policymakers, called for more debt and government intervention and more rapid action on climate change.[27]

The idea of radical reforms is unlikely to be welcomed by all. The World Economic Forum's Chairman Klaus Schwab in his book *The Great Reset* identifies the disruptive implications of the pandemic and need for reform, without spelling out the consequences for the redistribution of wealth. This no doubt would be opposed by many of the billionaires attending his annual Davos meetings – the extra wealth of just ten men globally increased by $540 billion during the pandemic.[28] Journalist Fareed Zakaria, author of *Ten Lessons for a Post-Pandemic World*, cautions against radical thinking by saying, 'We understand the deficiencies and the ways to address them';[29] this is optimistic, as most societies, experts and leaders do not have sufficient insight into either the failures or solutions. However, with sufficient will, solutions can be found.[30]

The pandemic has allowed politicians to exercise a bigger role by stealth rather than via the ballot box. The challenge now is to turn the emergency response to the pandemic into a strategic agenda that attracts public support.

During the pandemic there has been a rewriting of the social contract in many spheres. Our freedoms have been curtailed and personal expectations have changed. But so too have our expectations of each other and of governments. The appetite for change has grown everywhere.

When things move very fast, so should minds. Channelling the desire for change into policies and politics is the next step. While the lesson of the pandemic should be that we need to cooperate more, history teaches us that during recessions, the political appeal of protectionism grows. The disastrous rise of protectionism and fascism in the 1930s came out of the Great Depression. More recently, it is the financial crisis that gave us Brexit in Britain, Trump in the White House, populist rule in Italy, Greece and Spain, and rising nationalism and protectionism in the countries that were worst affected. Whether this time is different depends in no small part on who we vote for and what we demand of our leaders.

The word 'respair' according to the Oxford English Dictionary is both a noun and a verb, meaning the return of hope after a period of despair. First recorded in the fifteenth century, it has not been widely used since the Renaissance but now, fittingly, is being evoked to reflect a new optimism that the pandemic can give way to a better world.

The bleak outlook facing many of us, not least young people, coupled with the failure of many democracies to manage the pandemic, has thankfully not infected voters with political cynicism.[31] On the contrary, the record turnout in the US 2020 Presidential election confirms global survey results regarding an increase in activism.

Public opinion surveys show that nine out of ten people around the world show 'a profound and widespread desire for change rather than a return to how things were before the Covid-19 pandemic'.[32] Russia and Colombia top the list of twenty-seven countries surveyed, with 94 per cent of people agreeing that the world should 'change significantly and become more sustainable and equitable', and support for this is similarly strong in Peru, Mexico, Malaysia, South Africa and Brazil.[33] In the UK 87 per cent of respondents expressed this desire for change, with Europeans in most countries similarly eager for change, and eight out of ten surveyed in the US expressed their desire for major changes rather than a return to how things were before the pandemic.[34]

In considering the content of change, research conducted by the Centre on International Cooperation at New York University revealed that there is widespread support for redistributive policies aimed at tackling inequity, regardless of whether the respondents themselves stand to benefit. In Europe, looking after the most vulnerable is the top priority of both Britons and Germans, while 73 per cent of Spaniards support a basic income for the most vulnerable.[35] In Canada, over 80 per cent of the population want the government to use empty hotels to house the homeless.[36] In Colombia, 97 per cent of those surveyed approved of the government channelling economic support directly to the most vulnerable.[37] In Pakistan, 91 per cent of people support their government's cash transfer initiative (and just 4 per cent think it is 'bad') even though only 7 per cent reported actually receiving any assistance from the programme.[38] The social programme that Kenyans find most useful is the one that gives cash directly to the poor.[39] In Argentina, 81 per cent approve of the provision of subsidies to informal workers, and Bangladeshis state that COVID-19 response measures cannot succeed if the poor cannot afford to eat.[40]

Clearly the desire for change exists. This needs to be acted on before the impact of the pandemic fades and we are lulled into complacency by the welcome return of the normalcy of our pre-pandemic world. It is no accident that the design of a new world happened during, not after, the horrors of the Second World War and long before the wounds had healed. Our greatest risk is that our yearning for our past life might dull our hunger for a better world. Unlike in the wars, during the pandemic the entire human race has fought a common unseen enemy. If this does not unite us in our determination to work together, nothing will.

Rescue offers no guarantee of a better life, but it does make it possible. Like refugees whose rescue from a cataclysmic fate allows them to envisage a better future, we now have the potential to create a better world. First, though, we have to traverse a no-man's-land; we are leaving the old pre-pandemic world but have not yet entered into a new one. This will naturally create anxiety and a desire to return to familiar territory. This is the greatest danger, and recalls the words of Jay Gatsby in Scott Fitzgerald's *The Great Gatsby*: 'Can't repeat the past? Why, of course you can!'[41] Set in the Jazz Age of the Roaring Twenties, the depiction of the exuberance following from the devastating pandemic of 1918 and the First World War could well be repeated, as the pent-up desire to socialise and spend creates a roaring 2020s. A century ago, that ended in tears, with the Great Depression, the rise of fascism and the Second World War.

We have been provided with a once-in-a-lifetime window of opportunity to escape from the downward spiral of ever-worsening global crises. While we celebrate the return of a semblance of normalcy following the pandemic, it is imperative that we seize the opportunity and redouble our efforts to break what otherwise will be an inevitable escalation of risks.

We cannot help others if we ourselves are feeling incapable. In our homes and communities there is an urgent need to overcome the crisis of loneliness and despair. Each of us can contribute in our own way to the creation of a better and happier society. We can join the amazing army of volunteers, reduce our carbon footprint and pay our fair share of taxes.

There is a battle of ideas raging and we need to enlist. Apathy and individualism are the enemy of societal change and allow our politics and social media to be overrun by populists, angry extremists, fake news and bad ideas.

The pandemic has revealed the strengths and weaknesses of societies as well as what is important and what is possible.[42] It has shown that competence in leadership and government matters. That international institutions matter. That research is vital and underfunded. That we require access to timely data as well as that its analysis is open to abuse by politicians and pundits.

The spell of great powers has been broken as the richest countries with the most sophisticated expertise have been overwhelmed by the virus and much poorer ones with little expertise have been able to fight back. The need for expertise from the humanities and social sciences to complement that of scientific experts has been widely demonstrated. Interdisciplinary perspectives and an understanding of human behaviour and the broader consequences of the pandemic and wide range of cures needed has become essential to address the crisis. At the same time, the creation of vaccines at record speed, within just a year, is a tribute to the power of collaborative science and new technologies in assisting humanity in meeting our critical global challenges.

The pandemic has shattered oppressive taboos. As individuals we are more able to change our behaviour, discuss our work–life balance and highlight concerns regarding mental illness and loneliness. Governments have found the means to break the spell of austerity and act speedily and forcefully to help workers and firms in need.

The extraordinary solidarity within our societies has been demonstrated in the sacrifices of the young for the old, in essential workers putting themselves at risk, and in the outpouring of volunteering, as evidenced by three times as many people volunteering for the UK National Health Service in 2020 than it called for.

But solidarity has also been shown to have its limits, as the pandemic has revealed and exacerbated the inequalities within and between countries. This widening rift needs urgently to be bridged; a more inclusive world with greater social cohesion is essential to overcome global crises and create a sustainable world.

At a time when poor people around the world face the biggest development setback of our lifetimes the global response has been utterly inadequate, with aid in 2020 lower than before the pandemic. The high-income countries need to do much more to provide aid and empower the international agencies to greatly increase their support for development, for the good of all of us. The longer it takes to distribute vaccines globally, the greater the risk of mutation of Covid-19 and the slower the health and economic recovery. Establishing a more inclusive and sustainable world is not easy. But Covid-19 has demonstrated the necessity and appetite for change. The time has come to prioritise people and our planet.

The pandemic has shown that it is much less costly to stop a crisis than to respond to one that is raging. In just one day in 2020 governments spent more responding to the pandemic than they had in ten years of pandemic prevention. The fact that a pandemic was inevitable and we failed to prevent or prepare for it is surely as loud a wake-up call as could be sounded. If this is finally heard, Covid-19 could rescue humanity and provide a portal to a better future. Whether we now commit to a new and improved world or remain set in our dangerous ways is the historic choice confronting us.

The stakes have never been higher. It is our turn to answer the call that has been invoked over the generations: If not now, then when? If not us, then who?

Acknowledgements

This book has been the most intense I have written, in terms of both the immediacy of the issues and the tight deadlines, making the support of others more essential than ever. Karolina Sutton first suggested I undertake this project, at the height of the coronavirus gloom, encouraging me to envisage a better future. I am most fortunate to be in the hands of such an enormously supportive and talented guide, who deservedly has been recognised as literary agent of the year.

My greatest debt is to Juliet Brooke, my superb editor at Sceptre, whose extraordinarily perceptive comments, incisive direction, constructive engagement and editing are reflected in every page. Thanks also are due to Jacqui Lewis, for excellent copy-editing, and to Zoe Paskett, who very helpfully read and improved an early draft. Alex Copestake and Fiona Kasperk provided timely research assistance.

Above all I am grateful to my wife, Tess Webber Goldin, who provides unconditional love and support. In addition to suggesting the title and greatly improving the manuscript, Tess has raised my awareness of the importance of wellbeing. Together with her psychiatrist brother, Ian, she provided expert advice for the chapter on mental health. My thanks are due too to my children Olivia and Alex, and sister Jacqui who never cease to widen my emotional and intellectual horizons. Alex provided very thoughtful comments on an early draft. In writing this book I have consulted with dozens of business leaders and health experts and interviewed over two dozen individuals from a wide range of backgrounds. Their unstinting willingness to share their experiences has informed and enriched this book, as has their ability to rise above their personal difficulties to offer perspectives on how others are doing. Sarah Cliffe has been particularly helpful in sharing insights on essential workers, Vittorio Colao on the relation between technology and Covid-19, Margaret MacMillan on the lessons from history, Nick Stern on the relationship between climate and Covid-19, and Tasmin Little on the arts. My VC Jericho cycling group, when circumstances allowed, offered much needed exercise, while Russell Brimelow kept me appraised of legal developments related to Covid-19. None of the many people who have helped to improve the book are responsible for its contents, and I alone am responsible for the remaining errors and omissions.

The Oxford Martin School has offered a wonderfully nurturing environment for ideas, and the depth of expertise on pandemics and vaccines in the School has helped ensure that I have been able to access scholars who are at the forefront of these and other fields. Max Roser and the Our World In Data team have provided an unparalleled source of information, as have colleagues in Balliol College and across Oxford University. Particular thanks are due to Andrew Pitt, the head of research at Citi, whose support for the Oxford Martin programmes on the Future of Work and Technological and Economic Change has given essential substance to the pursuit of my research ideas.

The book draws on interviews I conducted for my BBC Radio series *The Pandemic that Changed the World*, with the rich insights of Larry Brilliant, Peter Piot, Ngozi Okonjo-Iweala, Kristalina Georgieva, Achim Steiner, Arundhati Roy, Clare Wenham, Zanny Minton-Beddoes and Joe Stiglitz seeding the arguments that are the foundation of this book.

Given the contemporaneous nature of the book I relied more than usual on news and current affairs sources and commentaries. I am deeply indebted to the journalists and contributors to the *Financial Times, The Economist,* the *Guardian, New York Times,* BBC and a wide range of other publications, blogs and social media posts that provided a daily deluge of fresh insights and data that informed and stimulated my thinking. I am grateful to the editors of *Finance and Development* for agreeing to my use of parts of my article published in their journal.

My hope in writing this book is that it contributes to throwing light on the deep failures in our current national and global systems that led to the pandemic and are causing deepening inequalities and suffering. I will have succeeded if I manage to convince readers that going back to business as usual is a dangerous idea and that we need to redouble our efforts to create a better world. That is the only way to ensure that all the suffering that the pandemic has caused will not be in vain.

Select Bibliography

Atkinson, Anthony. *Public Economics in an Age of Austerity.* (Routledge, London, 2014).

Atkinson, Anthony. *Inequality: What Can Be Done?* (Harvard University Press, Cambridge, Mass., 2015).

Baldwin, Richard. *The Globotics Upheaval: Globalisation, Robotics and the Future of Work.* (W&N, London, 2019).

Bew, John. *Citizen Clem: A Biography of Attlee.* (Riverrun, London, 2016).

Case, Anne, Angus Deaton. *Deaths of Despair and the Future of Capitalism.* (Princeton University Press, 2020).

Collier, Paul, John Kay. *Greed is Dead: Politics After Individualism.* (Penguin, London, 2020).

Fitzgerald, F. Scott. *The Great Gatsby.* (Chatto & Windus, London, 1925).

Goldin, Ian, Mike Mariathasan. *The Butterfly Defect: How Globalization Creates Systemic Risks, and What to Do About It.* (Princeton University Press, 2014).

Goldin, Ian, Christopher Kutarna. *Age of Discovery: Navigating the Storms of Our Second Renaissance.* (Bloomsbury, London, 2018).

Goldin, Ian, Robert Muggah. *Terra Incognita: 100 Maps to Survive the Next 100 Years.* (Century, London, 2020).

Hazareesingh, Sudhir. *Black Spartacus: The Epic Life of Toussaint Louverture.* (Allen Lane, London, 2020).

Hertz, Noreena. *The Lonely Century: Coming Together in a World that's Pulling Apart.* (Sceptre, London, 2020).

Khanna, Parag. *The Future is Asian: Commerce, Conflict, and Culture in the Twenty-First Century*. (W&N, London, 2019).

Krastev, Ivan. *Is It Tomorrow Yet?* (Allen Lane, London, 2020).

Lonergan, Eric, Mark Blyth. *Angrynomics*. (Columbia University Press, New York, 2020).

Mahbubani, Kishore. *Has the West Lost It?: A Provocation* (Penguin, London, 2018).

Mahbubani, Kishore. *Has China Won?: The Chinese Challenge to American Primacy* (Public Affairs, New York, 2020).

Mazzucato, Mariana. *The Entrepreneurial State: Debunking Public vs Private Sector Myths*. (Penguin, London, 2018).

Micklethwait, John, Adrian Wooldridge. *The Wake-Up Call: Why the Pandemic has Exposed the Weakness of the West – and How to Fix it*. (Short Books, London 2020).

Piketty, Thomas. *Capital in the Twenty-First Century*. (Harvard University Press, Cambridge, Mass., 2014).

Pope Francis. *Let Us Dream: The Path to a Better Future*. (Simon & Schuster, London, 2020).

Putnam, Robert, Shaylyn Romney Garrett. *The Upswing: How We Came Together a Century Ago and How We Can Do it Again*. (Simon & Schuster, London, 2020).

Raghuram, Rajan. *The Third Pillar: The Rival of Community in a Polarised World*. (Penguin, London, 2020).

Rawls, John. *A Theory of Justice*. (Harvard University Press, Cambridge, Mass., 2017).

Sandel, Michael J.. *The Tyranny of Merit: What's Become of the Common Good?* (Allen Lane, London, 2020).

Scheidel, Walter. *The Great Leveler: Violence and the History of Inequality from the Stone Age to the Twenty-First Century*. (Princeton University Press, 2017).

Schwab, Klaus, Thierry Malleret. *Covid-19: The Great Reset*. (Forum Publishing, Geneva, 2020).

Sen, Amartya. 1999. *Development as Freedom*. (Oxford University Press, 1999).

Sen, Amartya. *The Idea of Justice*. (Allen Lane, London, 2009).

Susskind, Daniel, Richard Susskind. *The Future of the Professions.* (Oxford University Press, 2017).

Woodcock, Jamie, Mark Graham. *The Gig Economy: A Critical Introduction.* (Polity, London, 2019).

Zakaria, Fareed. *Ten Lessons for a Post-Pandemic World.* (Allen Lane, London, 2020).

Notes

INTRODUCTION

1 Statement by Franklin D. Roosevelt welcoming participants
   at the Bretton Woods Monetary Conference. Department of
   State. *United Nations Monetary and Financial Conference: Bretton
   Woods, Final act and related Documents*, 29 June 1944.

CHAPTER I
Reducing Inequality

1 Walter Scheidel. *The Great Leveler*. (Princeton University
   Press, 2017).
2 Thomas Piketty. *Capital in the Twenty-First Century*. (Harvard
   University Press, Cambridge, Mass., 2014).
3 *How to Fix Economic Inequality?* Peterson Institute for
   International Economics. 2020.
4 'A new look at the declining labor share of income in the
   United States.' McKinsey Global Institute, May 2019.
5 'Italy's informal workers fall back on charity.' *The Economist*,
   6 June 2020.
6 'Protect a Generation: The impact of COVID-19 on children's
   lives.' Save the Children, 10 September 2020.
7 Juan Palomino, Juan Rodriguez, Raquel Sebastian. 'Wage
   inequality and poverty effects of lockdown and social
   distancing in Europe.' *European Economic Review*, October
   2020.

8 'America's huge stimulus is having surprising effects on the poor.' *The Economist*, 6 July 2020.

9 'Falling through the cracks.' New Economics Foundation, 30 November 2020.

10 'Build Back Fairer: The COVID-19 Marmot Review.' *Institute of Health Equity*, 15 December 2020.

11 'COVID-19 has shone a light on racial disparities in health.' *The Economist*, 21 November 2020.

12 Ibid.

13 'COVID-19: The risk to BAME doctors.' British Medical Association, 13 November 2020.

14 'COVID-19 has shone a light on racial disparities in health.' *The Economist*, 21 November 2020.

15 'Total household wealth by ethnicity of household reference person, Great Britain, July 2010 to June 2016.' Office for National Statistics, 28 September 2018.

16 'More than half of Black-owned businesses may not survive COVID-19.' *National Geographic*, 17 July 2020.

17 'Pandemic aid is exacerbating US inequality.' *Financial Times*, 6 August 2020.

18 Ibid.

19 Claire Kramer Mills, Jessica Battisto. 'Double Jeopardy: COVID-19's concentrated health and wealth effects in black communities.' Federal Reserve Bank of New York, August 2020.

20 Ian Goldin. *Development: A Very Short Introduction*. (Oxford University Press, 2018).

21 The Global Gender Gap Report. World Economic Forum, 2018.

22 'The narrowing, but persistent, gender gap in pay.' Pew Research Center, 22 March 2019.

23 The Global Gender Gap Report. World Economic Forum, 2018.

24 'Whose time to care: Unpaid care and domestic work during COVID-19.' UN Women, 25 November 2020.

25 'Downturns tend to reduce gender inequality. Not under Covid-19'. *The Economist*, 4 June 2020. 'The US economy lost 140,00 jobs in December. All of them were held by women.' *CNN Business*, 9 January 2021.

26 'Sector shutdowns during the coronavirus crisis: which workers are most exposed?' Institute for Fiscal Studies, 6 April 2020.

27 Abi Adams-Prassl et al. 'Inequality in the Impact of the Coronavirus Shock: Evidence from Real Time Surveys'. IZA Discussion Papers, Institute of Labor Economics (IZA), April 2020.

28 Daniela Del Boca et al. 'Women's work, housework, and childcare before and during COVID-19.' VoxEU & CEPR, 19 June 2020.

29 'Challenges stack up for Italian women.' *Financial Times*, 7 October 2020.

30 Global Gender Gap Report 2020. World Economic Forum, 2020.

31 Ghazala Azmat, Lena Hensvik, Olof Rosenqvist, Olof. 'Presenteeism at work and gender inequality.' VoxEU & CEPR, 4 October 2020.

32 Almudena Sevilla, Sarah Smith. 'Baby Steps: The Gender Division of Childcare During the Covid-19 Pandemic.' IZA Discussion Paper, June 2020.

33 'Parents, especially mothers, paying heavy price for lockdown.' Institute for Fiscal Studies, 27 May 2020.

34 'How are mothers and fathers balancing work and family under lockdown?' Institute for Fiscal Studies, 27 May 2020. 'UK school closures mean mothers take twice as much unpaid leave as fathers.' *Guardian*, 8 January 2021.

35 2 in 5 working mums face childcare crisis when new term starts – TUC poll. Trades Union Congress, 3 September 2020.

36 'Why the pandemic is forcing women out of the workforce. *New Yorker*, 23 October 2020.

37 'Reopening UK offices risks excluding women and minorities, says business chief.' *Guardian*, 13 September 2020.

38 'CMI chief: Return to office could create two-tier workforce.' *Personnel Today*, 14 September 2020.

39 'Pandemic boost to tech and digital industries worsens gender job divide.' *Financial Times*, 22 November 2020.

40 Ibid.

41 'Worldwide covid-19 is causing a new form of collective trauma.' *The Economist*, 29 August 2020.

42 'Northern lockdowns shine a light on Britain's landscape of inequality.' *The Conversation*, 14 October 2020.

43 'One-in-three jobs in parts of Britain at risk due to Covid-19 – local data reveals.' RSA House, 26 April 2020.

44 'New Child Poverty Data Reveals True Extent of Levelling Up Challenge.' End Child Poverty, 14 October 2020.

45 Ibid.

46 'State of the North 2020/21: Power up, level up, rise up.' IPPR, 7 December 2020.

47 'The land that time forgot: months of lockdown grate in northern England.' *Guardian*, 2 October 2020.

48 'How covid-19 exacerbates inequality.' *The Economist*, 26 March 2020.

49 Ibid.

50 'Asia's migrant workers are having a rough time under covid-19.' *The Economist*, 19 September 2020.

51 'Riding the storm, Billionaires insights 2020.' *UBS*, October 2020.

52 Updates: Billionaire Wealth, U.S. Job Losses and Pandemic Profiteers. Inequality.org, 9 December 2020.

53 'US Billionaires added $1 trillion to their collective wealth since the start of the pandemic.' *Forbes*, 27 November 2020. 'Updates: Billionaire Wealth, U.S. Job Losses and Pandemic Profiteers.' Inequality.org, 9 December 2020

54 Ibid.

55 'Billionaire Bounceback: 10 Tycoons Gained $126 Billion Over the Past Month.' *Forbes*, 25 April 2020.

56 Author's calculation from Our World in Data and World Bank.

57 Report by Joint Committee on Taxation. Congress of the
    United States, 9 April 2020.

58 'Millionaires to reap 80% of benefit from tax change in US
    coronavirus stimulus.' *Guardian*, 15 April 2020.

59 Chuck Collins, Omar Ocampo, Sophia Paslaski. 'Billionaire
    Bonanza 2020: Wealth windfalls, tumbling taxes, and
    pandemic profiteers.' Institute for Policy Studies,
    23 April 2020.

60 Ibid.

61 Robert Reich. Twitter, 29 November 2020.

62 Batchelder: Tax the Rich and their Heirs. TaxProf,
    26 June 2020.

63 Lily Bachfelder. 'Leveling the Playing Field between Inherited
    Income and Income from Work through an Inheritance Tax.'
    The Hamilton Project, 28 January 2020.

64 Dedrick Asante-Muhammed, Chuck Collins. 'The Pandemic
    is Accelerating the Racial Wealth Divide. Here's How We
    Turn It Around.' Institute for Policy Studies, 27 June 2020.

65 Wealth Tax Commission. London School of Economics,
    9 December 2020. 'A wealth tax packs a powerful fiscal
    punch.' *Financial Times*, 10 December 2020; author's
    calculations.

66 Wealth Tax Commission. London School of Economics,
    9 December 2020.

67 Ibid.

68 Gabriel Zucman. Twitter, 7 December 2020.

69 This section draws on Ian Goldin, Robert Muggah. *Terra
    Incognita*. (Century, London, 2020).

70 Christine Lagarde. Twitter, 17 June 2015.

71 'Seven charts that show how the developed world is losing its
    edge.' *Financial Times*, 19 July 2017.

72 Lifting the Small Boats Speech by Christine Lagarde. IMF,
    17 June 2015.

73 'How Fair is the World? Social Inequality and Economic
    Growth.' ifo Institut, 2018.

74 'The economic origins of the populist surge.' *Financial Times*, 27 June 2017.

75 Anthony Atkinson. *Inequality: What Can Be Done?* (Harvard University Press, Cambridge, Mass., 2015).

76 Ibid.

77 Annual Results Report 2017 Education. UNICEF, January 2018.

78 'Oxbridge uncovered: More elitist than we thought.' BBC News, 20 October 2017.

79 Elitist Britain 2019. The Sutton Trust, 2019.

80 See, for example The productivity and equality nexus. OECD, 2016.

81 Manuel Funke, Moritz Schularick and Christoph Trebesch. 'The political aftermath of financial crises: going to extremes.' VoxEU & CEPR, 21 November 2015.

82 'What is Human Development?' United Nations Development Reports, 2020.

83 Robert Reich. Twitter, 16 November 2020.

84 Income Inequality. Our World in Data, October 2016.

85 Ibid.

86 Christopher Ingraham. Twitter, 10 September 2020.

87 'Bolsa Familia: Brazil's Quiet Revolution.' The World Bank, 4 November 2013.

88 Bolsa Familia in Brazil. Centre for Public Impact, 2 September 2019.

89 'Bolsa Familia: Changing the Lives of Millions.' The World Bank, 2019.

90 Conditional Cash Transfers in Brazil, Chile and Mexico: Impacts upon Inequality. International Poverty Centre, April 2007.

91 Income Inequality in Brazil: new evidence from combined tax and survey data. UN World Social Science Report, 2016

92 Gini index (World Bank estimate). The World Bank, 2018.

93 These countries are doing the most to reduce inequality. World Economic Forum, 10 October 2018. The Commitment

to Reducing Inequality Index 2018. Development Finance International and Oxfam Report, 2018. Rebecca Simson. 'Mapping recent inequality trends in developing countries.' LSE, May 2018.

94 'Georgetown Study: Wealth, Not Ability, The Biggest Predictor of Future Success.' WNPR, 15 May 2019.

CHAPTER 2
Solidarity of Young and Old

1   To inform, not persuade. Winton Centre for Risk and Evidence Communication, University of Cambridge, 2020.

2   'The peril and the promise.' *The Economist*, 8 October 2020.

3   Young workers in the coronavirus crisis. Resolution Foundation, 18 May 2020.

4   Ibid.

5   Ibid.

6   'The magnifying glass: How Covid revealed the truth about our world.' *Guardian*, 11 December 2020.

7   'Generation Covid' hit hard by the pandemic, research reveals. BBC News, 26 October 2020.

8   '"I'm stuck in limbo": will the Covid generation of young people face long-term fallout?' *Guardian*, 30 May 2020.

9   'Coronavirus lays bare the trauma of losing your job.' *The Conversation*, 24 March 2020.

10 'Nasty politics returns to Spain.' *The Economist*, 16 April 2020.

11 An intergenerational audit for the UK. Resolution Foundation, 7 October 2020.

12 'Covid-19 will blight the prospects of a generation.' *Financial Times*, 19 May 2020.

13 Ibid.

14 Ibid.; 'The pandemic tests a new generation of graduate trainees.' *Financial Times*, 18 January 2021.

15 'Pandemic highlights "the aspiration gap" as young people lose hope.' Prince's Trust, 29 September 2020.

16 Zang Zhijie, Du Guodong. Out of School Out of Job, *China Report*, 1 August 2020.

17 Kathleen Henehan. Class of 2020. Resolution Foundation, May 2020.

18 'She Spent Her Last Month of College Lifting Bodies in a Morgue.' *New York Times*, 19 May 2020.

19 Author interviews with Deliveroo and online delivery drivers and job applicants September–October 2020.

20 Youth & COVID-19: impacts on jobs, education, rights and mental well-being. International Labour Organization, 11 August 2020.

21 An intergenerational audit for the UK: 2019. Resolution Foundation, June 2019.

22 Ibid.

23 'Universal credit: "I felt guilty claiming benefits for the first time."' BBC 15 December 2020.

24 'Wall Street will soon have to take millennial investors seriously.' *Economist*, 20 October 2020.

25 'The risks of keeping schools closed far outweigh the benefits.' *Economist*, 18 July 2020.

26 Ofsted: Children hardest hit by COVID-19 pandemic are regressing in basic skills and learning. Office for Standards in Education, Children's Services and Skills, 10 November 2020.

27 Elisabeth Grewenig et.al. 'COVID-19 school closures hit low-achieving students particularly hard.' VoxEU & CEPR, 15 November 2020.

28 '"Generation Covid" hit hard by the pandemic, research reveals.' BBC News, 26 October 2020.

29 'Covid: How Marcus Rashford Campaign changed free school meals.' BBC News, 9 November 2020.

30 The Food Foundation.

31 Marcus Rashford. Twitter, 21 October 2020.

32 'Marcus Rashford in "despair" as MPs reject free school meal plan.' *Guardian*, 21 October 2020. 'Marcus Rashford welcomes

school holiday support climbdown.' BBC News,
8 November 2020.

33   Reversing the Inequality Pandemic: Speech by World Bank
Group President David Malpass. World Bank Group,
5 October 2020.

34   150 million additional children plunged into poverty due to
COVID-19, UNICEF Save the Children say. UNICEF,
17 September 2020.

35   'Measuring poverty in the midst of America's covid-19
epidemic.' *Economist*, 3 October 2020.

36   'The end of $600 stimulus checks has left unemployed
Americans facing financial ruin.' CNN Business,
3 November 2020.

37   UNICEF Executive Director Henrietta Fore's remarks at a
press conference on new updated guidance on school-related
public health measures in the context of COVID-19. UNICEF,
15 September 2020.

38   'The risks of keeping schools closed far outweigh the
benefits.' *Economist*, 18 July 2020.

39   Progress on drinking-water, sanitation and hygiene in
schools. World Health Organization, 13 August 2020.

40   UNICEF Executive Director Henrietta Fore's remarks at a
press conference on new updated guidance on school-related
public health measures in the context of COVID-19. UNICEF,
15 September 2020. 'As Covid-19 Closes Schools, the World's
Children Go to Work.' *New York Times*, 8 October 2020. Save
our Education: Protect every child's right to learn in the
COVID-19 response and recovery. Save the Children,
13 July 2020.

41   The Global Girlhood Report 2020: How COVID-19 is putting
progress in peril. Save the Children, 1 October 2020.

42   Ibid.

43   Simulating the Potential Impacts of the COVID-19 School
Closures on Schooling and Learning Outcomes: A set of
Global Estimates. The World Bank, 18 June 2020.

44 The Age of Secular Stagnation. Council on Foreign Relations, 15 February 2016.

45 Antoine Bozio, Rowena Crawford and Gemma Tetlow. The history of state pensions in the UK: 1948 to 2010. Institute for Fiscal Studies, 2010.

46 'Coronavirus puts the squeeze on retirement hopes.' *Financial Times*, 12 June 2020. 'Britain's over-50s rethink plans as virus takes toll on retirement.' *Financial Times*, 30 September 2020. The coronavirus pandemic and older workers. Institute for Fiscal Studies, 30 September 2020.

47 Ibid.

48 Ibid.

49 'Youth organisations in England face wholesale closure.' *Guardian*, 3 January 2021.

50 'Vocation, vocation should be UK middle class's new mantra.' *Financial Times*, 2 October 2020. Evan Cunningham. Profession certifications and occupational licenses: evidence from the Current Population Survey. US Bureau of Labor Statistics, June 2019.

51 'Another promise to improve vocational education in Britain.' *Economist*, 3 October 2020.

52 Ibid.

CHAPTER 3
Overcoming Global Poverty

1 COVID-19 to Add as Many as 150 Million Extreme Poor. The World Bank, 7 October 2020.

2 Reversing the Inequality Pandemic: Speech by World Bank Group President David Malpass. The World Bank, 5 October 2020.

3 COVID-19, Informal Workers and WIEGO's Work during the Crisis. WIEGO, 2020.

4 Shania Bhalotia, Swati Dhingra, Fjolla Kondirolli. City of dreams no more: The impact of Covid-19 on urban workers

in India. CEP LSE, September 2020. 'How coronavirus piled misery on India's workers.' *Guardian*, 6 September 2020.

5   Ibid.

6   The impact of COVID-19: An opportunity to reaffirm the central role of migrants' human rights in sustainable development. Economic Council for Latin America and the Caribbean, November 2020.

7   'China's poorest pay the price of coronavirus outbreak.' *Financial Times*, 15 March 2020.

8   NIDS-CRAM Wave 1 & 2 reports. CRAM, 2020.

9   Ibid.

10   Ibid.

11   Ibid.

12   'Data analysis: How the poorest countries are losing out on Covid-19 relief funds.' *New Statesman*, 21 September 2020.

13   Official Development Assistance (ODA) spending for 2020: First Secretary of State's letter. UK Government, 22 July 2020.

14   How Does COVID-19 Pandemic Affect Emerging Market Currencies? FXCM, June 2020.

15   'Africa's debt crisis hampers its fight against covid-19.' *Economist*, 11 April 2020.

16   'Developing nations squeezed as virus fuels public spending.' *Financial Times*, 20 July 2020.

17   Heavily Indebted Poor Countries (HIPC) Initiative and Multilateral Debt Relief Initiative (MDRI) – Statistical Update. International Monetary Fund & World Bank, 6 August 2019.

18   'Africa's debt crisis hampers its fight against covid-19.' *Economist*, 11 April 2020.

19   'G20 readies limited extension of debt relief for poorest nations.' *Financial Times*, 13 October 2020. Defusing Debt: Creating comprehensive solutions. The World Bank, 13 October 2020.

20   Ibid.

21 'Zambia resists Chinese pressure on arrears.' *Financial Times*, 13 October 2020.

22 'African governments face a wall of debt repayments.' *Economist*, 6 June 2020.

23 Reversing the Inequality Pandemic: Speech by World Bank Group President David Malpass. The World Bank, 5 October 2020.

24 'Emerging economies plead for more ambitious debt relief programmes.' *Financial Times*, 12 October 2020.

25 'Why the Covid economic crisis has hit poorer countries less deeply than feared.' *Guardian*, 14 December 2020.

26 'Which emerging markets are in most financial peril?' *Economist*, 2 May 2020.

27 'Borrow to fight economic impact of pandemic, says World Bank's chief economist.' *Financial Times*, 8 October 2020. 'How can governments recover faster from insolvency?' *Economist*, 21 November 2020.

28 Fiscal Monitor – Policies for the Recovery. IMF, October 2020. Daniel Munevar, Arrested Development, Eurodad, 6 October 2020.

29 Ibid.

30 Valentin Lang, David Mihalyi, Andrea Presbitero. 'Borrowing costs after debt relief.' VoxEU & CEPR, 14 October 2020.

31 'How a UK aid budget cut will hollow out a world reeling from COVID-19.' Thompson Reuters Foundation News, 20 November 2020.

32 'Please Spend as Much as You Can, but Keep the Receipts'. Globsec, 15 June 2020.

33 'From Catastrophe to Catalyst.' Oxfam, 4 December 2020.

CHAPTER 4
Work for All

1 ILO Monitor: COVID-19 and the world of work. Fifth edition. International Labour Organization, 30 June 2020.

2   Jack Blundell, Stephen Machin and Maria Venura. 'Covid-19
    and the self-employed: Six months into the crisis.' Centre for
    Economic Performance, November 2020.

3   Non-standard employment around the world. International
    Labor Organization, 2016. COVID-19 and the New
    Leadership Agenda. *Boston Consulting Group*, 2020.

4   Neele Balke, Thibaut Lamadon. Productivity Shocks, Long-
    Term Contracts and Earnings Dynamics. BFI Working Paper,
    9 November 2020. Jose Maria Barrero, Nicholas Bloom nd
    Steven Davis. COVID-19 is also a reallocation shock. National
    Bureau of Economic Research Working Paper, May 2020.

5   Earnings Outlook Q1 2020. Resolution Foundation,
    16 July 2020.

6   'Unemployment down but so is pace of job gains.' Jared
    Bernstein Blog, 4 September 2020.

7   Sector shutdowns during the coronavirus crisis: which
    workers are most exposed? Institute for Fiscal Studies,
    6 April 2020.

8   'The Richest Neighbourhoods Emptied Out Most as
    Coronavirus hit New York City.' *New York Times*,
    15 May 2020.

9   'Covid-19: Record traffic around Paris as second French
    lockdown begins.' BBC News, 30 October 2020.

10 An unprecedented but essential pledge to underwrite wages
    and strengthen the safety net. Resolution Foundation,
    20 March 2020.

11 Technology at work v5.0. Citi GPS: Global Perspectives &
    Resolutions, June 2020.

12 The effects of the coronavirus crisis on workers. Resolution
    Foundation, 16 May 2020.

13 Ability to work from home: evidence from two surveys and
    implications for the labor market in the COVID-19 pandemic.
    U.S. Bureau of Labor Statistics, June 2020.

14 'The potential for teleworking in Europe and the risk of a
    new digital divide.' VoxEU & CEPR, 14 August 2020.

15 Ibid.

16 Ibid.

17 Stanford research provides a snapshot of a new working-from-home economy. Stanford University, 29 June 2020.

18 Richard Susskind, Daniel Susskind. *The Future of the Professions*. (Oxford University Press, 2017).

19 Richard Baldwin. *The Globotics Upheaval: Globalisation, Robotics and the Future of Work*. (W&N, London 2019).

20 Jamie Woodcock, Mark Graham. *The Gig Economy: A Critical Introduction*. (Polity, 2019).

21 'Do not let homeworking become digital piecework for the poor.' *Financial Times*, 15 September 2020.

22 Kotara Hara et al. A Data-Driven Analysis of Workers' Earnings on Amazon Mechanical Turk. CoRR, 28 December 2017.

23 'Blue-collar openings recover faster than office jobs in UK.' *Financial Times*, 9 September 2020. KPMG and REC, UK report on jobs. KPMG & REC, 9 September 2020.

24 Alexander Bartik et al. Measuring the labor market at the onset of the COVID-19 crisis. BFI Working Paper, 3 August 2020. Iona Elena Marinescu, Daphne Skandalis and Daniel Zhao. Job Search, Job Posting and Unemployment Insurance During the COVID-19 Crisis. SSRN, 30 July 2020.

25 Dana Scott et al. Employment Effects of Unemployment Insurance Generosity During the Pandemic. Yale University, 14 July 2020.

26 Corina Boar, Simon Mongey. Dynamic Trade-offs and Labor Supply under the CARES Act. BFI Working Paper, 19 August 2020.

27 '1m more British workers set to lose jobs this year, warn economists.' *Financial Times*, 25 September 2020. 'Young and minorities hardest hit after UK job support schemes end.' *Financial Times*, 27 October 2020. Jobs, jobs, jobs. Resolution Foundation, 27 October 2020.

28 New Food Foundation Survey: Three million Britons are
    going hungry just three weeks into lockdown. The Food
    Foundation, April 2020. Rachel Loopstra. Vulnerability to
    food insecurity since the COVID-19 lockdown. King's College
    London, 14 April 2020.

29 New report reveals how coronavirus has affected food bank
    use. Trussell Trust, 14 September 2020.

30 UK Poverty: Causes, Costs, and Solutions. Joseph Rowntree
    Foundation, 29 May 2020.

31 Ibid.

32 On Notice: Estimating the impact on redundancies of the
    Covid-19 crisis. Institute for Employment Studies, September
    2020. 'Unemployment: Planned redundancies twice the rate
    of last recession.' BBC News, 13 September 2020.

33 Benefits in unemployment, share of previous income.
    OECD, 2020.

34 'Mass unemployment threatens Britain.' *Economist*,
    20 August 2020.

35 Evan DeFilippis et al. Collaborating During Coronavirus:
    The Impact of Covid-19 on the Nature of Work. National
    Bureau of Economic Research Working Paper,
    4 August 2020.

36 Nicholas Bloom et al. Does working from home work?
    Evidence from a Chinese experiment. National Bureau of
    Economic Research Working Paper, 2014.

37 'Covid-19 has forced a radical shift in working habits.'
    Economist, 12 September 2020. Bonnie Gariety and Sherrill
    Shafer, Wage differentials associated with working at home,
    U.S. Bureau of Labor Statistics, Monthly Labour Review,
    March 2007.

38 Jose Maria Barrero, Nick Bloom and Steven Davis. 60 Million
    Fewer Commuting Hours Per Day: How Americans Use
    Time Saved by Working from Home. BFI Working Paper,
    18 September 2020.

39 Ibid.

40 Interview AP, 10 October 2020. 'Where's the spark? How lockdown caused a creativity crisis.' *Financial Times*, 18 January 2021.

41 Matthew Claudel et al. An exploration of collaborative scientific production at MIT through spatial organization and institutional affiliation. *PLoS ONE*, 22 June 2017.

42 Technology at Work v5.0 – A New World of Remote Work. Oxford Martin School, 22 June 2020.

43 Ibid.

44 'The reasons behind America's new wave of lay-offs.' *Economist*, 8 October 2020.

45 'Millions of Americans Have Lost Jobs in the Pandemic – And Robots and AI are Replacing Them Faster Than Ever.' *TIME*, 6 August 2020.

46 Ibid.

47 Ibid.

48 Ian Goldin, Robert Muggah. *Terra Incognita*. (Century, London, 2020).

49 'Millions of Americans Have Lost Jobs in the Pandemic – And Robots and AI are Replacing Them Faster Than Ever.' *TIME*, 6 August 2020.

50 'Britain's call centres are overwhelmed and overhauling how they work.' *Economist*, 4 April 2020.

51 Ibid.

52 'Coronavirus: will call centre workers lose their 'voice' to AI?' *Financial Times*, 23 April 2020.

53 'Millions of Americans Have Lost Jobs in the Pandemic – And Robots and AI are Replacing Them Faster Than Ever.' *TIME*, 6 August 2020.

54 The Future of Jobs Reports 2020. World Economic Forum, 20 October 2020.

55 Don't fear AI. It will lead to long-term job growth. World Economic Forum, 26 October 2020.

56 A jobs crisis in the cultural and creative industries. Creative Industries Policy & Evidence Centre, 10 December 2020.

57 'Covid-19 is forcing the arts in Europe back into the arms of government.' *Economist,* 29 October 2020.

58 Ibid.

59 ITV News, 6 October 2020.

60 'Photographer "devastated" by government-backed "Fatima" dancer advert.' BBC News, 15 October 2020.

61 Contribution of the arts and culture industry to the UK economy. Centre for Economics and Business Research, 17 April 2019.

62 Ibid.

63 Louise McMullan, Equity Deputy Secretary General communication with Andy de la Tour, 2 November 2020.

64 'More calls for help for arts freelancers who "face using food banks".' BBC News, 5 November 2020.

65 Financial services firms look to a future that balances remote and in-office work. PricewaterhouseCoopers, June 2020.

66 'The view from outside the echo chamber: Working from home isn't working.' *City A.M.*, 3 November 2020.

67 Ibid.

68 'How to make the hybrid workforce model work.' *Financial Times*, 12 October 2020.

69 The enterprise guide to closing the skills gap. IBM, 2019.

70 Ibid.

71 Discussion, Sir Tim Berners-Lee, Oxford Martin School, 26 November 2020.

72 Bloom, Nicholas; Davis, Steven; Zhestkova, Yulia. COVID-19 Shifted Patent Applications Toward Technologies that Support Working from Home. University of Chicago, Becker Friedman Institute for Economics Working Paper, 22 September 2020.

73 Sabina Dewan, Ekkehard Ernst. Rethinking the World of Work, Finance & Development IMF, Winter 2020.

74 Sir Tim Berners-Lee, Oxford Martin School, 26 November 2020.

75 'The lockdown in our minds will be the last restriction to be lifted.' *Guardian*, 28 April 2020.

CHAPTER 5
Economies for Shared Prosperity

1   'The threat of long economic Covid looms.' *Financial Times*,
    20 October 2020.

2   Fiscal Monitor: Policies for the Recovery. IMF, October 2020,
    p.31, 40.

3   Ibid.

4   Ibid.

5   David Cutler, Lawrence Summers. The COVID-19 Pandemic
    and the $16 Trillion Virus. Jama Network, 12 October 2020.

6   'Universal basic income gains momentum in America.'
    Economist, 8 August 2020.

7   Impacts of minimum wages: review of the international
    evidence. HM Treasury & Department for Business, Energy
    & Industrial Strategy, 5 November 2019.

8   'Housing was the business cycle.' *Economist*, 18 July 2020.

9   Building a post-Brexit immigration system for the economic
    recovery. IPPR, 3 November 2020.

10 'Be bold like FDR and create jobs directly.' *Financial Times*,
    29 September 2020.

11 World Economic Outlook, October 2020: A Long and
    Difficult Assent. IMF, October 2020.

12 Public Investment for the Recovery. IMF Blog,
    5 October 2020.

13 Are there $1.6 trillion in tax loopholes? Committee for a
    Responsible Federal Budget, 10 July 2019.

14 Nicholas Shaxson. Tackling Tax Havens. Finance &
    Development, IMF, September 2020.

15 Ibid.

16 'Opinion: It is time to levy a one-time pandemic wealth tax
    on billionaires' windfall gains.' Market Watch,
    20 August 2020.

17 'Call for windfall tax on PPE firms to fund £500 bonus for
    frontline staff.' *Guardian*, 6 December 2020.

18 Samuel Bowles, Wendy Carlin. 'The coming battle for the COVID-19 narrative.' VoxEU & CEPR, 10 April 2020.

19 Franklin D. Roosevelt. Second Inaugural Address, Inaugural Addresses of the Presidents of the United States (1989).

20 'Reweaving the social fabric after the crisis.' *Financial Times*, 24 April 2020.

21 Ibid.

22 Raghuram Rajan. *The Third Pillar*. (William Collins, London, 2020).

23 'Volunteers Rushed to help New York hospital. They found a bottleneck.' *New York Times*, 8 April 2020.

24 '"A devastating loss of funds": UK Charities Count the Cost of Covid.' *Guardian*, 12 November 2020.

25 'Which is the best market model?' *Economist*, 12 September 2020.

26 Austerity – COVID's little helper. British Medical Association, 8 October 2020.

27 Ibid.

28 'Boris Johnson: PM lays out vision of post-Covid UK.' BBC News, 6 October 2020.

CHAPTER 6
Better Business

1 The Economic Case for Biden. Project Syndicate, 21 September 2020.

2 'Watchdog criticises government over awarding of £17bn Covid contracts.' *Financial Times*. 18 November 2020. 'The magnifying glass: how Covid revealed the truth about our world.' *Guardian*, 11 December 2020.

3 Vast sums spent, no one knows why: COVID reveals why UK transparency law must change. Open Democracy, 13 July 2020.

4   Government Procurement Scandal Continues with £43.8 Million PPE Contract for dormant firm. Byline Times, 2 September 2020. 'UK government paid £1.7bn to private groups for coronavirus contracts.' *Financial Times*, 4 June 2020.

5   How much do US presidential elections cost in 2020? TRT World, 3 November 2020.

6   Lobbying Data Summary. Open Secrets.org, 23 October 2020. How much does it cost to become president? Investopedia, 6 November 2020.

7   'Covid-19 Is Dividing the American Worker.' *Wall Street Journal*, 22 August 2020.

8   16.6 Million UK jobs at risk if entrepreneurs and SMEs cannot sustain their businesses. King's Business School, 25 October 2020. 'Covid leaves 6m UK small businesses and 16m jobs in "precarious position".' *Guardian*, 26 October 2020.

9   'Is it Insane to Start a Business During Coronavirus? Millions of Americans Don't Think So.' *Wall Street Journal*, 26 September 2020.

10   'Jeff Bezos is now twice as rich as Mark Zuckerberg.' *Business Insider*, 29 August 2020. 'Jeff Bezos Becomes The First Person Ever Worth $200 Billion.' *Forbes*, 26 August 2020.

11   'Many Companies Won't Survive the Pandemic. Amazon Will Emerge Stronger Than Ever.' *TIME*, 28 July 2020.

12   'Can Amazon keep growing like a youthful startup?' *Economist*, 18 June 2020.

13   Apple is valued at $2 trillion as investor confidence grows. World Economic Forum, 20 August 2020.

14   'New technological behaviours will outlast the pandemic.' *Economist*, 16 November 2020.

15   'Pandemic boosts automation and robotics.' *Financial Times*, 20 October 2020.

16   'Peloton will rally another 18% as profits trounce expectations over next year, Bank of America says.' *Business Insider*, 9 September 2020.

17 'Covid recovery will stem from digital business.' *Financial Times*, 4 October 2020.

18 Economic Conditions and the Path of Monetary Policy. Federal Reserve Bank of Dallas, 29 September 2020.

19 'Is Google Advertising Revenue 70%, 80%, or 90% of Alphabet's Total Revenue?' *Forbes*, 24 December 2019. Revenue of Alphabet from 1st quarter 2014 to 3rd quarter 2020. Statista Statistics, 12 December 2020.

20 'Covid recovery will stem from digital business.' *Financial Times*, 4 October 2020.

21 CSIRO scientists publish new research on SARS-COV-2 virus 'survivability'. CSIRO, 12 October 2020. Shane Riddell et al. 'The effect of temperature on persistence of SAS-CoV-2 on common surfaces.' *Virology Journal*, 7 October 2020.

22 'How the digital surge will reshape finance.' *Economist*, 8 October 2020.

23 Ibid. 'Could coronavirus hasten the death of cash?' *Financial Times*, 13 October 2020.

24 Ibid.

25 Ibid.

26 Ibid.

27 'Flower power: Covid restrictions fuel boom in plant and bulb sales.' *Guardian*, 31 October 2020.

28 Ibid.

29 'Pandemic sets off a scramble to snap up outdoor heaters.' *Financial Times*, 4 November 2020.

30 'The pandemic shock will make big, powerful firms even mightier.' *Economist*, 26 March 2020.

31 'WeWork's valuation has fallen from $47 billion last year to $2.9 billion.' *Business Insider*, 18 May 2020.

32 'The sharing economy will have to change.' *Economist*, 4 June 2020.

33 'The post-Covid consumer: is back-to-basics shopping here to stay?' *Financial Times*, 1 November 2020.

34 'Why reinsurance is booming after pandemic disaster.'
     Financial Times, 14 August 2020.

35 Ibid.

36 'Private jets take off as wealthy flyers seek to avoid virus.'
     Financial Times, 25 October 2020.

37 'Which sectors are likely to win or lose from the pandemic?'
     Financial Times, 3 November 2020.

38 Interview with Andrew P., 10 October 2020.

39 'The pandemic shock will make big, powerful firms even
     mightier.' *Economist*, 26 March 2020.

40 Marco Pagano, Christian Wagner and Josef Zechner. Disaster
     Resilience and Asset Prices. CEPR Discussion Paper,
     28 May 2020.

41 'Bubble-hunting has become more art than science.'
     Economist, 19 August 2020.

42 'Epic S&P 500 Rally Is Powered by Assets You Can't See or
     Touch.' *Bloomberg*, 21 October 2020.

43 'Corporate dealmakers emerge from pandemic
     hibernation.' *Economist*, 25 July 2020. 'Global banks generate
     record $125bn fee haul in 2020.' *Financial Times*, 29 December
     2020.

44 'The pandemic bankruptcy wave has been delayed, not
     avoided.' *Financial Times*, 3 December 2020.

45 'The number of new businesses in America is booming.'
     Economist, 10 October 2020.

46 'The pandemic shock will make big, powerful firms even
     mightier.' *Economist*, 26 March 2020.

47 'Pandemic seals dominance of UK's biggest banks.' *Financial
     Times*, 9 August 2020.

48 Ibid.

49 'The virus has crushed the challenger bank dream.' *Financial
     Times*, 2 November 2020.

50 'America's two-track economy: the small business crunch.'
     Financial Times, 14 December 2020.

51 Ibid.

52 Ian Goldin et al. The Productivity Paradox: reconciling rapid
    technological change and stagnating productivity. Oxford
    Martin School Programme on Technological and Economic
    Change, May 2019.

53 The Coming Equity Shortage. Project Syndicate,
    9 October 2020.

54 'Larry Ellison hosts Trump fundraiser, but has contributed to
    both sides.' *The Desert Sun*, 19 February 2020.

55 Discussion with David Craig, CEO Refinitiv,
    11 November 2020.

56 '50 years later, Milton Friedman's shareholder doctrine is
    dead.' *Fortune*, 13 September 2020.

57 Letter: Rules must change on pursuit of quick profits.
    Financial Times, 11 December 2020.

58 'The Corporate Response To COVID-19 And Inequality: A
    Big Data Analysis.' *Forbes*, 23 September 2020.

59 Ibid.

60 Council of Institutional Investors Responds to Business
    Roundtable Statement on Corporate Purpose. Council of
    Institutional Investors, 19 August 2019.

61 '50 years later, Milton Friedman's shareholder doctrine is
    dead.' *Fortune*, 13 September 2020.

62 'The new social contract.' *Financial Times,* 6 July 2020.

63 Missing Profits of Nations, Missingprofits.org. https://
    missingprofits.world

64 'Milton Friedman was wrong on the corporation.' *Financial
    Times*, 8 December 2020.

65 'Opioid maker Purdue Pharma agrees $8b US settlement.'
    Financial Times, 21 October 2020.

CHAPTER 7
Governments That Serve

1 Fiscal Monitor Database of Country Fiscal Measures in
   Response to the COVID-19 Pandemic. IMF, October 2020.

2   Outlook for the public finances. Institute for Fiscal Studies,
      13 October 2020. Rishi Sunak: Read the Chancellor's Keynote
      Speech in full. Conservatives, 5 October 2020.
3   Verbatim of the remarks made by Mario Draghi. European
      Central Bank, 26 July 2020.
4   'Rich countries try radical economic policies to counter
      Covid-19.' Economist, 26 March 2020.
5   Ibid.
6   'Government handouts threaten Europe's single market.'
      Economist, 28 May 2020.
7   'EU recovery deal to "alter permanently" bloc's crisis-fighting
      approach.' Financial Times, 11 December 2020.
8   'EU reveals plan to regulate Big Tech.' BBC News,
      15 December 2020.
9   Oscar Jorda, Sanjay Singh, and Alan Taylor. Longer-Run
      Economic Consequences of Pandemics. Federal Reserve
      Bank of San Francisco Working Paper Series, June 2020.
10   Julian Kozlowski, Laura Veldkamp and Venky
      Venkateswaran. Scarring Body and Mind: The Long-Term
      Belief-Scarring Effect of Covid-19. FRB St. Louis Working
      Paper, April 2020.
11   'Ranking the effectiveness of worldwide COVID-19
      government interventions.' Nature Human Behaviour,
      16 November 2020.

CHAPTER 8
Cities For the Future

1   'Working life has entered a new era.' Economist, 30 May 2020.
2   Ibid.
3   Long-term trends in UK employment: 1861 to 2018. Office for
      National Statistics, 29 April 2019.
4   The Future is Flexible: Employees want greater ownership
      and choice in the new world of work. Cisco,
      14 October 2020.

5   'Is the office finished?' *Economist*, 12 September 2020.

6   Ibid.

7   Ibid. Jonathan Dingel, Brent Neiman. How Many Jobs Can be Done at Home? National Bureau of Economic Research Working Paper, June 2020.

8   Ian Goldin et al. Migration and the Economy: Economic Realities, Social Impacts and Political Choices. Citi-Oxford Martin School, 9 September 2020.

9   'Is the office finished?' *Economist*, 12 September 2020.

10 Ibid.

11 Home-working here to stay, new IoD figures suggest. Institute of Directors, 5 October 2020.

12 Chris Herd. Twitter, 5 October 2020.

13 Rewiring how we work; building a new employee experience for a digital first world. Slack, 7 October 2020.

14 'Is the office finished?' *Economist*, 12 September 2020.

15 'Cities count cost of lasting exodus from offices.' *Financial Times*, 14 September 2020.

16 'Why workers in some countries are returning to the office.' *Financial Times*, 24 August 2020.

17 'City of London suffers crushing blow from second lockdown.' *Financial Times*, 6 November 2020. 'London property: Out of office.' *Financial Times*, 4 January 2021.

18 'Traders set to don virtual reality headset in their home offices.' *Financial Times*, 18 September 2020.

19 'What will be the new normal for offices?' *Economist*, 9 May 2020. 'Law firms ditch trophy office moves as pandemic reshapes City.' *Financial Times*, 4 January 2021.

20 Is flexible working here to stay? We asked 6 companies how to make it work. World Economic Forum, 26 August 2020.

21 'What will be the new normal for offices?' *Economist*, 9 May 2020.

22 'Is the office finished?' *Economist*, 12 September 2020.

23 Stanford research provides a snapshot of a new working-from-home economy. Stanford News, 29 July 2020.

24 Chris Herd. Twitter, 5 October 2020.

25 Ibid.

26 'What It Might Mean If We All Work From Home?' *Forbes*, 10 September 2020.

27 Interview, Russell Brimelow, 17 October 2020.

28 'Goodbye to the "Pret economy" and good luck to whatever replaces it.' *Financial Times*, 1 September 2020.

29 'Coronavirus drives shop closures to new record.' BBC News, 20 October 2020. Store Openings and Closures – 2020. PricewaterhouseCoopers, 20 October 2020.

30 'Nearly 60% of West End shop rents left unpaid.' *Guardian*, 25 September 2020.

31 'Cities count cost of lasting exodus from offices.' *Financial Times*, 14 September 2020.

32 Ibid.

33 'What It Might Mean If We All Work From Home?' *Forbes*, 10 September 2020.

34 DiNapoli: Restaurant Industry Critical to New York City's Economy. New York State Comptroller, 1 October 2020. 'New York could lose 159,000 restaurant jobs due to pandemic.' *Financial Times*, 1 October 2020.

35 'More Than 14,500 Stores are Closing In 2020 So Far – A Number That Will Surely Rise.' *Forbes*, 6 July 2020.

36 'Shopping for Fashion, Six Months On.' *New York Times*, 18 September 2020.

37 'A nation of shopkeepers shaken by the shift online.' *Financial Times*, 15 August 2020.

38 Ibid.

39 'Sainsbury's to cut 3,500 jobs and close 420 Argos stores.' BBC News, 5 November 2020.

40 'Co-op gears up for retail expansion with £130m autumn stores surge.' *Talking Retail*, 4 September 2020. 'M&S job cuts: How many job losses are there and will there be store closures?' *Heart*, 20 July 2020.

41 'Convenience stores may benefit from covid-19 – if they adapt.' *Economist*, 17 October 2020.

42 'Shopping malls need to travel back to the future.' *Financial Times*, 13 November 2020.

43 'Ode to the shopping mall.' *Economist*, 9 May 2020.

44 'From peak city to ghost town: the urban centres hit hardest by Covid-19.' *Financial Times*, 15 October 2020.

45 'Is investors' love affair with commercial property ending?' *Economist*, 25 June 2020.

46 'Britain's coming commercial property slump.' *Economist*, 24 September 2020.

47 Ibid.

48 'From peak city to ghost town: the urban centres hit hardest by Covid-19.' *Financial Times*, 15 October 2020.

49 'Is investors' love affair with commercial property ending?' *Economist*, 25 June 2020. 'British Land collects less than half of rent.' *Financial Times*, 11 January 2021.

50 Technology at Work v5.0 – A New World of Remote Work. Oxford Martin School, 22 June 2020.

51 'Landlords slash rents by up to 20% as tenants quit city centres in pandemic.' *Guardian*, 20 September 2020.

52 'Manhattan Empties, Brooklyn Hangs on as Renters Prioritize Space, Amenities Over Commute in Pandemic Economy.' *The City*, 12 November 2020.

53 'Escape to the country: how Covid is driving an exodus from Britain's cities.' *Guardian*, 26 September 2020. 'How coronavirus has shaped the home of tomorrow.' *Financial Times*, 1 January 2021.

54 Ibid.

55 'Cities count cost of lasting exodus from offices.' *Financial Times*, 14 September 2020. 'House prices rise as Covid sparks rural relocation.' BBC News, 18 November 2020.

56 Interview, Savills, 13 October 2020.

57 'Covid-19 has forced a radical shift in working habits.'

Economist, 12 September 2020.

58 'Londoners look to properties beyond suburbs.' *Financial Times*, 18 September 2020.

59 'Booming house prices spell more trouble for the social contract.' *Economist*, 3 October 2020.

60 'Housing Boom: Sales of Million-Dollar Homes Double.' *NPR*, 22 October 2020.

61 Ibid.

62 Ibid.

63 An Intergenerational Audit for the UK: 2019. Intergenerational Center Resolution Foundation, June 2019.

64 Anne Case, Angus Deaton. *Deaths of Despair and the Future of Capitalism.* (Princeton University Press, 2020).

65 'Unemployment Problem Includes Public Transportation That Separates Poor From Jobs.' *Huffington Post.* 7 November 2012.

66 'Britain's experiment in radical rail privatisation is over.' *Economist*, 26 September 2020.

67 Sadiq Khan and Boris Johnson strike London transport rescue deal. *Financial Times*, 1 November 2020.

68 'Boris Johnson blames London mayor for TfL "bankruptcy" before Covid-19.' BBC News, 21 October 2020.

69 'America's biggest transit system is in trouble.' *Economist*, 3 September 2020.

70 Ibid.

71 Ibid.

72 'Why the pandemic is pushing city dwellers towards cars.' *Financial Times*, 4 August 2020.

73 'UK lockdown measures drive used car prices to record growth.' *Financial Times*, 2 October 2020.

74 'Why the urban poor will be forced to leave big cities.' *Financial Times*, 22 October 2020.

75 Edward Glaeser, Matthew Resseger. The Complementarity Between Cities and Skills. National Bureau of Economic Research Working Paper, June 2009.

76 Patricia Melo, Daniel Graham and Robert Noland. A Meta-Analysis of Estimates of Urban Agglomeration Economies. *Regional Science and Urban Economics*, May 2009.

77 Jorge De la Roca, Diego Puga. Learning by Working in Big Cities. *Review of Economic Studies*, 2017.

78 'Cities are too resilient to be killed by Covid.' *Financial Times*, 29 September 2020.

79 The Multiplier Effect of Innovation Jobs. *MIT Sloan Management Review*, 6 June 2012.

80 'It's 'back to the 50s' as day trips replace the UK rail commute.' *Guardian*, 18 September 2020.

81 'What will be the new normal for offices?' *Economist*, 9 May 2020.

82 'City of London seeks to "reinvent itself" after pandemic.' *Financial Times*, 19 October 2020.

83 'High streets can be resurrected if communities are empowered.' *Financial Times*, 12 December 2020.

84 'Why cities are not as bad for you as you think.' BBC Future, 1 December 2020.

CHAPTER 9
Improving Mental Health

1   'The family unit has shaped people's experience of Covid-19.' *Economist*, 4 June 2020.

2   Is there a loneliness epidemic? Our World in Data, 11 December 2019.

3   '"I'm stuck in limbo": will the Covid generation of young people face long-term fallout?' *Guardian*, 30 May 2020.

4   A majority of young adults in the U.S. live with their parents for the first time since the Great Depression. Pew Research Center, 4 September 2020.

5   'The pandemic and the parent trap.' *Financial Times*, 16 September 2020.

6   Katherine Hill et al. Young adults living with their parents in low to middle income families. Centre for Research in Social Policy Loughborough University, September 2020. '"Boomerang trend" of young adults living with their parents is rising study says.' *Guardian*, 18 October 2020.

7   What next? Priorities for Britain. Renew Normal: The People's Commission on Life After Covid-19, September 2020.

8   Ibid.

9   'Universal credit: "I felt guilty claiming benefits for the first time."' *Guardian*, 15 December 2020.

10 'Coronavirus: Domestic violence "increases globally during lockdown".' BBC, 17 August 2020.

11 '"The worst year": domestic violence soars in Australia during Covid-19.' *Guardian*, 30 November 2020.

12 'Domestic abuse surged in lockdown Panorama investigation finds.' *Guardian*, 17 August 2020.

13 Ofsted Chief Inspector Amanda Spielman at NCASC 2020. National Children and Adult Services Conference, 6 November 2020. '"Toxic lockdown" sees huge rise in babies harmed or killed.' BBC News, 6 November 2020.

14 'Divorce Lawyer to the wealthy: "The pandemic has been a real wake-up call".' *Financial Times*, 12 October 2020.

15 'The decline of the office romance.' *Economist*, 15 August 2020.

16 'Virtual dating on the rise as users seek lockdown love, says Match chief.' *Financial Times*, 18 June 2020.

17 Ibid.

18 Socrates. *Respectfully Quoted: A dictionary of quotations.* 1989.

19 Co-SPACE study early results – increase in mental health difficulties among children during COVID-19 Lockdown. NHS, 24 June 2020. Report 04: Changes in children and young people's emotional and behavioural difficulties through lockdown. Co-SPACE study, 16 June 2020.

20 'How covid-19 exacerbates inequality.' *Economist*,

26 March 2020.

21 Care homes in England had greatest increase in excess deaths
    at height of the COVID-10 pandemic. University of Stirling,
    August 2020.

22 'How will humans, by nature social animals, fare when
    isolated?' *Economist*, 4 April 2020.

23 Leo Sher. The impact of the COVID-19 pandemic on suicide
    rates. *QJM: An International Journal of Medicine*, Volume 113,
    Issue 10, October 2020.

24 Carmen Moreno et al. How mental health care should
    change as a consequence of the COVID-19 pandemic. *The
    Lancet Psychiatry*, 16 July 2020.

25 Leo Sher. The impact of the COVID-19 pandemic on suicide
    rates. *QJM: An International Journal of Medicine*, Volume 113,
    Issue 10, October 2020.

26 Jia Ru et al. Mental health in the UK during the COVID-19
    pandemic: cross-sectional analyses from a community cohort
    study. *BMJ Open*, 25 August 2020.

27 Mental Health, Substance Use, and Suicidal Ideation
    During the COVID-10 Pandemic – United States, June 24–30,
    2020. Centre for Disease Control and Prevention,
    14 August 2020.

28 Co-SPACE study early results – increase in mental health
    difficulties among children during COVID-19 Lockdown.
    NHS, 24 June 2020. Report 04: Changes in children and
    young people's emotional and behavioural difficulties
    through lockdown. Co-SPACE study, 16 June 2020.

29 Coronavirus: The divergence of mental health experiences
    during the pandemic. Mental Health Foundation, 2 July 2020.

30 'Job losses in white and blue collar workers.' Centre for
    Monitoring Indian Economy, 14 September 2020. *Financial
    Times*, 6 October 2020.

31 'Depression to suicide.' *Business Standard*, 13 September 2020.
    'Increasing Rate of Suicides Indicates Youth At Grave Risk of
    Losing Mental Equilibrium.' *Outlook*, 10 September 2020.

32   Suicide cases rise by 57% in Malawi-Police. Helpline Malawi,
     15 September 2020.
33   COVID-19 disrupting mental health services in most countries,
     WHO survey. World Health Organization, 5 October 2020.
34   Ibid.
35   Ibid.
36   Ibid.
37   COVID-19 Continuing to Impact Behavioural Health
     Organizations In Need of Relief. National Council for
     Behavioural Research, 1 September 2020.
38   Ibid.
39   Maxime Taquet et al. Bidirectional associations between
     COVID-19 and psychiatric disorder: retrospective cohort of
     62354 COVID-19 cases in the USA. *The Lancet Psychiatry*,
     9 November 2020. 'Antidepressant use in England soars as
     pandemic cuts counselling access.' *Guardian*, 1 January 2021.
40   'Covid could cause "tsunami of cancelled NHS operations".'
     BBC News, 5 October 2020.
41   Ibid.
42   'In Covid's shadow, another UK health crisis looms.' *Financial
     Times*, 6 November 2020.
43   Ibid.
44   Ibid.
45   Jan-Emmanuel De Neve, Christian Krekel. Cities and
     Happiness: A Global Ranking and Analysis. World Happiness
     Report, 20 March 2020.
46   'Half of child psychiatrists surveyed say patients have
     environment anxiety.' *Guardian*, 20 November 2020.
47   'The pandemic may be encouraging people to live in larger
     groups.' *Economist*, 5 December 2020.
48   Ibid.
49   'Nearly half of NHS critical care staff report PTSD,
     depression or anxiety.' *Guardian*, 13 January 2021.
50   Governor Cuomo Commends Mental Health Professionals
     Working as Volunteers to Address Mental Health Needs

Related to Coronavirus. Governor New York State,
25 March 2020.

CHAPTER 10
Politics and Power Shifts

1 'Throughout history, pandemics have had profound economic effects.' *Economist*, 14 March 2020.

2 'China–US rivalry and threats to globalisation recall ominous past.' *Financial Times*, 26 May 2020.

3 Serving the Country and Contributing to the World: China's diplomacy […], Address by H. E. Wang Yie. Ministry of Foreign Affairs of the People's Republic of China, 11 December 2020.

4 *Terra Incognita.* p.436.

5 'European support for populist beliefs falls, YouGov survey suggests.' *Guardian*, 26 October 2020.

6 'Southern Europe's millennials suffer two huge crises by their mid-30s.' *Economist*, 18 April 2020.

7 Ibid.

8 Ibid.

9 An intergenerational audit for the UK. Resolution Foundation, 7 October 2020.

10 'Covid-19 drives 50% of students in UK to become "more political".' *Guardian*, 12 December 2020.

11 'The Coronavirus is rewriting our imagination.' *New Yorker*, 1 May 2020.

12 How Trump Won the Unhappiness Vote. HAI Stanford University, 18 September 2020.

13 'As Trump equivocates on White Supremacy, the FBI Warns of Right-Wing Terror.' *The Nation*, 30 September 2020.

14 U.S. firearms sales: 2020 year-to-date sales set new high. *Small Arms Analytics*, 3 October 2020. 'Americans have bought record 17m guns in year of unrest, analysis finds.' *Guardian*, 30 October 2020.

15 The Curse of Falling Expectations. Project Syndicate, 25 September 2020.

16 '"I can't breathe": why George Floyd's words reverberate around the world.' *Guardian*, 8 June 2020.

17 'Six months after mass protests began, what is the future of BLM?' *Economist*, 12 December 2020.

18 Eric Lonergan Mark Blyth. *Angrynomics*. (Columbia University Press, New York, 2020).

19 'Would-be autocrats are using covid-19 as an excuse to grab more power.' *Economist*, 23 April 2020.

20 Ibid. Azerbaijan. Human Rights Watch, 18 December 2020.

21 Molly Morgan Jones, Dominic Abrams and Aditi Lahiri. Shape the Future: how the social sciences, humanities and the arts can SHAPE a positive, post-pandemic future for peoples, economies and environments. *Journal of the British Academy*, 2 October 2020.

22 'Why Covid is bad for global democracy.' *Financial Times*, 2 October 2020.

23 Democracy under Lockdown, Special Report 2020. Freedom House, 2020.

24 'The pandemic has eroded democracy and respect for human rights.' *Economist*, 17 October 2020.

25 'Boris Johnson and Priti Patel "should apologise for lawyer attacks".' BBC News, 26 October 2020.

26 'Have countries led by women coped better with Covid-19?' *Financial Times*, 2 December 2020.

27 The Post-Pandemic Recovery's Missing Link. Project Syndicate, 18 September 2020.

28 Sarah Cliffe, 4 October 2020.

29 'Building back better requires systemic shifts.' *Financial Times*, 30 July 2020.

30 'Vacancy: rule-breakers for post-Covid politics.' *Financial Times*, 17 September 2020.

31 Ibid. The New Normal? More in Common, 2020.

32 Ibid. Ibid.

33 'Young people's attitudes toward protests should worry Republicans.' *Washington Post*, 12 June 2020.

34 The New Normal? More in Common, 2020.

35 'A better society can emerge from the lockdowns.' *Financial Times*, 15 April 2020.

36 'The Pandemic's Economic Lessons.' *Atlantic*, 6 April 2020.

CHAPTER 11
Inclusive Globalisation

1 How deglobalization is hurting the world's emerging economies. World Economic Forum, 29 September 2020.

2 Ibid.

3 World Economic Situation and Prospects: September 2020 Briefing, No. 141. UN Department of Economic and Social Affairs, 1 September 2020. World Bank Predicts Sharpest Decline of Remittances in Recent History, World Bank, 22 April 2020.

4 Risk, resilience, and rebalancing in global value chains. McKinsey Global Institute, 6 August 2020.

5 Setting up a pharmaceutical manufacturing supply chain is a complex and lengthy process. Catalyst, 14 May 2020.

6 'The reasons behind America's new wave of lay-offs.' *Economist*, 8 October 2020.

7 Turning hope into reality, OECD Economic Outlook. OECD, December 2020.

8 Global Asset Managers in China – Riding the waves of reform. Oliver Wyman, 2018.

9 'Is Wall Street winning in China?' *Economist*, 3 September 2020.

10 Ibid.

11 'Beijing and Wall Street deepen ties despite geopolitical rivalry.' *Financial Times*, 27 October 2020.

12 Ibid.

13 'Beijing's first bond offer to US investors draws record

demand.' *Financial Times*, 15 October 2020.

14 Review of Maritime Transport 2020. UNCTAD, 2020.

15 'The great uncoupling: one supply chain for China, one for everywhere else.' *Financial Times*, 6 October 2020.

16 Parag Khanna. *The Future is Asian: Commerce, Conflict, and Culture in the Twenty-First Century*. (Simon & Schuster, London, 2019).

17 'China's prodigious exporters have some new tricks.' *Economist*, 25 June 2020.

18 Ibid.

19 Exports of goods and services (% of GDP). The World Bank, 2020.

20 'Covid-19's blow to world trade is a heavy one.' *Economist*, 14 May 2020.

21 'China's prodigious exporters have some new tricks.' *Economist*, 25 June 2020.

22 'The great uncoupling: one supply chain for China, one for everywhere else.' *Financial Times*, 6 October 2020.

23 'Covid-19's blow to world trade is a heavy one.' *Economist*, 14 May 2020.

24 'Why coffee has been caught up in the coronavirus sell-off.' *Financial Times*, 5 February 2020.

25 Globalization Comes to the Rescue: How Dependency Makes Us More resilient. ECIPE, September 2020.

26 Ibid.

27 Ibid.

28 Ibid.

29 Richard Baldwin, Simon Evenetti. COVID-19 and Trade Policy: Why Turning Inward Won't Work. VoxEU & CEPR, 29 April 2020.

30 'The world's food system has so far weathered the challenge of Covid-19.' *Economist*, 9 May 2020.

31 Amartya Sen. Property and Hunger. Cambridge University Press, 5 December 2008.

32 'Coronavirus and globalisation: the surprising resilience of

container shipping.' *Financial Times*, 17 September 2020.

33 'How Covid-19 put wind in shipping companies' sails.'
Economist, 10 October 2020.

34 'Coronavirus and globalisation: the surprising resilience of
container shipping.' *Financial Times,* 17 September 2020.

35 'How Covid-19 put wind in shipping companies' sails.'
Economist, 10 October 2020. 'Demand for Chinese Goods Is
So Strong There's a Container Shortage.' *Bloomberg News,* 7
January 2021.

36 Ibid. Parag Khanna. The next wave of globalization: Asia in
the cockpit. *Nikkei Asia,* 13 January 2021.

37 'Demand for Chinese Goods Is So Strong There's a
Container Shortage.' *Bloomberg News,* 7 January 2021.

38 Steven Altman, Philip Bastian. DHL Global Connectedness
Index 2020. DHL, December 2020.

39 'The death of the business trip?' *Financial Times,*
25 September 2020.

40 'Half UK's true carbon footprint created abroad, research
finds.' *Guardian,* 16 April 2020.

41 William Gibson. The future is already here – it's just not
evenly distributed.

42 Antonio Guterres Address to the Opening of the General
Debate. United Nations General Assembly,
22 September 2020.

CHAPTER 12
Responding to the Climate Emergency

1 Experts support UN Secretary General's call for major effort
in 2021 to achieve the $100-billion climate finance goal.
United Nations, 11 December 2020.

2 'What is a 'mass extinction' and are we in one now?' *The
Conversation,* 12 November 2019.

3 *Terra Incognita,* p.341–7.

4 'The real scandal isn't what China did to us. It's what we did

to ourselves.' *Washington Post*, 7 May 2020.

5   SARS-CoV-2 mink-associated variant strain – Denmark.
     World Health Organization, 6 November 2020. 'Is a
     dangerous new coronavirus strain circulating in farmed
     mink?' *New Scientist*, 6 November 2020.

6   'Eat less meat: UN climate-change report calls for change to
     human diet.' *Nature*, 8 August 2019.

7   Corinne Le Quéré et al. Temporary reduction in daily global
     CO2 emissions during the COVID-19 forced confinement.
     Nature Climate Change, 19 May 2020.

8   COVID-19 crisis causes 17 per cent drop in global carbon
     emissions. University of East Anglia, 19 May 2020.

9   Secretary General Statement, Border Carbon Adjustment:
     What shape in the post-COVID geopolitical and economic
     landscape? OECD, 20 October 2020.

10   New NASA Research Projects Probe COVID-10 Impacts.
     NASA's Earth Science News, 27 July 2020.

11   Andrew Hook et al. A systematic review of the energy and
     climate impacts of teleworking. *Environmental Research Letters*,
     19 August 2020.

12   Majority of people expect government to make environment
     a priority in post COVID-19 recovery. IPSOS, 4 June 2020.

13   Jessica Long, Lizzie Gordon and Ruth Townend. Now what?
     Climate change & coronavirus. IPSOS, June 2020.

14   Why celebrate the bicycle? United Nations, 3 June 2020.

15   'Shopping for Fashion, Six months on.' *New York Times*,
     18 September 2020.

16   'Is it the end of the oil age?' *Economist*, 17 September 2020.

17   Renewables 2020 Analysis and forecast to 2025. IEA,
     November 2020.

18   Solar is now 'cheapest electricity in history', confirms IEA.
     CarbonBrief, 13 October 2020.

19   Renewables 2020 Analysis and forecast to 2025. IEA,
     November 2020.

20   'A renewable-energy boom is changing the politics of global

warming.' *Economist*, 14 March 2020.

21   Ibid.

22   'UK renewables prove a shining success during pandemic.'
     Financial Times, 17 May 2020.

23   'Sony warns it could move factories over Japanese energy
     policy.' *Financial Times*, 27 November 2020.

24   *Observatorio do clima*, 2020.

25   'The epidemic provides a change to do good by the climate.'
     Economist, 26 March 2020.

26   China's plan to launch the world's largest carbon trading
     scheme by 2025. World Economic Forum, 12 November 2020.

27   New Energy Outlook 2020. BloombergNEF, 2020.

28   'Revealed: Covid recovery plans threaten global climate
     hopes.' *Guardian*, 9 November 2020.

29   Ibid.

30   14 straight months of rising Amazon deforestation in Brazil.
     Mongabay, 12 June 2020.

31   Oluniyi Fadare and Elvis Okoffo. Covid-19 face masks: A
     potential source of microplastic fibers in the environment.
     The Science of the Total Environment, 16 June 2020.

32   'Face masks and gloves found on 30% of UK beaches in
     clean-up.' *Guardian*, 6 November 2020.

33   West Coast fires will cost US economy dearly. Deutsche
     Welle, 17 September 2020. See Australia fires. BBC News,
     18 December 2000.

34   Air pollution costs European economies US$ 1.6 trillion a
     year in diseases and deaths, new WHO study says. WHO
     Europe, 28 April 2015.

35   *Terra Incognita.* pp.338–341.

36   Air pollution. World Health Organization, 2020.

37   10,000 air pollution-related deaths avoided in Europe as coal,
     oil consumption plummet. Centre for Research on Energy
     and Clean Air, 30 April 2020.

38   Ibid.

39   Marina Andrijevic et al. COVID-19 recovery funds dwarf

clean energy investment needs. *Science,* 16 October 2020.

40 How the global coronavirus stimulus could put Paris
    Agreement on track. World Economic Forum,
    20 October 2020.

41 Globalism Survey Results. YouGov, 2020.

42 'Just because it's digital doesn't mean it's green.' *Financial Times,*
    6 March 2019. The Digital Economy and the Green Economy:
    Compatible Agendas? PGI Working Paper, October 2019.

43 'E.U.'s Coronavirus Recovery Plan Also Aims to Fight
    Climate Change.' *Scientific American,* 28 May 2020. 'South
    Korea Doubles Spending Plan for "New Deal" to Reshape
    Economy.' *Bloomberg,* 14 July 2020.

44 'South Korea's Green New Deal.' *The Diplomat,* 29 May 2020.

45 'Labour to plan green economic rescue from coronavirus
    crisis.' *Guardian,* 17 May 2020.

CHAPTER 13
Stopping Global Crises

1 The Global Risks Report 2020. World Economic Forum,
   2020.

2 Future Risks Report. AXA & Eurasia Group, October 2020.

3 Ian Goldin. Rethinking Global Resilience. IMF: Finance and
   Development, September 2020.

4 Ibid.

5 *The Butterfly Defect: How Globalization Creates Systemic Risks,
   and What to Do about it.* Chapter 6.

6 Larry Brilliant. My wish: Help me stop pandemics. TED
   Talk, February 2006.

7 Ibid.

8 Jie Zhao, Peiquan Jin and Guori Hang. A Survey on
   Detecting Public Emergencies from Web Pages. *Advances on
   Information Sciences and Service Science,* 2011.

9 Ian Goldin. *Divided Nations.* (Oxford University Press, 2013).
   Ian Goldin. Rethinking Global Resilience. IMF: Finance and

Development, September 2020.

10 '£174 million reimbursement: Wimbledon and the insurance coup.' *Tennis Net*, 14 November 2020.

11 'Are we living at the "hinge of history"?' *BBC Future*, 24 September 2020.

12 'How pandemics change history.' *New Yorker*, 3 March 2020. Sudhir Hazareesingh. *Black Spartacus*. (Allen Lane, London, 2020). pp.93–94.

13 Nelson Mandela, Speech, 2001.

Conclusion

1 Failed safe? Enforcing workplace health and safety in the age of Covid-19. Resolution Foundation, 2 November 2020.

2 Ibid.

3 The speech: David Lloyd George, 23 November 1918, *The Scotsman*, 23 November 2007. Cited by Mark Carney in 'How the economy must yield to human values.' *Economist*, 16 April 2020.

4 John Maynard Keynes, How to pay for the war, in Elizabeth Johnson and Donald Moggridge (eds), *The Collected Writings of John Maynard Keynes*. (Cambridge University Press, 1978). Quote cited in 'The pandemic will leave the rich world deep in debt, and force some hard choices.' *The Economist*, 23 April 2020.

5 The IFS Deaton Review of Inequalities, 5 January 2021. 'UK "cannot duck" post-Covid inequalities.' BBC, 5 January 2021.

6 'The Coronavirus is rewriting our imaginations.' *New Yorker*, 1 May 2020.

7 The COVID Silver Linings Playbook. Project Syndicate, 15 September 2020.

8 Paul Collier, John Kay. *Greed is Dead: Politics After Individualism*. (Penguin, London, 2020).

9 Mark Carney. 'How the economy must yield to human

values.' *The Economist*, 16 April 2020.

10   Ibid.

11   Ibid.

12   'What Isn't for Sale?' *Atlantic*, April 2012.

13   Molly Morgan Jones, Dominic Abrams and Aditi Lahiri.
     Shape the Future: how the social sciences, humanities and
     the arts can SHAPE a positive, post-pandemic future for
     peoples, economies and environments. *Journal of the British
     Academy*, 2 October 2020.

14   'It will change everything.' *Nature*, 30 November 2020.

15   COVID-19 Primer, Primer.

16   '"I just want to go home" – how Covid-19 changed expat
     life.' *Financial Times*, 2 October 2020.

17   UNDP Future of Development High Level Strategy Lab:
     COVID-10. UNDP, 11 November 2020.

18   George Ward. Is happiness a predictor of election results?
     CEP Discussion Paper, LSE, 2015.

19   'Good genes are nice, but joy is better.' *Harvard Gazette*,
     11 April 2017.

20   'Africa Summit, Getting Africa Back to Business.' *Financial
     Times*, 12 October 2020.

21   Cameron Hepburn et al. Will COVID-19 fiscal recovery
     packages accelerate or retard progress on climate change?
     Oxford Review of Economic Policy, 4 May 2020.

22   Talking about a revolution? Gavin Kelly's blog, 29 July
     2020.

23   Ibid.

24   John Bew. 2016. *Citizen Clem: A biography of Attlee*. (Riverrun,
     London, 2016).

25   'Coronavirus: the moment for helicopter money.' *Financial
     Times*, 20 March 2020.

26   'Virus lays bare the frailty of the social contract.' *Financial
     Times*, 3 April 2020.

27   'Dawn breaks on a new age of economic thinking.' *Financial
     Times*, 11 October 2020.

28 The Inequality Virus, Oxfam, Oxford, January 2021.

29 'The pandemic upended the present. But it's given us a chance to remake the future.' *Washington Post*, 6 October 2020.

30 Ibid.

31 Talking about a revolution? Gavin Kelly's blog, 29 July 2020.

32 Around the world, people yearn for significant change rather than a return to a 'pre-COVID normal'. IPSOS, 16 September 2020.

33 Ibid.

34 Ibid.

35 El Pais, Estudio sobre la crisis del coronavirus II. 40dB, April 2020. COVID-19 Opinion Tracker. KEKST CNC, May 2020.

36 Survey on Stronger Measures Covid-19. IPSOS, April 2020.

37 Covid-19 and Public Support for Radical Policies. Centre for International Policies, New York University, 25 June 2020.

38 Leah Zanmore, Ben Phillips. COVID-19 and Public Support for Radical Policies. Center on International Cooperation New York University, June 2020.

39 The Covid-19 Global Pandemic in Nairobi's Low-Income Areas: Health, Socio-Economic and Governance Aspects. TIFA Research, 11 May 2020.

40 Trust, Institutions, and Collective Action. BIGD Policy Brief, 29 April 2020. Encuesta: crece la imagen positive de Alberto Fernández en medio de la pandemia. *PERFIL*, 26 March 2020.

41 Fitzgerald, F. Scott. *The Great Gatsby*, Chapter 6. Cited in John Harris, 'The dream of going "back to normal".' *Guardian*, 15 November 2020.

42 The COVID Silver Linings Playbook. Project Syndicate, 15 September 2020.

Index